The Free Fantasia and the Musical Picturesque

This book explores the late eighteenth-century free fantasia and its relationship to the aesthetics of landscape and the picturesque. A crucial category across all the arts in the late eighteenth century, the picturesque has lost its currency in modern musical criticism, in spite of its rich potential to shed new light on the fantastical elements of instrumental music in general and the genre of the free fantasia in particular. Just as English garden architecture, in which the picturesque found its origins, was changing the landscape of continental Europe, the fantastical elements of irregularity, temporal displacement, ambiguity, interruption and self-referentiality in the music of C. P. E. Bach, Haydn and Beethoven were both lauded and criticised in terms borrowed from the discourse of the picturesque. This study reaffirms the centrality of the free fantasia and fantastical gesture in late eighteenth- and early nineteenth-century musical culture through an interdisciplinary approach that combines the visual, the literary and the musical.

ANNETTE RICHARDS is Assistant Professor of Music and University Organist at Cornell University. She is coeditor of *Acting on the Past: Historical Performance Studies Across the Disciplines* (2000).

New perspectives in music history and criticism

GENERAL EDITORS

JEFFREY KALLBERG, ANTHONY NEWCOMB AND RUTH SOLIE

This series explores the conceptual frameworks that shape or have shaped the ways in which we understand music and its history, and aims to elaborate structures of explanation, interpretation, commentary and criticism which make music intelligible and which provide a basis for argument about judgements of value. The intellectual scope of the series is broad. Some investigations will treat, for example, historiographical topics, others will apply cross-disciplinary methods to the criticism of music, and there will also be studies which consider music in its relation to society, culture and politics. Overall, the series hopes to create a greater presence for music in the ongoing discourse among the human sciences.

ALREADY PUBLISHED

Leslie C. Dunn and Nancy A. Jones (eds.), *Embodied voices: representing female vocality in western culture*

Downing A. Thomas, *Music and the origins of language: theories from the French Enlightenment*

Thomas S. Grey, *Wagner's musical prose*

Daniel K. L. Chua, *Absolute music and the construction of meaning*

Adam Krims, *Rap music and the poetics of identity*

The Free Fantasia
and the Musical
Picturesque

ANNETTE RICHARDS

CAMBRIDGE
UNIVERSITY PRESS

PUBLISHED BY THE PRESS SYNDICATE OF THE UNIVERSITY OF CAMBRIDGE
The Pitt Building, Trumpington Street, Cambridge CB2 1RP, United Kingdom

CAMBRIDGE UNIVERSITY PRESS
The Edinburgh Building, Cambridge, CB2 2RU, UK
40 West 20th Street, New York, NY 10011-4211, USA
10 Stamford Road, Oakleigh, Melbourne 3166, Australia
Ruiz de Alarcón 13, 28014, Madrid Spain
Dock House, The Waterfront, Cape Town 8001, South Africa

http://www.cambridge.org

First published 2001

Printed in the United Kingdom at the University Press, Cambridge

Typeface 10/12pt Adobe Palatino   *System* QuarkXPress™   [SE]

A catalogue record for this book is available from the British Library

Library of Congress Cataloguing in Publication data

Richards, Annette.
The free fantasia and the musical picturesque / Annette Richards.
    p.   cm. – (New perspectives in music history and criticism)
Includes bibliographical references and index.
ISBN 0 521 64077 6 (hardback)
1. Art and music. 2. Fantasia. 3. Picturesque, The. 4. Music – Europe –
18th century – History and criticism. 5. Music – Europe – 19th century –
History and criticism.
I. Title. II. Series.
ML3849.R48 2000
784.18'94 – dc 21   00-028944

ISBN 0 521 64077 6 hardback

For David

CONTENTS

FIGURES

Figures

Figures

ACKNOWLEDGEMENTS

I would like to thank all the friends and colleagues who inspired, criticised and encouraged my work during the course of this project; I am
especially grateful to Karol Berger, Terry Castle, Laurence Dreyfus,
Thomas Grey, Christopher Hogwood, Jeffrey Kallberg, Anthony
Newcomb, James Webster, David Yearsley and Neal Zaslaw. Portions of
chapters 3 and 5 have appeared in anthologies edited by Jan and Aleida
Assmann, Mark Franko and Susan Brauchli, all of whom I thank for
suggestions that contributed to the improved and expanded versions.
Jan Assmann, Julia Annas and Gail Fine helped me to solve riddles that
profoundly affected the direction of my argument. Arthur Groos and
Tilman Skowroneck gave me invaluable help with the German translations, as did Paul Osterfield in copying the musical examples. My
thanks also to Penny Souster at Cambridge University Press, and to
Lucy Carolan, for her indispensible expertise and commitment to detail.

I am indebted to the Stanford Humanities Center, the Getty Research
Institute and the Society for the Humanities at Cornell for fellowships
that made this book possible.

1

Framing the musical picturesque

The picturesque catches the eye. Startling, often disturbing, it is a visual mode that functions to arouse curiosity, to pique the interest, to command and control vision. This programme of capturing and captivating the spectator is encapsulated by the frontispiece to the *Musikalischer und Künstler Almanach* of 1784, an engraving entitled 'The spirits of music and painting embrace before the bust of Nature', which offers a succinct visualisation of the sometimes unruly mixture of themes that constitutes this book (figure 1.1). A conventional representation of the ideal union of music and the visual arts, the image haunts my own exploration into late eighteenth-century ways of framing the musical imagination. The engraving's setting is a natural landscape, richly textured with trees of varied species and shapes, the sky darkened with cloud masses; the foreground is scattered with stones and enhanced by a climbing rose that partially screens the scene, and in the sunny middle ground, two cherubs, their wings decorated like those of butterflies, embrace beneath the spreading limbs of a majestic, leaning tree. One cherub clutches a paintbrush in his fist, the other has casually propped a lyre, the symbol of his art, against the nearby tree.

To the right, and a little behind the pair, stands a curious figure – part human sculpture, part abstract obelisk, a Grecian torso on an Egyptian base. And what a torso it is. Three luxuriant pairs of breasts draw the viewer's eyes away from the laurel-wreathed head from which a veil falls to shroud the demure, blank face and part of the torso. The goddess is mysterious, exotic, fecund. This late eighteenth-century image of nature fuses the polymastic Artemis of Ephesus with the veiled Isis, and advertises an overt femininity and fecundity while hinting at sublime and unknowable secrets – a tantalising combination satirised by William Hogarth's translation of the veil into a skirt in his engraving of 'Boys Peeping at Nature' (figure 1.2). But the presence of this figure in the frontispiece to the *Musikalischer und Künstler Almanach* points beyond a simple, natural context for the hopeful embrace of music and painting. Already the musical vehicle for a disconcertingly literal incarnation as a water organ in the gardens of the Villa d'Este at Tivoli (1568) (figure 1.3), this nature goddess inhabited many European landscape

1

Figure 1.1   'Music and Painting Embrace before the Bust of Nature',
Musikalischer und Künstler Almanach, Freyburg, 1784

Figure 1.2   Hogarth, 'Boys Peeping at Nature', subscription ticket for *A Harlot's Progress* (1731)

Figure 1.3   Water organ in the form of Isis, Villa d'Este, Tivoli (1568)

gardens of the later eighteenth century (figure 1.4);[1] and indeed, if you look again at the frontispiece to the *Musikalischer und Künstler Almanach* you can see that the setting it represents is not a natural woodland at all, but rather, as the rose trellis in the foreground implies, a landscape garden. Apparently wild and natural, it is in fact designed and culti-vated. In addition, it has been carefully, if somewhat crudely, framed for the viewer, with its darkened foreground and irregular shapes, its slant-ing tree, scattered rocks and broken clouds. Both the conflation of the wild and the cultivated that this landscape represents, and its presenta-tion for consumption by the viewer, exemplify the contemporary aesthetic of instability and surprise, rough textures and partial conceal-ments, as well as the invitation to spectatorship and aestheticised viewing, that is the picturesque.

The aesthetic of the picturesque was developed in England during the course of the eighteenth century and was articulated more formally in the 1780s and 1790s. Taken in its technical sense the picturesque is a complex aesthetic category which encompasses and encourages frag-mentation and disruption, contrast and variety, and problematises the limits of form and conventional expectation; in modern music criticism, however, the term has generally been taken colloquially to describe quaint or pastoral associations or obvious pictorialism.[2] Given the many intersections between music and aesthetic theory in the period, and especially music and the aesthetic of gardens, the picturesque has been curiously overlooked in recent scholarship on eighteenth-century

[1] On Isis as a personification of Nature, see Pierre Hadot, *Zur Idee des Naturgeheimnisses: Beim Betrachten des Widmungsblattes in den Humboldtschen 'Ideen zu einer Geographie der Pflanzen'* (Wiesbaden: Steiner, 1982), and also Hadot and Dirk Syndram, *Ägypten-Faszinationen: Untersuchungen zum Ägyptenbild im europäischen Klassizismus bis 1800* (Frankfurt am Main: Peter Lang, 1990), 216–19.

[2] The one study that deals with the picturesque and music in any detail is Roger Barnett Larsson, 'The Beautiful, the Sublime and the Picturesque in Eighteenth-Century Musical Thought in Britain' (Ph.D. diss., SUNY Buffalo, 1980); Larsson, whose study is confined to English sources, suggests that the colloquial use of 'picturesque' to mean 'pictorial' is compatible with the more formal usage associated with the aesthetic cate-gory – that both have similar meanings if different perspectives: English response to Haydn in the 1790s, for example, uses 'picturesque' to refer both to obvious pictorial-isms and to disjointed and surprising effects. But this is to gloss over a fundamental dif-ference between the two usages: where the colloquial picturesque is about representation, the formal picturesque is concerned with abstract qualities. As such, it lends itself well to the contemporary debate over the meaning of 'abstract' instrumen-tal music. See also Tilden A. Russell, 'Minuet, Scherzando, and Scherzo: The Dance Movement in Transition, 1781–1825' (Ph. D. diss., University of North Carolina, Chapel Hill, 1983) and his 'On "Looking over a Ha-Ha"', *Musical Quarterly* 71/1 (1985), 27–37; and A. Peter Brown, 'The Sublime, the Beautiful, and the Ornamental: English Aesthetic Currents and Haydn's London Symphonies', in *Studies in Music History pre-sented to H. C. Robbins Landon on his Seventieth Birthday*, ed. Otto Biba and David Wyn Jones (London: Thames and Hudson, 1996), 44–71.

5

Figure 1.4   Statue of Isis in the Neuer Garten, Potsdam (*c.* 1780–90)

musical culture, despite a resurgence of interest in the parallel categories of the sublime and the beautiful, and in late eighteenth-century
gardens and landscape in recent social, literary and art history. But in its
dialectical engagement with the natural and artificial, and its predilection for irregularity, unruly freedom and ambiguous borders, the picturesque was, and is, an important tool for the conceptualisation of
contemporary instrumental music, and especially that period's most
ambiguous genre, the free fantasia. Indeed, the forgotten category of the

6

musical picturesque allows for a reevaluation of the disordered and (apparently) irrational and offers a new way of looking at – and listening to – the complexities of the fantastical in late eighteenth- and early nineteenth-century music.

Although theorists of the picturesque derived their observations from the arts of landscape painting and, most especially, landscape gardening, not only did they cite picturesqueness as an attribute of contemporary music, but music consistently provided a rich source for the belated formulation of the theory itself. In his *Essay on the Picturesque* (1790) Uvedale Price, who described his three major preoccupations as 'pictures, scenery and music',[3] claimed a universal applicability for the picturesque across the arts: 'The English word picturesque naturally draws the mind towards pictures; and from that partial and confined view of the subject, what is, in truth, only an illustration of picturesqueness, becomes the foundation of it.' The quintessential attributes of the picturesque were to be found not only in the visual arts but in music as well. 'We no more scruple to call one of Handel's choruses sublime, than Corelli's Pastorale beautiful', Price writes,

But should a person and without qualifying expressions, call a capricious movement of Domenico Scarlatti, or Haydn, picturesque, he would, with great reason, be laughed at; for it is not a term applied to sounds: yet such a movement, from its sudden, unexpected, and abrupt transitions – from a certain playful wildness of character and appearance of irregularity, is no less analogous to similar scenery in nature than the concerto or the chorus to what is grand or beautiful to the eye.[4]

While acknowledging that the idea of 'picturesque' music may at first seem incongruous, Price asserts that this aesthetic is as clearly present in certain types of music as it is in landscape.

That the surprises and disjunctions of modern instrumental music could be subsumed under an unlikely aesthetic category originating in the visual arts was a startling notion. Yet music had already figured repeatedly in the more general discourse on the landscape garden, most often as an example of the successful manipulation of variety and surprise effects. In his *Elements of Criticism* (1762), Henry Home, Lord Kames compared the constant changes in mood and scene in the landscape garden to contrast in music. A free mixture of affects, designed to keep the emotions in flux and achieved, in part, by the alternation of the wild and rugged with the soft and cultivated, were integral to the

---

[3] Quoted in Stephanie Ross, *What Gardens Mean* (Chicago and London: University of Chicago Press, 1998), 127.

[4] Price, 'On the Picturesque', *Essays on the Picturesque, As Compared with the Sublime and the Beautiful; and, on the Use of Studying Pictures, for the Purpose of Improving Real Landscape*, 3 vols. (London, 1810) [Price's collected writings on the picturesque], I, 45–6.

success of compositions both in landscape gardens and in music. 'A field may be laid out in grand, sweet, gay, neat, wild, melancholy scenes', Kames writes,

and when these are viewed in succession, grandeur ought to be contrasted with neatness, regularity with wildness, and gaiety with melancholy, so as that each emotion may succeed its opposite: nay, it is an improvement to intermix in the succession rude and uncultivated spots as well as unbounded views, which in themselves are disagreeable objects . . . The greatest masters of music have the same view in their compositions: the second part of an Italian song seldom conveys any sentiment; and, by its harshness, seems purposely contrived to give a greater relish for the interesting parts of the composition.[5]

Kames chooses music as the garden's parallel art, though the example he goes on to adduce is not particularly inspired (or well informed) and seems to reduce the issue to one of boredom versus interest. More successfully, Uvedale Price illustrated the effectiveness of variety and contrast in landscape by likening it to the accompaniment of a beautiful melody with more daring harmonic progressions:

discords in music, which are analogous to sharp and angular objects of sight, are introduced by the most judicious composers, in their accompaniments to the sweetest and most flowing melodies, in order to relieve the ear from that languor and weariness, which long continued smoothness always brings on.[6]

Dissonance, of course, had long been recognised by theorists as a necessary relief to unabating consonance, and while these references to music offer little in the way of meaningful analysis or criticism, they point to a new fixation on piquant contrast. Price followed earlier writers in citing music as evidence that variety is essential if garden art is to arouse interest, that in order to excite the attention of the visitor the gardener must transgress the beautiful.

By the second half of the eighteenth century the aesthetics and practice of gardening had become the object of intense interest and debate in England and across Europe, and were eagerly taken up by critics in the other arts, not least music. Not only had gardening recently been recognised as a fine art, but it offered a uniquely accessible aesthetic experience. William Chambers opened his famous *Dissertation on Oriental Gardening* (1772) with the claim that 'Amongst the decorative arts there is none of which the influence is so extensive as that of gardening', and in contrast to the other arts, Chambers maintained, the garden could appeal even to those with little prior knowledge of its tropes. The experience of the landscape garden served to educate those who had access to it in the aesthetic that would be codified as the

---

[5] Henry Home, Lord Kames, *Elements of Criticism*, 9th edn, 2 vols. (Edinburgh, 1817), II, 272.   [6] Price, 'On the Picturesque', 110.

picturesque;[7] the new garden ideal drew on the irregularities of natural landscape, with its woods, rocks and rugged waterfalls – a 'natural' aesthetic that had been advocated early in the century by Addison, Shaftesbury and Pope, who called for contrast, surprise and partial concealments in garden art, as opposed to the predictable regularities and symmetrical patterns of the old formal garden. The new style boasted undulating lines in place of straight edges and geometrical shapes, and was epitomised by the landscapes of Lancelot 'Capability' Brown, in which wide grassy expanses were dotted with isolated clumps of trees, artificial lakes curved in serpentine forms, and sinuous drives and walks guided the visitor through the park.

Such gardens were supremely 'natural' by contrast with their old formal counterparts, but by the 1770s they too had come increasingly under attack. Chambers blamed Brown for wreaking havoc on the English countryside with his destructive thinning of woods, extravagant creation of artificial lakes and penchant for ugly stretches of bald lawn. In such landscapes, he claimed, the balance of art and nature had been misjudged, for they were practically indistinguishable from fields – they required even greater art, or at least more obvious artifice. Chambers proposed as an alternative model the mixture of art and nature that had been achieved by Chinese gardeners, who 'take nature for their pattern' and aim to imitate her 'in all her beautiful irregularities', without altogether concealing their work: for the Chinese 'are not so attached to [Nature] as to exclude all appearance of art'.[8]

The opposition between art and nature, which formed a pivotal issue in the reception of the musical fantasia, conspicuously governed the aesthetic of the landscape garden. The 'naturalness' of such gardens became, for Friedrich Schlegel, the cause of their failure as art: 'This inextricable mingling of nature and art could, it seems, only be so extraordinarily delightful in an age that does not acknowledge the necessity for strictly observing the eternal boundaries between them.'[9] It was a paradox articulated by Immanuel Kant, that 'nature proved beautiful when it wore the appearance of art; and art can only be termed beautiful where we are conscious of its being art, while yet it has the

---

[7] William Chambers, *A Dissertation on Oriental Gardening* (London, 1772), 1.

[8] Ibid., 14, 16. Chambers had twice visited China (in 1744 and 1748), and had previously published his views on the Chinese style in his *Designs for Chinese Buildings . . .* (London, 1757). But he appealed to the notion of the Oriental garden less in pursuit of authentic Chinese designs, than as a pretext for an attack on the landscapes of Capability Brown. The *Dissertation* had a considerable impact on the Continent, and it was in large part responsible for the reception of the English garden there as the 'Anglo-Chinese' garden.

[9] August Wilhelm Schlegel, *Vorlesungen über schöne Literatur und Kunst*, vol. I (Heilbronn, 1884; originally from 1801–2), 212. Quoted in Tilden A. Russell, 'On "Looking over a Ha-Ha"', 32.

appearance of nature'.[10] But by the 1790s, the theorists of the picturesque Uvedale Price and Richard Payne Knight had come to consider
the Brownian landscape not so much too lacking in art, as too obviously
artificial. In Brown's manifestly unnatural landscapes, they claimed, the
hand of the improver was too conspicuous and the result too ordered.
The disparity between the smooth style of Brown and the rugged picturesque proposed by Knight and Price was illustrated by Thomas Hearne
for Knight's didactic poem 'The Landscape' (1794) in a pair of engravings showing two versions of the same park (figures 1.5a and b). In the
park as 'improved' by Brown, a Palladian house is isolated in smooth
lawns that lead to a serpentine stream winding between elegantly
placed clumps of trees; the banks of the stream are cut and cleared and
a Chinese-style bridge gracefully spans the water. In the version that
represents the antithesis to modern 'improvement', and serves as the
ideal for the late and full-blown picturesque, the house is old and visu-
ally chaotic, and is surrounded by foliage that appears to have been left
to grow ragged and wild; a rustic bridge crosses the stream, whose
banks are obscured by vegetation, and whose course is rocky and clut-
tered. The picturesque garden is wild, various, intricate and (seemingly)
unconfined.

Uvedale Price condemned Brown's style for its rigid imposition of dis-
cipline, its fixed and intrusive boundaries and its coercive roads. Such
landscapes allowed no digression, and, more importantly, no space for
the exercise of the imagination: it was as if the improver had said

'You shall never wander from my walks – never exercise your own taste and
judgement – never form your own compositions; neither your eyes nor your feet
shall be allowed to stray from the boundaries I have traced.'[11]

From the picturesque perspective in the 1790s, the visitor invited to
'view' the Brownian park was not permitted to participate freely in it,
her imagination and interpretative freedom severely constrained. The
ideal picturesque garden, on the contrary, in which nature appeared to
be overtly 'untamed by art' despite the park's fundamental artificiality,
was a site of freedom and imagination, the place for unconstrained
indulgence in fantasy.[12]

Although the art of the landscape garden was understood as a kind
of painting, one using the trees, rocks and water of the real world rather

---

[10] Immanuel Kant, *The Critique of Judgement*, trans. James Creed Meredith (Oxford:
Clarendon Press, 1952), 167.

[11] Price, *An Essay on the Picturesque, As Compared with the Sublime and the Beautiful; and, On
the Use of Studying Pictures, for the Purpouse of Improving Real Landscape* (London, 1794),
278.

[12] This was, of course, Capability Brown's aim too, and, according to many, his great
achievement.

(a)

(b)

Figure 1.5a and b   Engravings by Thomas Hearne from Richard
Payne Knight, *The Landscape* (1794): plate I, 'In the distance, a
mansion-house with the ancient decorations'; plate II, 'The same
modernized'.

than their representations, it was seen to offer an aesthetic experience broader and more complex than that of painting – as if painting had exploded into three dimensions, and incorporated into itself a crucial temporal element. The picturesque, with its aversion to formal perfection, depends fundamentally on the representation of the passage of time, its effects bound up with the processes of decay or maturation (as a recent writer comments, 'the picturesque is never shiny and new');[13] for William Gilpin, the so-called 'Father of the Picturesque', author of numerous best-selling *Picturesque Tours*, and instructor in the art of landscape sketching, the picturesque was explicitly located in the irregular outlines, contrasting lights and shades and variegated colours of the ruin. The decay of classical order and balance was achieved, however, not only by the gentle passage of time but also by acts of artistic vandalism:

A piece of Palladian architecture may be elegant in the last degree . . . [but] should we wish to give it picturesque beauty, we must use the mallet instead of the chisel: we must beat down one half of it, deface the other, and throw the mutilated members around in heaps; in short, from a *smooth* building we must turn it into a *rough* ruin.[14]

The picturesque eye, and hand, pursued a textured and roughed-up beauty which verged on the disorderly realm of the sublime (figure 1.6).

While Gilpin considered the picturesque a sub-species of the beautiful, Uvedale Price insisted that it encompassed a distinct class of elements excluded from Burke's definitions of both the sublime and the beautiful. Inherently unstable, the picturesque occupies an uncertain space between or beyond the sublime and the beautiful, but is independent of both; frequently engaged in modifying one or the other, it corrects the languor of beauty or the horror of sublimity.[15] According to Price's assessment of both landscape and music, the relaxation caused by beauty's insipid sameness may lead to boredom unless counteracted by

---

[13] Dabney Townsend, 'The Picturesque', *The Journal of Aesthetics and Art Criticism* 55/4 (Fall 1997), 367.

[14] William Gilpin, 'On Picturesque Beauty', in *Three Essays: – On Picturesque Beauty; on Picturesque Travel; and, on Sketching Landscape: to which is added a Poem, on Landscape Painting* (London, 1792), 7.

[15] Essential studies of the picturesque include Christopher Hussey, *The Picturesque: Studies in a Point of View* (London: Putnam, 1927); Walter J. Hipple, *The Beautiful, the Sublime and the Picturesque in Eighteenth-Century Aesthetic Theory* (Carbondale, IL: Southern Illinois University Press, 1957); Martin Price, 'The Picturesque Moment', in *From Sensibility to Romanticism: Essays Presented to Frederick A. Pottle*, ed. Frederick W. Hilles and Harold Bloom (New York: Oxford University Press, 1965), 259–92; John Dixon Hunt, *Gardens and the Picturesque: Studies in the History of Landscape Architecture* (Cambridge, MA: MIT Press, 1992); Sidney K. Robinson, *Inquiry into the Picturesque* (Chicago: University of Chicago Press, 1991); and Stephen Copley and Peter Garside, eds., *The Politics of the Picturesque* (Cambridge: Cambridge University Press, 1994).

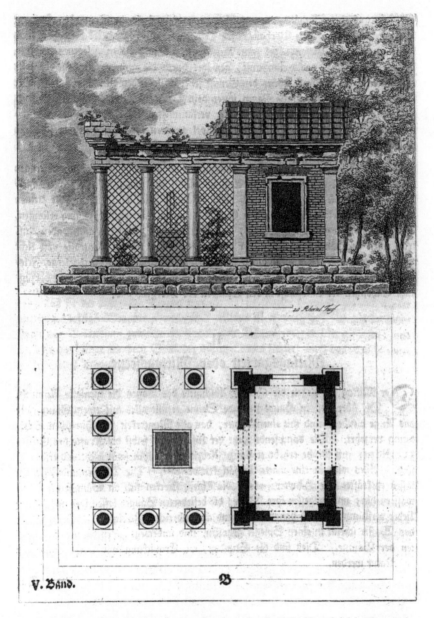

Figure 1.6   Design for garden temple, C. C. L. Hirschfeld, *Theorie der Gartenkunst*, vol. V (1785)

the lively irritation of the picturesque: the picturesque is 'the coquetry of nature; it makes beauty more amusing, more varied, more playful'. Likewise, it releases the paralysing wonder caused by the sublime, for 'by its variety, its intricacy, its partial concealment, [the picturesque] excites that active curiosity which gives play to the mind, loosening those iron bonds with which astonishment chains up its faculties'.[16] A category that embraced the overlooked and discarded, the picturesque was, not coincidentally, concerned with what might commonly be considered 'ruts and rubbish'. Indeed, in this process of reevaluating, of seeing anew, Price conceived of the primary effect of the picturesque as the stimulation of curiosity: it is a mode of active engagement, as opposed to passive enjoyment, and demands energetic involvement rather than the relaxation associated with the beautiful.[17] Precariously balanced, the picturesque works to blend the extreme categories of the sublime and the beautiful which, in a pure state, become unacceptable to a successful, 'tasteful' work. The picturesque was an acquired taste, piquant, perhaps peculiar, more highly flavoured and interesting than the merely beautiful, yet not so extreme as to become grotesque or decadent.

The picturesque is indeed predicated on the tension between the formed and deformed, between underlying coherence and surface disruption: it is this that makes it so pertinent to certain kinds of late eighteenth-century instrumental music. Uvedale Price, himself no great music critic, included music in his injunctions against the excessive irregularities that might put the fundamental stability of form at risk:

as the principles of harmony must be preserved in the wildest and most eccentric pieces of music, in those where sudden and quickly varying emotions of the soul are exposed, so that of breadth must be in scenes of bustle and seeming confusion, and where the wildest scenery or most violent agitations of nature are represented.[18]

By analogy with music, the curious detail and highly flavoured oddity must be controlled, in order to avoid a descent into meaningless chaos.

The musical picturesque is epitomised by the free fantasia, but not confined to this genre, just as pictures (and their living counterparts, gardens), for Price, exemplified but did not circumscribe the visual picturesque. Like the picturesque, the fantasy has tended to be marginalised in musicological writing. The fantasia as a genre has an ambiguous ontological status: is it the spontaneous 'natural' improvisation of genius speaking directly to the emotions of the listener? Or is it an artfully constructed composition designed as a simulacrum of that unmediated utterance, requiring all the more art in its apparent rejection of

---

[16] Price, *Essay* (1794), 86–7.   [17] Ibid., 19, 85, footnote.   [18] Ibid., 128–9.

usual compositional rule? The free fantasia is central to my study of the musical picturesque, for it crystallised many of the problematic complexities of instrumental music which could not be integrated into more conventional aesthetic theory of the period. More crucial, however, is the fact that the 'fantastic', both in the fantasia proper, and more generally as it intruded into other instrumental genres, played a key role in the formulation in the late eighteenth century of a notion of the musical picturesque. Both fantasy and picturesque share qualities of disruptedness and surprise; both problematise the opposition between art and nature, as the 'natural' garden mirrors the tension between improvisation and composition inherent in the fantasia. Moreover, the particularly self-conscious listening practice engendered by the musical fantastic, like certain types of eighteenth-century narrative, shares with the picturesque a peculiar concern with temporality, as well as a paradoxical tension between passionate sentiment and the potential ironical critique that is introduced by aesthetic distance. Beyond the well-pruned avenues of more conventional studies of eighteenth-century music a picturesque critical space beckons.

Like the picturesque, the fantasy has a certain post-modern appeal. Fragmentary, subjective, open-ended, it simultaneously resists interpretation and offers itself promiscuously to multiple readings; ambiguously placed between improvisation and composition, the fantasia pushes away from the constraints of musical notation, evading an obvious conformity to musical form, threatening the fakery and illusion associated with bewitching performance, evanescent and virtuosic display. Improvisation is an inherently problematic object of study for the historian: quintessentially ephemeral, it relies on no pre-existing text and leaves little record from which to conjure a recreation. Composed fantasies, and perhaps even improvisations, may occasionally be entirely 'free' but more often they subtly play against other more 'formal' genres, especially the sonata and rondo. The generic ambiguity inherent in the free fantasia and its hovering between ephemeral soundscape and fixed text can usefully be approached in terms of Tzvetan Todorov's definition of the literary fantastic. For Todorov the fantastic is a matter of hesitation, a blurred moment of indecision in which both the character in the story and the reader must choose between dream or reality, truth or illusion. Todorov points to the instability and ephemerality of the fantastic, which 'leads a life full of dangers' and 'may evaporate at any moment', located as it is on the frontier between the marvellous and the uncanny. Crucially, it exists only in a kind of performative here-and-now, like that of improvisation, for 'the hesitation which characterizes it cannot be situated, by and large, except in the present'. The sheer immediacy of the fantastic 'implies an integration of the reader into the world of the characters' and therefore highlights the genre's temporality: 'every work contains an indication as to the time of its perception; the narrative of the fantastic, which strongly emphasizes the process of uttering, simultaneously emphasizes this time of the reading itself'.[19] To listen to an improvisation, the musical performance of fantasy, is to hear utterance in the act of its invention; as I will discuss in chapter 3, the improvisation and its written-out representation draw attention to the realm of the imaginary and the process of creating new ideas – original thoughts, both opaque and unprecedented – which offer an open invitation to interpretation.

In both improvised and composed versions, but especially in the latter, like a second reading of a fantastic story, the fantasia carries with it a tendency towards meta-fantasy in the course of which 'we note the methods of the fantastic instead of coming under its spell';[20] the composed fantasy can be repeated, unlike the spontaneous improvisation (though Beethoven claimed to have been able to repeat his improvisations), and indeed, it must usually be rehearsed before it can be properly performed; in the process of repetition the effect of instantaneous surprise is compromised, the moment of hesitation irrecoverable, or made a conscious foundation of the listener's expectations.

Carl Philipp Emanuel Bach, whose idiosyncratic compositional style was imbued with the discontinuities and irregularities of the fantastic, stands at the centre of this study. His works, and his improvisations, both defined a fantasy tradition for well over half a century and contributed in crucial ways to the formulation of an aesthetic of the musical picturesque, serving in turn as a monument, or point of reference, for picturesque gestures by his contemporaries and successors, including Haydn and Beethoven. Contemporary accounts of free fantasy performances by C. P. E. Bach attest to the genre's potential for a compelling brilliance, and to Bach's status as the acknowledged master of the art. Charles Burney's description is perhaps the most famous of these, and bears repeating here to evoke again the lure of such performance: 'After dinner,' Burney recounts, '[Bach] played, with little intermission, till near eleven o'clock at night. During this time, he grew so animated and *possessed*, that he not only played, but looked like one inspired. His eyes were fixed, his under lip fell, and drops of effervescence distilled from his countenance. He said, if he were to set to work frequently, in this manner, he would grow young again.'[21] Similarly, to Carl Friedrich Cramer, editor of the *Magazin der Musik*, Bach's improvisations were

---

[19] Tzvetan Todorov, *The Fantastic: A Structural Approach to a Literary Genre*, trans. Richard Howard (Ithaca, NY: Cornell University Press, 1975), 42, 89.   [20] Ibid., 89.

[21] Charles Burney, *The Present State of Music in Germany, the Netherlands and the United Provinces*, 2nd edn, 2 vols. (London, 1775), II, 270–1.

wonders of artistry, daring, evocative and, crucially, erudite. 'Anyone who has heard the Herr Kapellmeister improvising on the fortepiano', he writes,

and who is something of a connoisseur will gladly admit that greater perfection in this art could scarcely be imagined. The greatest virtuosos who have been here in Hamburg, and stood beside him, when, in just the right mood, he improvised for them, have been astounded at his bold ideas and transitions, his daring, unprecedented, and yet technically correct modulations . . . they have rubbed their brow [in disbelief] and expressed regret that they did not possess *such knowledge* themselves.[22]

It is as if the listener were privy to a visitation from another world.

Despite the centrality of the fantasia in the late eighteenth-century repertoire and to the period's critical discourse, twentieth-century music historians have tended to shy away from 'informal' music such as this, which problematises the role of the texts upon which such history is based, and which evades the complex formal patterning which Adorno and others have attributed to the process of writing.[23] The classic model for understanding late eighteenth-century music has been a formal one, and the paradigmatic plot of sonata form in particular tends to stand as the template against which to hear and to 'understand' the music of the period. With its structures based on repetition and return, sonata form directly engages the memory of the listener, measuring past event against present, while the fantasia tends to evade clear harmonic trajectories, period structures and formal design; even when it is formally motivated, the fantasia treats such strategies mischievously. Generally notated without regular metre or barlines, the free fantasia presents a mosaic of rhapsodic, quick-changing effects, extravagant shifts of harmony and sudden changes of texture and dynamic level. Both sonata and fantasia play with form, the sonata overtly, the fantasia, more usually, covertly, but the latter tends to exploit to a much greater degree the sense of lost direction, of being immersed in a structure whose pattern is unclear, even undiscoverable. Composed (and even improvised) fantasias, especially those of C. P. E. Bach, may in fact

---

[22] Review of 'Claviersonaten und freye Phantasien, nebst einigen Rondos fürs Fortepiano, für Kenner und Liebhaber, componirt von Carl Philipp Emanuel Bach, Fünfte Sammlung . . .' in C. F. Cramer, *Magazin der Musik* 2/2 (5 August 1786), 871.

[23] Adorno writes that 'the complex forms by means of which succession is internally organized as such would be inadequate for any improvised, non-written music-making'. Theodor W. Adorno, *Quasi una Fantasia*, trans. Rodney Livingstone (London: Verso, 1992), 295–6. See also Lydia Goehr, *The Imaginary Museum of Musical Works* (Oxford: Oxford University Press, 1992). For the most comprehensive history of the free fantasia see Peter Schleuning, *Die Freie Fantasie: Ein Beitrag zur Erforschung der klassischen Klaviermusik* (Göppingen: Kümmerle, 1973), and his *The Fantasia*, trans. A. C. Howie, 2 vols. (Cologne: A. Volk Verlag, 1971).

be highly crafted with a carefully planned underlying logic – and yet such music threatens a drastic subversion of notions of progess and return through various means, including digression, incongruous local effects, surprising and affective moments. Points of formal articulation are often deliberately concealed, and the whole effect is one of intentional irregularity. Leonard Ratner has suggested that the fantasia played an important role in expanding the expressive range of sonata form, 'thrusting against the rhythmic and harmonic controls [of the form] with harmonic digressions and melodic elaborations to impart warmth and expressive color to the style',[24] and in this study more generally I take 'fantasia' to mean not only the genre itself, but a musical aesthetic that enters into, destabilises and complexifies other genres of instrumental music, as in the symphonies of Haydn discussed in chapter 4 or the sonatas of Beethoven in chapter 6. Mark Evan Bonds has incisively summarised the crucial distinction between sonata and fantasia in terms of genre: the status of the sonata as genre is dependent on the extent to which it fulfils the expectations of the listener – it has a certain teleology against which digression can be measured; the fantasia, by contrast, has no set expectations that the composer or listener can play with or against, and is, in this sense, an 'anti-genre'.[25]

The analogy between landscape and music by way of the picturesque was made with varying degrees of specificity by a number of authors, and aside from its power to explain and rehabilitate the free fantasia's musical procedures, the picturesque played an important part in the reception of instrumental music. In fact, the somewhat conflicted reception of C. P. E. Bach in recent years curiously manages to pinpoint this very aesthetic. Charles Rosen, who praised Bach's music in his influential *The Classical Style* as 'violent, expressive, brilliant, [and] continuously surprising', labelled it at the same time as uncontrolled, wayward and baffling: 'C. P. E. Bach's horizon is wider harmonically [than that of J. C. Bach or the young Mozart], but his practice is incoherent: he is more interested in local effects – he delights in harmonic shock, as did Haydn; but Haydn knew how to weld his effects together, and his most disparate harmonies are not only reconciled but even explained by what follows as well as implied by what precedes.'[26] Rosen unwittingly gives a good account of the musical fantastic in his notion of short-term effect

---

[24] Leonard Ratner, *Classic Music: Expression, Form and Style* (New York: Schirmer, 1980), 233.

[25] See Mark Evan Bonds, *Wordless Rhetoric: Musical Form and the Metaphor of the Oration* (Cambridge, MA: Harvard University Press, 1991), esp. 114–18. See also Gary Saul Morson, *The Boundaries of Genre: Dostoevsky's Diary of a Writer and the Traditions of Literary Utopia* (Austin: University of Texas Press, 1981).

[26] Charles Rosen, *The Classical Style: Haydn, Mozart, Beethoven* (London: Faber, 1972), 44, 79.

taking precedence over long-term continuity (though some of Bach's music is replete with subtle underlying long-term connections); that this could be seen as a virtue rather than as a fault is amply demonstrated by eighteenth-century writing on the picturesque, and Rosen's evaluation speaks to the enormous distance between those commentators and their modern counterparts.

A similar, if unwitting, distrust of the picturesque is presented by David Schulenberg, writing on the C major fantasia (H. 284) from C. P. E. Bach's fifth *Kenner und Liebhaber* collection. Schulenberg undertakes a formal analysis of the piece but ends up admitting that the fantasia's 'more mysterious parts' consist of 'little more than one thing after another'; coherence, he concludes warily, resides in a principle of 'progression by non-sequitur' which 'stretches the idea of formal connections to its limits'.[27] Indeed, when formal analysis has failed to find its version of coherence in the fantasia, it has tended to trivialise the genre and brush it aside, but the critic who wishes to hear form (as it might appear on paper) misses a 'hearing' of the fantasia that might reflect more closely the eighteenth-century listener's experience of fantasy performance, one founded on concepts of rhetoric and affect; as a number of recent commentators have shown, notions of form for late eighteenth-century listeners were neither thematically nor harmonically based (the late nineteenth- and earlier twentieth-century view), but relied on 'the experience of punctuation', the articulation of a composition into a 'hierarchy of parts'.[28] In her study of changing aesthetic views of instrumental music in eighteenth-century Germany, Bellamy Hosler registers a certain discomfort with the fantasia: 'The fantasy', she writes, 'although recognized as a viable art form, was nevertheless a theoretical anomaly. Did it effect the understandable communication of a passion? Certainly, it did not use the prescribed vehicle for the representation and arousal of a passion: simple, natural, lyrical utterance.'[29] The fantasia, with its principal objective of moving the listener, can be seen to exploit the possibilities of musical rhetoric without necessarily appealing to established formal categories, and yet, this rhetorical model is itself called into question by a kind of fantastic music in which

---

[27] See David Schulenberg, *The Instrumental Music of Carl Philipp Emanuel Bach* (Ann Arbor, MI: UMI Research Press, 1984), 157.

[28] See especially Bonds, *Wordless Rhetoric*, and Karol Berger, 'Toward a History of Hearing: The Classic Concerto, A Sample Case', in *Convention in 18th- and 19th-Century Music: Essays in Honor of Leonard Ratner*, ed. Wye J. Allenbrook, Janet M. Levy and William P. Mahrt (Stuyvesant, NY: Pendragon Press, 1992), 405–29.

[29] Bellamy Hosler, *Changing Aesthetic Views of Instrumental Music in 18th-Century Germany* (Ann Arbor, MI: UMI Research Press, 1981), 28. See also Arnold Schering, 'C. Ph. E. Bach und das redende Prinzip in der Musik', *Jahrbuch der Musikbibliothek Peters* 45 (1938), 13–29.

punctuation is deliberately obscure, even arbitrary. While the question of meaning, of the communication of something understandable or coherent, was the subject of much debate, the fantasia was praised as a highly original, personal expression, requiring active listening and even a physical response from the listener. In its problematisation of perception itself, the picturesque proffers a useful tool for unravelling some of the knotted debates over the status and meaning of instrumental music in the late eighteenth century.

Before looking more closely at the ways in which theories of gardens, landscape and music intersected in England and Germany in the long shadow of C. P. E. Bach, I would like first to present a late and, in fact, not very free fantasia of Bach's to illustrate the way in which the fantasia can be understood as a 'picturesque' vehicle for a critique of formal procedures and generic distinctions. The fantasia in B♭ major, H. 289 (*Kenner und Liebhaber* VI, 1787) paradigmatically exploits the freedom of the genre, with its hesitations and licence, and its manipulation of formal convention, while being, atypically, constructed around the tonal architecture and patterns of thematic return of sonata form. Here sonata principles are imported into the fantasia to create a 'fantasia quasi una sonata' instead of the sonata-infected-by-fantasy hybrid that was to become the object of consternation for German music critics in the next two decades, a transgression which I will investigate more closely in chapter 6.[30] The yoking-together of the fantasia, which revels in apparent formal freedom, and the significant pattern of fixed relationships in sonata form, results in a conscious display of artifice. It presents an overt challenge to the listener, seductively setting up expectations within the sonata paradigm, yet threatening at any moment to swerve off-course in the aberrant manner of the fantasia, pushing at both the formal tension necessarily inherent in the complex structure of the sonata, and the patchwork of surprises and effects that the fantasia exploits in its self-confessed freedom of expression.

The pattern of key relationships and reprise of thematic groups in this piece echo those of sonata form, but the fragmented, irregular and decidedly unperiodic thematic material, coupled with the audacious moments of harmonic experimentation, militate against balance and formal logic. Unlike the truly 'free' fantasia, this piece is measured throughout, with the exception of a short recitative passage heard in the first and last sections; in addition, it maintains one tempo, allegretto,

---

[30] Bach's sonatas themselves, of course, are hardly representative of classic Viennese sonata procedure – indeed, they are themselves heavily coloured by fantasia. On the 'fantastic' in genres other than Fantasia in Bach's music, see Matthew Head, 'Fantasy in the Instrumental Music of C. P. E. Bach' (Ph.D. diss., Yale University, 1995).

Example 1.1   C. P. E. Bach, Fantasia in B♭, H. 289, *Kenner und Liebhaber* VI (1787), bars 1–14

and unlike many of Bach's other fantasias it has no pivotal slow section or even any clearly defined section of contrasting material (see also example 1.1):

bars	1–6	7–35	31–41	43–71	72–109	109–15
'thematic' material	a	b	a	[b]	b	a
time signature	(C)	(3/4)	(C)	[3/4]	(3/4)	(C)
harmony	I	I	V	x	I	I

The template of sonata-allegro form, with its increase in tension as it moves towards the dominant, and subsequent relaxation and return to the tonic after excursions to more distant keys, forms the basic frame for the action of this fantasia, a piece in which the fantastic appears to be thoroughly shackled by the wholesale reprise of thematic material. In

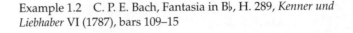

Example 1.2   C. P. E. Bach, Fantasia in B♭, H. 289, *Kenner und Liebhaber* VI (1787), bars 109–15

this sketch of harmonic and thematic patterning the fantastic seems indeed to have evaporated, its residue a skeletal version of the teleological narrative of the sonata. And yet, when the piece is performed, the ear is distracted from the underlying form by the disconcertingly fragmented surface, especially of the lengthy 'b' group, with its quirky, nervous discontinuities, its evasion of anything close to melody or thematic elaboration, its strange tendency to digress, its constant stops, starts and dramatic pauses. Even disregarding the fantastic surface, the pattern of reprise itself, at first sight anathema to improvisatory revelation, in fact contributes to the sense of generic hesitation that Todorov defines as peculiar to the fantastic; given the doggedly literal pattern of reprise in this piece, especially of the 'a' group, the exact repetition of the opening section at the end serves less to resolve a dramatic tension heightened during the progress of the piece, than, disconcertingly, to introduce the possibility of a continuation of the cycle of reiteration. Without any earlier reworking of the 'a' group, or even a concluding appendix, the sense of achievement, of final arrival, is diminished; indeed, despite the abrupt final tonic chord, in closing as it began (example 1.2) this piece threatens an elusive open-endedness that runs counter to the affirmative closure demanded by the conventional drama of sonata form, and suggests that what might have been 'development' was instead the usual wandering of fantasy, a generalised tension that was in no particular need of resolution. Teleological drive is negated, so that, although it seems to mimic a sonata narrative, the tale becomes a shaggy dog story.

But if the sonata is undone here, so too is the fantasia. Interruptions are short and contained, and digressions are instantly identifiable as temporary and parenthetical. The freedoms of the fantasia are curbed in a sonata-style continuity which incorporates the locally fragmented

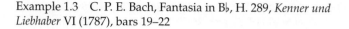

Example 1.3   C. P. E. Bach, Fantasia in B♭, H. 289, *Kenner und Liebhaber* VI (1787), bars 19–22

and capricious thematic materal into a relatively linear structure. Take, for example, the treatment of the most conspicuous digression in the piece, where, at bar 21, after a two-bar *cantabile* fragment in E♭, the texture is ruptured and instrumental recitative breaks out unconstrained by metre and in a strange key (G♭ major, coloured by its relative minor, over a diminished triad on F; example 1.3); this is a moment of pure fantasy, a sudden relinquishing of control in favour of an overflow of passion, the instantaneous expression of a fleeting idea. But is it? The seemingly improvisatory passage not only returns in the 'recapitulation', but is incorporated into the ordered harmonic trajectory of the piece; transposed down a fourth to D♭ major (the relative major of the tonic parallel minor) it leads logically to the untransposed passage that follows (bars 86–7), which now provides the tonic resolution to the concluding half-cadence of the recitative (example 1.4). Even the chaotic interruption is legitimised, as it takes on a conventional and controlled thematic significance – it can no longer be interpreted as evanescent or improvisatory.[31]

In its overt exploration of generic ambiguity, C. P. E. Bach's B♭ fantasia exemplifies in heightened terms one of the principal preoccupations of the picturesque. For the picturesque is predicated on the ambiguous placement and concealment of boundaries, the veiled articulation of the distinction between inside and out that sets up a continual tension

---

[31] Peter Schleuning hears the recitative itself as a quote from the E major polonaise of Wilhelm Friedemann Bach (Fk 12/7, 1765) and suggests that this B♭ major fantasy may have been intended as a memorial for C. P. E. Bach's elder brother, who had died two years before its publication; he suggests also that the C minor fantasy of the *Versuch* (1753) may have reflected on the death of J. S. Bach. See Schleuning, *Freie Fantasie*, 250.

Example 1.4   C. P. E. Bach, Fantasia in B♭, H. 289, *Kenner und Liebhaber* VI (1787), bars 84–7

between formal order and its dissolution. Uvedale Price asserted that the fundamental distinction between the sublime and the picturesque lay in their opposed relationship to borders and margins: where the sublime is grand and infinite, the picturesque (which may indeed be grand) contains and controls the sublime, framing it in a picture, commodifying it as an object of touristic appreciation, enclosing it in a landscape garden. 'Infinity', Price writes,

is one of the most efficient causes of the sublime; the boundless ocean, for that reason, inspires awful sensations: to give it picturesqueness you must destroy that cause of its sublimity; for it is on the shape and disposition of boundaries that the picturesque in great measure must depend.[32]

The quintessential emblem of its unstable borders is the ha-ha, the sunken ditch that enabled the natural landscape outside a park to be incorporated into the effect of the garden. The ha-ha owed its curious name, in popular early eighteenth-century French and English tradition, to the 'astonishment of the visitor/spectator on coming suddenly upon it',[33] an 'Ah!Ah!' moment that contained within it the humour of pleasantly frustrated expectation – a 'Ha-Ha' moment. As you stand at the edge of the ha-ha, the ditch falls away sheer on the inside (the observer's side) but slopes gently on the far side, providing an impassable and, from a distance, invisible barrier between the cultivated area within and the wild one outside. Unwanted intruders (both human and animal) can be kept out (or, as Jane Austen hinted, unwilling members

---

[32] Price, *Essay* (1794), 77.

[33] Antoine Joseph Dézallier D'Argenville, *The Theory and Practice of Gardening*, trans. John James (London, 1712) from *La Théorie et la pratique du jardinage* (Paris, 1709), in *The Genius of the Place: The English Landscape Garden 1620–1820*, ed. John Dixon Hunt and Peter Willis (London: Paul Elek, 1975), 130.

of the household kept in),[34] and the formal boundaries of the property set and marked without any obvious imposition of form. Thanks to the illusory lack of division between the enclosed and the wild, the strict and the free, the 'artful confusion' of the 'natural' garden can be made to blend seamlessly with the truly natural landscape, the internal and the external imperceptibly joined. The ha-ha allows the visitor to the landscaped park a sense of freedom to go where she will; it creates an enclosed form without imposing a sense of closure. Of a walk in Lord Hamilton's park at Painshill, Uvedale Price explained how he was 'highly pleased with it' for its apparent naturalness,

not from what *had*, but from what had *not* been done to it; it had no edges, no borders, no distinct lines of separation; nothing was done except keeping the ground properly neat, and the communication free of obstruction; the eye and the footsteps were equally unconfined.[35]

Yet the freedom of the English landscape garden was, like that of many 'free' fantasias, an artfully constructed illusion – and could be insidiously deceptive. Humphry Repton noted that 'where the ground is subdivided by sunk fences, imaginary freedom is dearly purchased at the expense of actual confinement'.[36] The picturesque, like Bach's B♭ fantasia, relies on confinement, on a sophisticated awareness of form, while proffering the ideal of unlimited freedom.[37]

The picturesque garden, with its all-important perspectives, mediates between the private experience and the public space and draws attention to the act of viewing, the position in nature of the subject, and the subjective response which negotiates between the interiority of private feeling

---

[34] See Jane Austen, *Mansfield Park* (London, 1814), and the introduction by Tony Tanner to the Penguin edition (Harmondsworth, 1966), 24–6. See also Russell, 'On "Looking over a Ha-Ha"', 28.   [35] Price, *Essay* (1794), 276–7.

[36] Humphry Repton, *An Enquiry into the Changes of Taste in Landscape Gardening* (London, 1806), 171.

[37] Despite the subtlety of its effects, the boundary provided by the ha-ha is firmly present. In an essay on what might be termed the musical ha-ha, Tilden Russell has suggested that the theme of freedom versus restraint in the landscape garden, epitomised by the ha-ha, provides an intriguing parallel to those late eighteenth- and early nineteenth-century musical works in which 'the centrifugal force of directionality confronts the centripetal force of containment'. Russell discusses dance movements with deliberately ambiguous patterns of repetition, but the comparison can as easily, and perhaps better, be made with more fantastical music, which, like the picturesque garden, confronts the dialectic between art and nature, freedom and constraint, both in the tension between underlying order and surface disorder, and in a more overt, humorous-ironic confrontation with form itself. On the paradoxical and contradictory nature of the picturesque's freedoms see especially Simon Pugh, *Garden, Nature, Language* (Manchester: Manchester University Press, 1988) and his 'Received Ideas on Pastoral', in *The Architecture of Western Gardens: A Design History from the Renaissance to the Present Day*, ed. Monique Mosser and Georges Teyssot (Cambridge, MA: MIT Press, 1991), 253–60.

and the reality of the exterior world. In so doing it introduces aesthetic distance and potential ironic critique. Just as the picturesque's attention to the processes of maturation and decay paradoxically intimates temporal distance, so its safe representation of the natural for the pleasure of the viewer establishes a critical distance. Indeed, the picturesque has been theorised as the crucial contributor to the formulation of ideas of aesthetic distance in the late eighteenth century. Devotees of this aesthetic admired the fragmented outlines and chiaroscuro of ragged beggars and broken-down hovels in dehumanised landscapes, as the practical and useful garden was replaced by one that imitates nearly uninhabitable wild nature; in its disinterestedness and distance, the picturesque played an important role in separating the aesthetic from the moral.[38] 'The autonomous aesthetic of spectatorhood and distance', writes one recent critic,

leads to theories of aesthetic expression that replace the dominant 18th-century theories of imitation. In addition to introducing distance and detachment, both physically and emotionally, the picturesque provides a way to identify expressive qualities in nature.[39]

The picturesque tension created by the ghostly form underlying surface discontinuities which predominates in Bach's B♭ fantasia performs an ironical commentary on the formal process. In music, a picturesque 'hesitation' between genres actively engages the listener in making choices; unable to rely on the imperatives of form against which to measure expectation, the listener is instead subject to the whim of the composer/performer, forced into high consciousness of the process of utterance and reception. One of the central themes of my study is the way in which, in its picturesque dialectic between freedom and constraint, its disguised connections and hidden lines of demarcation, the musical fantastic draws attention to the act of interpretation, of reading itself, and threatens to undermine, and render impossible, the naive engagement of sensibility; the humorous-ironic mode of late eighteenth-century instrumental music draws attention to the artifice of the work encouraging a free critique of the act of listening – as in musical jokes which catch the listener out – but also of the act of composing.

In his *Essay on Modern Gardening* (1770), Horace Walpole remarked that the principal imitators of the English landscape garden would be the

---

[38] Critics of the picturesque condemned it for what was seen as a dangerous and irresponsible immorality, aestheticising beggars, bandits and cripples, the disfigured and extremely poor. See Ann Bermingham, *Landscape and Ideology: The English Rustic Tradition, 1740–1850* (Berkeley: University of California Press, 1986); John Barrell, *The Dark Side of the Landscape: The Rural Poor in English Painting, 1730–1840* (Cambridge: Cambridge University Press, 1980), and Copley and Garside, eds., *The Politics of the Picturesque*.   [39] Townsend, 'The Picturesque', 372.

'small princes of Germany'. In the 1760s and 1770s many German aristocrats travelled to England, returning home to 'improve' their own parks in the English style, especially in the North where the connections with the ducal House of Hanover (the English royal family) were especially strong. The first and best known of such parks in Germany was that started at Wörlitz in 1764 by the young Prince von Anhalt-Dessau; the garden was begun after a long English tour in the company of the architect von Erdmannsdorff and the prince's head gardener, Eyserbeck, and the work pushed forward with new energy after a tour by the prince to Italy in 1765–7 in the company of Erdmannsdorff and the English writer Laurence Sterne.[40] The park at Wörlitz, open to exploration by boat or by foot, was organised as a dramatic succession of scenes, arranged for maximum contrast and variety; Italian landscapes alternated with English grottoes, evocations of the German Middle Ages, dreamy lakes, and mysterious groves. Densely equipped with temples, monuments and buildings covered with inscriptions, the park was designed to be, quite literally, read. As the visitor to the landscape garden is immersed in its entangled plan the conspicuous presence in it not just of artfully constructed views, but also of objects such as temples, monuments and ruins replete with texts of various sorts, inspires pleasurable reflection that is simultaneously that of introspection and of interpretation.

Journeys made through landscape gardens such as these were both literal and literary. Many parks were open to visitors; they offered the experience of a sentimental and affective wander through varied landscape, an escape from the everyday and a retreat into nature neatly packaged where feeling could be examined in solitude; but this was equally an experience to be gleaned from novels (such as Rousseau's *La Nouvelle Héloise* and, later, Goethe's *Die Wahlverwandschaften*), guide books and extensive published descriptions of gardens. The literature on gardens in the second half of the eighteenth century was plentiful, not just in England but also in Germany, where many English texts circulated in translation, amplified by and summarised in the magisterial *Theorie der Gartenkunst* (1779–85) of Christian Cay Lorenz Hirschfeld.[41] Hirschfeld's

---

[40] On the art of the landscape garden in eighteenth-century German-speaking lands see Alfred Hoffmann, *Der Landschaftsgarten* (Hamburg: Broschek, 1963); Adrian von Buttlar, *Der Landschaftsgarten: Gartenkunst des Klassizismus und der Romantik* (Cologne: DuMont, 1989); Siegmar Gerndt, *Idealisierte Natur: Die literarische Kontroverse um den Landschaftsgarten des 18. und frühen 19. Jahrhunderts in Deutschland* (Stuttgart: J. B. Metzler, 1981); and Géza Hajós, *Romantische Gärten der Aufklärung: Englische Landschaftskultur des 18. Jahrhunderts in und um Wien* (Vienna and Cologne: Böhlau, 1989).

[41] Important English texts on gardens and gardening translated into German included Henry Home, Lord Kames' *Elements of Criticism* (Edinburgh, 1762, trans. Leipzig, 1771), Thomas Whately's *Observations on Modern Gardening* (Dublin, 1770, trans. Leipzig, 1771), William Chambers, *A Dissertation on Oriental Gardening* (London, 1772, trans.

Figure 1.7   Reading alone among ruins in a garden, C. C. L.
Hirschfeld, *Theorie der Gartenkunst*, vol. III (1780)

Theorie, like similar English works, combines aesthetic theory and practical advice with literary aspiration and it was a favourite of the German reading public, who praised it as much for its fine descriptions of nature and elegant prose as for its elaborate investigation into garden art and its theory. Indeed, as a work of literature, Hirschfeld's *Theorie* effected a mapping of the experience of the garden onto that of reading itself; his aim, he claimed, was for the reader of his book to be able 'to step into an enchanted maze, without losing [the] way', as if in an ideal picturesque garden.[42] While private reading, like the private music making I will discuss in chapter 5, offered an escape from society, even a temporary imaginary flight from the confines of domestic space (for novel-reading women in particular), to read literary evocations of gardens was doubly pleasurable. In fact, the picturesque garden itself offered the perfect site for solitary reading (see figure 1.7), and might even incorporate into itself an actual library, disguised perhaps as a thatched hut or log

Footnote 41 *(cont.)*

    Gotha, 1775), William Mason, *The English Garden* (London, 1772–81, trans. Leipzig, 1779–83), Joseph Heely, *Letters on the Beauties of Hagley, Enville and the Leasowes. . .* (London, 1777, trans. Leipzig, 1779). Walpole's *Essay On Modern Gardening* (1770) was first translated by Hirschfeld in his *Taschenbuch für Gartenfreunde* (Braunschweig, 1789).

[42] 'in einem zauberischen Irrgarten zu treten, ohne sich zu verirren' (I, 80). See Linda Parshall, 'C. C. L. Hirschfeld's Concept of the Garden in the German Enlightenment', *Journal of Garden History* 13/3 (1993), 125–71.

cabin.[43] I take up this theme of solitude, sentiment and irony in chapter 5, for as Nature framed within the garden was yet further enclosed by text in Hirschfeld's *Theorie*, and in the landscape gardens he described and proposed as the locus for solitary communing with nature, such gardens merged passionate engagement with ironical distance.

The extent to which German landscapes had been colonised by English ideals is illustrated by the fact that already in the 1770s 'over-Englished' parks could represent icons of exaggerated sensibility. Gardens that encompassed excessive artifice within a supposedly natural frame provided extravagant stage-settings for the emotions, such as that satirised in Goethe's *Triumph der Empfindsamkeit* (1778) where a large section of Hell, ironically called 'Paradise', is revealed to be an extreme version of an English-style park, staffed with obelisks, temples, grottoes, pagodas, graves and ruins.[44] Goethe's comedy was anticipated by Justus Möser's satire of 1768–9, 'Das englische Gärtgen', in which a fanatically anglophile German couple transform grandmother's vegetable garden into a grotesque miniature version of an anglo-chinese landscape garden (a 'garden of scenes'). The fictive writer of the account, Anglomania Domen (Cathedralia), describes in a letter to her grandmother the 'improvements' underway: the cabbage patch has become a 'Shrubbery, or as others call it, an English thicket' ('oder wie andre sprechen, ein englisches Boßkett'). A small hill has been constructed, upon which

one sits under a Chinese canopy, over which there is a sun-shade of gilded metal. A Chinese bridge will soon come to lie close by, for which my husband has got the newest design from England, and which is ready to be put in place. On the other side of the bridge, just there where, grandmama, your bleaching shed was, there is going to be a darling little gothic cathedral, since my husband is called Gothick Cathedral. I gather that he got the idea from the garden at Stowe, in which Lord Temple has constructed so many temples. The cathedral will indeed not be much larger than the sentry-box in which Uncle Toby commanded the sieges in his garden with Corporal Trim (but of course, you won't understand this, you haven't read Tristram Shandy). But the gothic work in it will indeed attract the eye of the curious, and above it will be placed a fetish. In short, your fine garden, grandmama, now seems like an enchanted island, in which one finds everything which one does not seek there, and in which what one seeks, one does not find . . . we are going to travel to Schevelingen before the winter, to see the English garden . . . From Schevelingen we are perhaps going to England, and then on to China. . . [45]

---

[43] Parshall, 'Hirschfeld's Concept of the Garden', 134.

[44] See Gerndt, *Idealisierte Natur*, 85–8.

[45] Justus Möser, 'Das englische Gärtgen', *Patriotische Phantasien* II (1775), in *Sämtliche Werke: Historisch-kritische Ausgabe*, ed. Ludwig Schirmeyer and Werner Kohlschmidt, 14 vols. (Oldenburg: Gerhard Stalling Verlag, 1944), V, 281–3. Cited in Hoffmann, *Der Landschaftsgarten*, 66–7. See also Willy Richard Berger, *China-Bild und China-Mode im Europa der Aufklärung* (Cologne: Böhlau, 1990), especially 245–9.

Criticising profuse ornament, social pretension and adulation of all things English, including fashionable reference to Sterne's *Tristram Shandy*, Möser's attack on the slavish imitation of the 'Anglo-Chinese' garden by the North German bourgeoisie is an indication of the enormous influence of the new art of *Gartenkunst* on contemporary culture, as well as that art's rootedness, like the musical fantasia, in the cult of sensibility, and its tendency to excess.

In 1778 the Berlin artist (and acquaintance of C. P. E. Bach) Daniel Chodowiecki conjoined sensibility and landscape, depicting the appreciation of nature as the quintessential opportunity for the expression of sentiment in a set of engravings representing the opposition between 'Natural and Affected Conduct' (see figures 1.8a–c).[46] In matters ranging from comporting oneself well in bad weather and looking good on a horse to more general behaviour in the display of taste (*Geschmack*), connoisseurship (*Kunstkenntnis*), and the all-important sentiment (*Empfindung*), the series proposes an ideal of naturalness over the contortions of artifical decorum. Here good taste is acted out against a backdrop of natural *Gartenkunst*, the opposition between Nature and Artifice epitomised by the contrast between a stiff and overdressed *ancien régime* couple strutting along the allées of a French-style garden, and a modest modern pair, wandering through an English-style landscape. Not only is good taste subtly underscored in this series of engravings by a preference for natural gardens, but Sentiment itself, the sensitivity and sensibility upon which honest, "natural" conduct is predicated, is epitomised by the act of viewing nature. In the vignette representing *Empfindung* the affected couple contort themselves with loud enthusiasm for the scene before them, while their more tasteful counterparts allow themselves to be quietly filled with emotion as they observe a sweeping vista flooded by the light of the setting sun. But as if irony were inherent in the project of sensibility itself, Chodowiecki cheekily undermines the very "Natural" that he proposes as an ideal: in his opening vignette, courtly artifice is opposed not to the humble decorum of the modestly-dressed, but instead to a subtle excess of display, as a latter-day Adam and Eve exhibit their half-covered bodies (breasts exposed) to the viewer's gaze; it is as if the artist were offering, perhaps inadvertently, yet another weird version of the many-breasted nature goddess herself.

In bringing together the fantastic imaginary of late eighteenth-

---

[46] On 22 September 1781, Chodowiecki wrote 'In eight or ten days' time I am thinking of riding to Hamburg, in order to visit Meyer, Klopstock, Amus and Bach'. Cited in Hans Gunter Ottenberg, *C. P. E. Bach*, trans. Philip J. Whitmore (Oxford: Oxford University Press, 1987), 148.

century instrumental music and the aesthetics of the landscape garden, I take as my backdrop contemporary attitudes towards the representation and commodification of nature; merging the virtual realm of the imagination with the visual and musical, I explore the conjunction of ideas and themes that constitutes the picturesque in music and its critical literature in the eighteenth and early nineteenth centuries. In chapters 2 and 3 I investigate the ways in which C. P. E. Bach's musical fantasy was framed in terms of English landscape gardens in contemporary German critique, reading these approaches against theories of genius, landscape sketching, fantasy machines and imaginary cloudscapes. Instrumental music in this context was understood to call for imaginative interpretation predicated on an active listening practice, one that celebrates the ambiguity, even irony, inherent in fantasia and instrumental music. I take up the notion of the picturesque as a humorous mode in chapter 4, arguing that its articulation as the 'ornamental style' in London in the 1790s was founded on the music of Haydn and C. P. E. Bach, and the parallel literary practice of Laurence Sterne's sentimental novels; in return, the picturesque carried important implications for the conception of the comic in contemporary German writing on music. The humorous in this sense is not necessarily a public or extroverted discourse, and in chapter 5 I explore the notion of sensibility as an inward expression of the picturesque mode; here, I draw parallels between domestic music-making on the most intimate of instruments, the clavichord, and the wanderings of the solitary figure in the landscape amongst the ruins of sentiment. Finally, in chapter 6 I trace the echoes of Bach's fantasy practice in early nineteenth-century Beethoven criticism, as the uncanny return of the picturesque garden refocusses attention on the figure of the veiled Isis, and the invention of self in early nineteenth-century reception of Beethoven's fantasy.

The fantasia as a genre exploits ellipsis and digression, and any inquiry into its aesthetic necessarily encounters ambiguities and complex connections between diverse elements; my account of the musical picturesque takes for its inspiration Sterne's *Tristram Shandy*, which provides a suggestive literary analogue for the musical fantastic: 'I defy the best cabbage planter that ever existed to go on coolly, critically, and canonically, planting his cabbages one by one, without ever and anon straddling out, or sidling into some bastardly digression.'[47] Sterne's narrative is so stretched and baggy with digression that the connecting thread only just manages to tell a coherent story; while I aim

[47] Laurence Sterne, *The Life and Opinions of Tristram Shandy, Gentleman*, 9 vols. (London: R. & J. Dodsley, 1760–7), VIII (1765), chapter 1, p. 2.

(c)

Geschmack
Gout

Geschmack
Gout

Figure 1.8a–c   Daniel Chodowiecki, 'Natürliche und affectierte
Handlungen des Lebens', second series (1778), plates 1-6

to lay my cabbages out in a 'tolerable straight line' instead of the elaborate arabesques of Sterne's tale, this project's juxtaposition of music
with the picturesque situates itself, like Tristram Shandy's errant
adventures, in that 'clear climate of fantasy and perspiration'[48] which
might just permit a cabbage planter the odd erratic loop and fantastic
curlicue.

[48] Ibid. See vol. VI (1762), chapter 40, pp. 152–3 for Sterne's disquisition on the loopy
course of his narrative.

2

C. P. E. Bach and the landscapes of genius

The picturesque eye ranges after nature untamed by art, and
bursting wildly into all its available forms.

William Gilpin, *Observations on the Mountains and
Lakes of Cumberland and Westmoreland* (1786)

With him order always seems disordered, and disorder carries with it
a surprising regularity.   Longinus, *On the Sublime*, trans. W. Smith (1752)

I

In 1783 C. P. E. Bach's fourth collection of keyboard music for *Kenner und
Liebhaber* was published by Breitkopf in Leipzig. The subscribers
included a collection of wealthy amateurs, high-minded critics and professional musicians, among them Sarah Itzig in Berlin, Baron von
Grotthuß in Courland, Johann Nikolaus Forkel in Göttingen, Carl
Friedrich Cramer in Kiel, Charles Burney in London, Kapellmeister
Ernst Wilhelm Wolf in Weimar, the publisher Artaria and Baron van
Swieten in Vienna. For the first time in the *Kenner und Liebhaber* series,
this volume contained two free fantasias in addition to sonatas and
rondos, a novelty that not only caught the attention of the critics, but
seems to have been considered by Bach as a particular selling point for
the volume: the notice placed in the *Hamburgischer unpartheyischer
Correspondent* on 15 October 1782 opened with the announcement that
'Our Herr Capellmeister Bach has composed some new free fantasias,
and after much urging from various friends of music, who have heard
these masterpieces, he has decided to add a pair of them to his fourth
collection for *Kenner und Liebhaber.*'[1] A year later, a review in the same
paper predicted that the fantasies would be 'eagerly taken up and
studied' by expert and non-expert alike; they offered a glimpse of that
fabulous art for which Bach was so renowned, giving an idea of the way
in which 'the great man' manages to transport his listeners 'to general
wonder' in his improvisations; finally, these pieces offered proof of 'the

---

[1] In Ernst Suchalla, ed., *Carl Philipp Emanuel Bach: Briefe und Dokumente, Kritische
Gesamtausgabe*, 2 vols. (Göttingen: Vandenhoeck & Ruprecht, 1994), II, 941.

creative genius of the composer, who alone, with his knowledge of harmony, supported by the liveliest imagination, could produce such masterpieces'.[2] And yet Bach had been unsure of the market for such music. Writing to Forkel in February 1775 he had explained that he was unenthusiastic about the publication of fantasias, for 'how many are there who love, understand, and play that sort of thing well?'[3] By the early 1780s his attitude had softened, though he still found it necessary to justify to Breitkopf the admission of fantasias into his latest collection, writing in October 1782 that 'My friends insisted on having two fantasias included, so that after my death one could see what a Fantasist I was [welche Fantast ich war].'[4]

Bach was stating the obvious when he admitted that his fantasias were not to everyone's taste. For his critics they were the source of all that was difficult, strange and overly artificial in the famous Bach style, epitomising a dubious predilection for the bizarre. When the Mannheim Kapellmeister Georg Joseph Vogler published a critique of Bach under the guise of a comparison between Bach and Alberti, he focussed on an affected disorder that resulted from a mistaken effort at originality:

Maestro, your taste is incorrect: you love forced artificiality, you wish to be learned, and forget the simple; conspicuous in all your works is the anxious quest to say something entirely unique, entirely new, completely different from anything ever said before; you distance yourself too far from the well-planned.[5]

Pairing Bach with Scarlatti, whose music was also contrived, involved, 'full of difficult modulations, of bizarre, complex, raving fantasias and furious fugues', Vogler's diagnosis for the undue artificiality of Bach's style was that the composer was indeed a recalcitrant 'Fantast', a deluded artist who had misjudged the limits of fantasy, for 'between simplicity and matter-of-factness, variety and confusion, between a high flight, original brushstrokes and fantasy, caricature, bizarre nonsense, ie:, between musical imagination [musikalischer Fantasie] and a high fever, there is a world of difference'.[6]

Even Burney commented that 'it must be owned, that the style of this author is so uncommon, that a little habit is necessary for the enjoyment of it . . . Complaints have been made against his pieces, for being long,

[2] *Hamburgischer unpartheyischer Correspondent*, 19 September 1783. In Suchalla, ed., *Bach: Briefe*, II, 978.

[3] C. P. E. Bach to Forkel (10 February 1775); in Suchalla, ed., *Bach: Briefe*, II, 486. Translation from Stephen L. Clark, *The Letters of C. P. E. Bach* (Oxford: Clarendon Press, 1997), 77.

[4] C. P. E. Bach to Breitkopf (15 October 1782); in Suchalla, ed., *Bach: Briefe*, II, 939. Translation based on Clark, *Letters*, 187.

[5] G. J. Vogler, 'Eingeschickte Frage. Wie verhalten sich die zwei großen Clavierspieler C. P. E. Bach und Alberti von Rom gegen einander?' *Betrachtungen der Mannheimer Tonschule*, 4 vols. (Mannheim, 1780; reprint edn. Hildesheim: Olms, 1974), III, 153.

[6] Vogler, *Betrachtungen*, 158, 156.

difficult, fantastic and far-fetched.'[7] For Vogler and others, if Bach's style was bizarre, the problem lay in an over-indulgence in the fantastic. The eccentric Bach admirer C. F. D. Schubart reported that 'what people complain of in [Bach's] pieces is capricious taste, frequently also bizarreness, affected difficulty, obsessively idiosyncratic notation . . . and an unyielding resistance to fashionable taste'.[8] With its mercurial temperament, the bizarre functioned negatively as a sign for the problematic quick-changing affective contrasts of modern instrumental music. In his *Musikalisches Lexicon* (1802) Heinrich Christoph Koch defined *Bizarria* as 'a kind of *fantasia* in which the player abandons himself to his own mood',[9] while John Hoyle's *Complete Dictionary of Music* (London, 1791) fixated on variety of affect in a definition of *Bizarro* as 'a fanciful kind of composition, sometimes strong, slow, soft, fast, etc. according to the fancy of the composer';[10] likewise, in an essay published in 1803, J. K. D. P. Reimold alluded to a notion of the bizarre in the visual arts – 'marked and violent colour contrasts', 'sharp juxtapositions' for which no attempt is made to blend, and in which differences are made to stand out more starkly than usual – to locate the musical bizarre in 'random groups of notes', the work of 'musical hacks' who,

lacking the ability to select, or even to join together contrasting ideas by means of unifying transitional passages . . . create a patchwork jacket for a musical dandy from totally unrelated scraps: heat and cold, height and depth, joy and sorrow, all are thrown together, provided that the time-signature fits.[11]

Perhaps the most pressing problem of the fantastic style was its deliberate caprice, its extreme changes of affect, its failure to order emotions and their discourse; whether or not it represented 'hack-work', it failed to conform to the conventional parameters expected of the lasting work of art. For Johann Nikolaus Forkel music must avoid random changes of affect, striving for unity and coherence rather than sudden transitions between extremes; 'without order and a suitable sequence, or gradual progress in our emotions', he writes, 'no real artistic expression is possible'. Instrumental music that eschews such control risks degenerating

---

[7] Charles Burney, *The Present State of Music in Germany, the Netherlands and United Provinces*, 2nd edn, 2 vols. (London, 1775; reprint edn., New York: Broude Bros., 1969), II, 266.

[8] C. F. D. Schubart, *Ideen zu einer Ästhetik der Tonkunst*, ed. Ludwig Schubart (Vienna: Degen, 1806, written 1784–85; reprint edn, Hildesheim: Olms, 1973), 179.

[9] Heinrich Christoph Koch, *Musikalisches Lexicon* (Offenbach am Main, 1802), col. 259, s.v. 'Bizarrerie'.

[10] John Hoyle, *Complete Dictionary of Music* (London, 1791; reprint edn, Geneva: Minkoff, 1976), 12.

[11] J. K. D. P. Reimold, 'Etwas über den Grundsatz der schönen Künste', *Apollon* 1/7 (Penig, 1803), 17–25; in Peter le Huray and James Day, eds., *Music and Aesthetics in the Eighteenth and Early Nineteenth Centuries* (Cambridge: Cambridge University Press, 1981), 283.

into empty nonsense, though it might, at best, manage the recognisable effects of the fantasia: 'Without it our impassioned depictions become ecstatic visions [Schwärmereyen], mostly without meaning or power, and only very rarely somewhat tolerable fantasias.'[12]

That Forkel should grudgingly admit the possibility of at least 'tolerable' fantasias, notwithstanding his admiration for J. S. Bach's Chromatic Fantasy (BWV 903),[13] is an indication of the status of the genre, for to dismiss it outright would be too reactionary in the contemporary climate; it is not that the conservative critic advocates the admission of only one affect in a piece of music – for in this same essay he celebrates the natural diversity and contrast inherent in human emotions, their changeability and irregularity[14] – but a certain order, or plausible sequence must prevail in their artistic representation, and such coherence is, in his view, definitively anathema to musical fantasias. In Forkel's theory the fantasia lurks on the margins of rational communication in music, a kind of shadowy double, or mysteriously unstable alter ego, the accidental by-product of a failed sonata. If the sonata should present an impassioned but logical sequence of emotions, it is the failure of that attempt at order that engenders fantasias. The sonata, he declares, is like the poetic ode, for in both impassioned creativity has been controlled and curbed by art; both consist of passionate ideas expressed in a 'suitable' order, and in both the artist is prevented from wandering off the straight path into random digressions – the random digressions that constitute fantasias:

A sequence of most animated ideas, which follow each other after the principles of an inspired imagination, is an ode. Just such a sequence of lively, expressive musical ideas, when they follow one another as prescribed by a musically inspired imagination, is a sonata in music. Indeed, inspiration alone cannot produce this musical Ode (Sonata). Especially with moderate affects [inspiration] would be an unsuitable leader, without the guide of art, that is, without a

---

[12] J. N. Forkel, 'Ueber eine Sonate aus Carl Philipp Emanuel Bachs dritter Sonaten-sammlung für Kenner und Liebhaber, in F moll . . . Ein Sendschreiben an Hrn. von ***', in Forkel, *Musikalischer Almanach für Deutschland* (1784), 21.

[13] Hans T. David and Arthur Mendel, eds., *The New Bach Reader: A Life of Johann Sebastian Bach in Letters and Documents*, revised and enlarged by Christoph Wolff (New York: Norton, 1998), 468.

[14] Forkel writes 'When one observes that in Nature everything is subject to a perpetual fluctuation, everything gradually emerges, fades away, and likewise emerges again, the aesthetician can easily come to the conclusion that the sentiments, just like physical things, are subject to this inevitable course of Nature. From that follows the principle of diversity in the depiction of our emotions.' Forkel, *Musikalischer Almanach* (1784), 31–2. Cited in Bellamy Hosler, *Changing Aesthetic Views of Instrumental Music in 18th-Century Germany* (Ann Arbor, MI: UMI Research Press, 1981), 180; Hosler points to this as one of the most forward-looking aspects of Forkel's aesthetic theory, and notes its importance for the changing status of instrumental music in Germany in the eighteenth century. See Hosler, ibid., 177–87.

suitable sequence and order of emotions. It would lead the composer, like the poet, off the track, permit visions [Schwärmereyen], it would connect emotions which bear too little relation to each other, and it would generally perhaps produce beautiful musical fantasias or poetic rhapsodies, but no sonatas or odes.[15]

The fantasia, although it may by accident be successful, is of secondary value, probably without much meaning and certainly not the highest form of art.

Far from accepting the potentially thrilling power of the fantasia's penchant for the seemingly random, Forkel cites Lessing's famous strictures against unmotivated juxtapositions of affect in music, published more than a decade earlier in the twenty-seventh section of the *Hamburgische Dramaturgie:*

'He who wishes to speak to our hearts and to awaken sympathetic stirrings in them, must just as well observe coherence, as one who thinks to entertain and instruct our reason. Without coherence, without the innermost connection of each and every part, the best music is a flimsy sandheap, which is capable of making no lasting impression; only a proper connection makes it into firm marble on which the hand of the artist can immortalize itself.'[16]

Forkel, via Lessing, asserts that clarity in the representation of emotion is essential if music is to move or persuade – and it is persuasion that forms the basis for music's lasting status as art; indeed, Lessing had claimed that while poetry or drama might make sense of sudden changes and strange mixtures of affect, such goings-on in instrumental music could only ever appear unmotivated and incoherent: perhaps superficially interesting, even amusing, but never able truly to touch the heart of the listener. By the 1780s, of course, such notions were receding into a conservative past, and yet they formed the basis for an ongoing debate; both popularists and elitists alike could attack the fantasia for its transgressive nature.

II

But according to devotees of the genre such strictures misrepresented musical fantasies. Writers more sensitive to the genre understood fantasies precisely as musical odes, in which disorder was only a semblance, the disguise of a secret order. J. A. P. Schulz, the Berlin theorist and admirer of C. P. E. Bach, referred to the cogent irregularities of the Pindaric ode when he wrote that 'Just as there is in fact always a secret order tied to the Pindaric disorder, likewise this must be introduced

---

[15] Forkel, 'Ueber eine Sonate', 27.
[16] Ibid., 25. G. E. Lessing, *Hamburgische Dramaturgie*, 2 vols. (Hamburg: s.n., 1769), section 27 (31 July 1767), I, 214.

into melody without metre through the art of the composer.' In setting the irregular metres of the ode to music, he writes, the composer might be forced beyond the accepted procedures of composition – yet would not abandon metrical regularity altogether. Such music would not verge on the senseless, for music without metre would be constructed by interpolating regular metrical patterns such that the disorder would 'never be real disorder but has its foundation in order'. The potential coherence of such rhapsodic musical utterance may be seen, Schulz declares, in 'good fantasias in purely instrumental music, which are comprehensible to every educated ear'.[17] Given the charges of incoherence clinging to Bach's free fantasias this comes as some suprise: indeed, it illuminates the way in which the fantasia's seemingly anarchic tendencies could be understood, like the rhapsodic excesses of ode poetry, to yield not rambling and self-indulgent rhetoric, but high art.

What appeared so irregular in the fantasia, according to contemporary understanding of coherent musical syntax, was its fundamental independence of usual thematic process, harmonic plan or rhythmic structure. The fantasia relied on a variety of thematic ideas rather than the manipulation and development of a single theme (*Hauptsatz*) or a limited number of related ideas.[18] Thus for Türk,

a fantasia is called free when its creator holds neither to a certain main subject (theme) [Haupsatz] nor to metre or rhythm (although for some thoughts a metre could be used), when he expresses various and often contrasting characters, in short, when he follows his whims completely without attempting to work out a specific plan.[19]

Türk characterised the paratactic and digressive fantasia as the antithesis of conventional composition, since it was not formally planned but responded to the mood of the moment. A music of continuous invention rather than elaboration, the fantasia consists of an effusion of ideas, one that is not chaotic, but deliberately fails to follow conventional patterns. Koch summed up half a century of views on the subject in his *Musikalisches Lexicon* (1802), emphasising the freedom from conventional rule that characterised fantasia, its looseness or lack altogether of

---

[17] Quoted by C. F. Cramer, announcement for 'Flora. Eine Sammlung Compositionen für das Clavier und den Gesang . . . ', in Cramer, *Magazin der Musik* 2/2 (22 June 1787), 1361, footnote.

[18] This take on the fantasia is based on Mark Evan Bonds' succinct summary in *Wordless Rhetoric: Musical Form and the Metaphor of the Oration* (Cambridge, MA: Harvard University Press, 1991), 114–16.

[19] D. G. Türk, *Klavierschule, oder, Anweisung zum Klavierspielen für Lehrer und Lernende* (Leipzig, 1789; reprint edn, Kassel: Bärenreiter, 1967), 395. Translation based on that by Raymond H. Haggh, *School of Clavier Playing, or, Instructions in Playing the Clavier for Teachers and Students* (Lincoln: University of Nebraska Press, 1982), 388.

formal order, the freedom of its tonal structure and its potential for endless variety. In the fantasia, he writes,

one binds oneself neither to form nor main key, neither to the adherence to the same metre nor to the retention of a particular character but portrays his sequence of ideas sometimes in truly coherent melodic sections, sometimes more loosely arranged, and sometimes also simply as diversely arpeggiated chords following one another.[20]

According to Heusinger's *Handbuch der Aesthetik* (1797), an 'entirely free fantasia' has 'neither a theme nor an intention', and it 'sometimes surprises artists when its imagination flees the reins of understanding'.[21] Thus even the creator can be spurred to astonish himself, for an element of self-revelation cleaves to the genre at its highest level. Given its lack of structural stereotype the fantasia makes little sense when judged on the same terms as other genres.

C. P. E. Bach's free fantasias revel in unpredictable juxtapositions, presenting as they do a mosaic of discontinuous ideas, and diverse fragmentary figures. Contrast and variety, Bach explained in the *Versuch über die wahre Art das Clavier zu spielen* (1753, 1762), are the principal features of the fantasy, which, in its freedom to carry the listener along in surprising twists and shocking turns, to move abruptly from one affect to another, constitutes the highest form of keyboard art. Bach's theory of fantasy turns on the central role of extravagant harmonic procedures – clever detours, extreme digressions, outlandish modulations. 'A free fantasia', he writes, 'consists of varied harmonic progressions which can be expressed in all manner of figuration and motives'(II, 326). Indeed, 'strange and profuse' modulations constitute the essence of the genre, with the effect of these 'rational deceptions' enhanced by avoided cadences and ellipses, so that the listener is deliberately misled; logical progressions masquerade as surprising and inexplicable digressions (II, 330).

Built into the metaphorical language used to describe this kind of harmonic adventuring is a notion of space, of distance – more specifically, the topography of harmonic experiment is conceived as landscape. Bach gives his reader an up-to-date version of this image in figuring the inventor of the fantasy as a wanderer in a landscape, its harmonic digressions and round-about routes pictured as twisting paths winding across varied scenery:

When one adds to this the harmonic artistry and rare progressions discussed in the preceding chapters, what an endless vista of harmonic variety opens up

---

[20] Koch, *Musikalisches Lexicon* cols. 554–5, s.v. 'Fantasie'.
[21] J. H. G. Heusinger, *Handbuch der Aesthetik*, 2 vols. (Gotha: Justus Perthes, 1797), I, 153. Cited in Bonds, *Wordless Rhetoric*, 117.

before us! Does it still seem difficult to move wherever we will? No, for one need only decide whether to make many detours or none at all. (II, 335)[22]

Not unrelated to the notion of the harmonic labyrinth, the image capitalises on the spatial metaphor underlying modulation itself (close and distant keys); in a similar vein Johann Samuel Petri referred in his *Anleitung zur praktischen Musik* (1782) to bold modulations as 'the secret tricks . . . whereby with one or two chords one can immediately get to the most distant key', tactics which could lead the listener astray, perhaps lose him completely: 'one can make such abrupt transitions through leaping and running figures, in unison in all voices, that the listener himself does not know how he happened to be brought so very quickly into a totally foreign key'.[23]

The skilful use of harmony in the free fantasias of Bach's fifth collection *Für Kenner und Liebhaber* (1785) earned particular praise from Carl Friedrich Cramer, who admired the 'daring, unprecedented, and yet technically correct modulations' and 'great wealth and variety of harmony' in these pieces, figuring the modulations as intricate paths, sometimes furtively creeping along, sometimes boldly leaping great voids:

The connoisseur will indeed be able to see from these fantasias the way in which this composer [accomplishes such modulations], by which particular paths he sometimes slowly steals from one key to another, sometimes as it were vaults across through a *salto mortale*, how he prepares the bold modulations, and changes tempi, as his genius thinks fit for a free fantasia.[24]

Bach was the rare genius who could trade in such volatile musical materials; others experimented at their peril. That this was widely attempted and often resulted in confusion was hinted at in Cramer's criticism of Charles Frederick Horn's *Six Sonatas for the Piano-Forte, or Harpsichord, with an Accompaniment for a Violin and Violoncello* (1786); Horn, Cramer remarks,

seems on the whole to have a certain shortage of ideas; and that seems to be the reason why he loses himself so often in more distant harmonies, in which, as they stand there so baldly, and are stripped of virtually all the charm of a beautifying melody, we do not find the delight excited by a Haydn or a Clementi, etc., when, deviating from the wide highway, they lead us sideways into hidden romantic regions.[25]

[22] C. P. E. Bach, *Versuch über die wahre Art das Clavier zu spielen*, 2 vols. (Berlin: C. F. Henning, 1753, 1762), II, 335.

[23] J. S. Petri, *Anleitung zur praktischen Musik*, revised and enlarged edn (Leipzig, 1782), 269, 281.

[24] Review of 'Claviersonaten und freye Phantasien . . . Fünfte Sammlung', in Cramer, *Magazin der Musik* 2/2 (5 August 1786), 872.

[25] Review of 'Six Sonatas for the Piano-Forte, or Harpsichord, with an Accompanyment for a Violin and Violoncello . . . by Charles Frederick Horn', in Cramer, *Magazin der Musik* 2/2 (24 April 1787), 1283.

Cramer's commentary is saturated with picturesque imagery, both in its reference to digression within landscape, and in its language of concealment and disguise.

Although the fantastical terrain seemed vast, a theorist as able as Bach offered practical advice on exploring it. Bach provided a short example of the basic procedures of the fantasy in the *Versuch* (vol. II, 1762), giving first a figured bass 'sketch', and then a worked-out realisation of the fantasia (see figure 2.1), accompanied by a commentary which takes the reader step by step through the harmonic progressions. For Bach, the surprises of fantasy are grounded in explainable procedures, and his description makes the following points about the diminutive fantasia: (1) at the beginning and the end marks long prolongations on and preparations for the tonic; (2) indicates a modulation to the dominant, A 'on which the performer remains for some time' until at (x) a $\sharp$6 chord (F$\sharp$–A–D$\sharp$) on F$\sharp$ and then a dominant seventh on B, indicate a move towards E minor; what follows, however, is a 6-4-2 chord on B$\flat$ at (3), and Bach describes this moment, the basic pivot device used in the fantasies and the prime source of their harmonic surprise, as an ellipsis (*eine Ellipsin*), for there are no common elements between the two chords. Crucially, theorising such ellipses itself required imaginative interpretation: in this instance Bach suggests two likely possibilities for the absent intervening chord – an E minor (6-4) chord or a C major chord (deceptive cadence) both of which share common tones with the 6-4-2 on B$\flat$. Another surprise comes at (4), where a dominant seventh on A is succeeded not by a D minor chord, but instead a 6-4-2 on C with an F$\sharp$ at (5); in a further diversion from the expected, a G minor chord is substituted for the anticipated G major at (6), which is followed, Bach states, 'by largely dissonant relationships leading back to the principal tonality, on which the fantasia ends over an organ point'(II, 341).

This neatly explained miniature of rational deception provides a model upon which a student may construct an improvisation; the harmonic 'deceptions', at first hearing surprising, are shown to be grammatical. Indeed, Heinrich Schenker (never one to underestimate the organic unity to be found in the works of geniuses), provided with Bach's own reductive analysis, highlighted the predominance of coherence and order in the piece. In his essay on 'The Art of Improvisation' Schenker commented that 'we see that Bach persists in most precise orderliness even in the diminution of a free fantasia, and he conceals this orderliness purely for the sake of the fantasia under the guise of disorder; it is precisely this which constitutes the inimitable in his art.'[26]

---

[26] Heinrich Schenker, 'The Art of Improvisation', in Sylvan Kalib, 'Thirteen Essays from the Three Yearbooks Das Meisterwerk in der Musik by Heinrich Schenker: An Annotated Translation', 3 vols. in 2 (Ph.D. diss., Northwestern University, 1973), II, 30.

Figure 2.1   Figured bass 'sketch' for a free fantasia, with realisation.
C. P. E. Bach, *Versuch über die wahre Art das Clavier zu spielen*, vol. II
(1762), 341.

Example 2.1   C. P. E. Bach, Fantasia in G minor, H. 225, *Musikalisches Vielerley* (1770)

Example 2.1 (*cont.*)

Schenker's analytical method is directed towards finding a concealed plan, but this is also the point of Bach's exercise here: the piece is an example of the basic structure of the fantasia, which consists of a more or less extended sequence of chords. The example is short, and illustrates Bach's rule that 'when one has little time to display one's abilities in preluding, it is better not to wander into too remote keys, for the performance must soon come to an end' (II, 327).

A longer fantasia in G minor (H. 225), written in 1766 and published in the anthology *Musikalisches Vielerley* (1770), gives a somewhat more adventurous example of the harmonic digressions and deceptions that animate Bach's fantasy style, in a setting that more nearly evokes the musings and effusions of the improvisation, though still not as extended as his full-blown essays in the genre (example 2.1). The piece is primarily an exercise in harmonic action and subtle slippage among remotely related keys – the characteristically oblique yet sophisticated progress of fantasy. The transition away from the stable G minor harmony of the opening three systems is achieved by an enharmonic reinterpretation of the bass note of a 6-4-2 on F as E♯; thus the dominant of C minor is reinterpreted as the dominant of F♯ minor, and leads in turn to B minor; as the bass descends by step a subsequent 6 chord (with F♯) on A prepares the ear for G major harmony, but that expectation is thwarted as the bass slips down a half-step to A♭, and the harmony is redirected towards C minor with a C–B appoggiatura in the context of a diminished seventh chord with A♭ in the bass. In a move typical of the fantasia, the appoggiatura resolves melodically but not harmonically as Bach relies on the A♭ common tone suddenly and surprisingly to displace the expected C minor harmony with A♭ minor. A♭ minor arpeggios lead to a dominant seventh on E♭, followed by a leap up a tritone to a diminished chord on A♮ (a characteristic example of ellipsis), and a turn towards F♯ minor. A chromatic ascent in the bass from C♯ to A♭, encompasses a veiled enharmonic modulation, and the arrival at the dominant of C minor; however, the tonic itself is, perhaps predictably by now, avoided. Finally, a short excursion towards B♭ minor, although here again the dominant is not resolved; this is seemingly remote harmonic territory, but in the world of Bachian fantasy transportation between keys (especially minor ones) a minor third apart is readily provided by the diminished seventh, leading via an enharmonic modulation (G♭ becomes F♯) back to G minor.

This fantasia, in which contrasting and dislocated thematic fragments are dispersed over the wide-ranging harmonic relationships, displays Bach's exploitation of the polymorphous potential of the diminished seventh chord, not only at surprise moments of discontinuity but incorporated into the fundamental structure of the piece. It opens and closes with two long sections in the tonic, but these frame a central oscillation between the subdominant C minor and F♯ minor. These two keys, a tritone apart, are mirror images of one another in the diminished harmony that so characterises Bach's fantasy style. Though they are chromatic and at times disconcertingly adventurous, the harmonic deceptions in the G minor fantasia (a piece published in an anthology for amateurs) are logical and grammatical, easily explained in the manner of Bach's D major sketch in the *Versuch*. They provide a coherent if complex foundation for the elaborate surface disjunctions of the fantastic style. The tension between wildness and control, the rhetoric of shock and bewilderment framed within recherché and highly skilled manipulation of harmony such as this constitute an alternative coherence to that of conventional thematic

Example 2.2   C. P. E. Bach, Fantasia in C minor, H. 75/iii, *18 Probestücke* (1753)

development. Indeed, the melodic surface is deliberately fantastic and fragmentary, veiling, concealing and distorting even the short-term harmonic relations.

The celebrated C minor fantasia (H. 75/iii) published as the last of the *18 Probestücke* that accompanied the first part of the *Versuch* in 1753, epitomises this tendency towards obfuscation. Not far into the piece a minim E♭ in the soprano is held over an arpeggiated diminished triad A♭–D–F; the clashing D is let go in the left hand and the resolution of the A♭ comes late, as the sonority fades. The resulting harmony implies a 6-4-2 chord on A♭ (without the B♭), and thus a move from the key of A♭ to its dominant, but what follows instead is an outlandish hiccup that enables a move to a 6-4 chord on A, an apparent leap away from the expected key of E♭ major into D major (example 2.2). So the diminished chord D–F–A♭ has a potential function as V of E♭, but it is reinterpreted as V/V in D major: the leading note, D♮, instead of rising a semitone to E♭, is reiterated and abruptly recast as a tonic note, leading to a resolution a whole tone lower than the one expected. This resolution too is avoided – the stasis of arrival is a rare luxury in Bach's fantasias, since it deflates the restive harmonic movement which drives the fantasist forward; in the sudden rest and fermata the listener's awareness of the moment is heightened as the composer/performer reinterprets the chord, his attention searching for the harmony that will lead off in surprising directions. The strangeness of the move is exaggerated by the jagged and impulsive reiteration of the hemidemisemiquaver d^2s and by a sudden plunge of two and a half octaves – an impossibly short repetition followed immediately by a portentously held bass note. This note, A, sounded alone, is itself ambiguously isolated until the entry of the tenor voice and ensuing D major arpeggio. After a long passaggio the listener is again brought up short by a deft side-step in which a full A7 chord is cut off abruptly by an apparently unmotivated C♮ in the bass, as if the performer had missed the D and landed one step too low, thoroughly strange-sounding, though grammatical as the seventh of the dominant seventh of G major but without the remaining

Example 2.3   C. P. E. Bach, Fantasia in C minor, H. 75/iii, *18 Probestücke* (1753)

constituents of the harmony (the D major triad) which would clarify the harmonic context. Here, then, is yet another example of inspired, if disconcerting, ellipsis. When the harmonic context does come it is in the form of a rapid D major scale which rushes up to c^3 at the upper end of the keyboard, before resolving the seventh three octaves above its original statement in a slowing descent to a whispered arrival at the new tonic note g^2 (example 2.3).

The C minor fantasia maintains the semblance of freely discursive improvisation within a controlled and ordered structure (it is tripartite, with a central measured section in the relative major). Like H. 225, it combines complex harmonic procedures (ellipses and enharmonic modulations) with confusing and obfuscatory surfaces that maximise the affective contrast. The whole piece is peppered with sudden rests, puncturing silences. Even the score of this piece, a masterpiece of engraving where every articulation, ornament, fingering and dynamic change is specified, highlights the complex and irregular geography of Bach's musical fantasy, giving a visual representation of the wild spontaneities of improvisation (figure 2.2). The choreography of surprise could not be more minutely directed, although of course the score leaves as many questions open as it answers: before one even begins to play one is confronted with the problem of ascertaining the meaning of Allegro moderato without the beat or steady tempo marked out by barlines.

Such music may indeed seem bizarre, difficult, far-fetched and fantastic, yet it is precariously balanced between the coherent and incoherent, the rational and crazed. Each of these fantasias is animated by the tension between apparent chaos and underlying order, between the random juxtaposition of contrasting emotions and their artistic representation. Charles Burney wrote with insight when he claimed that Bach's irrationality was rooted in compositional artifice, that wildness was a carefully crafted semblance rather than true loss of control:

for as to their being *fantastical*, and *far-fetched*, the accusation, if it be just, may be softened by alleging that his boldest strokes, both of melody and modulation, are always consonant to rule, and supported by learning; and that his flights are not the wild ravings of ignorance or madness, but the effusions of cultivated genius.[27]

Bach's irregular, disrupted surfaces are predicated on an underlying formal order and harmonic logic, although the complexity of the immediate musical topography problematises the relation between means and end. The heightened expression of emotion, the illusion of immediacy, is achieved through the use of clever devices that threaten to become an end in themselves as disruption draws the attention of the listener away from the balance between the surface and the substructure; indeed, where the B♭ fantasia, H. 289 overtly problematises form, what matters in the C minor fantasia is less the listener's sense of possible directedness, than the sheer pleasure of disorientation.

The picturesqueness of the fantasia is perhaps epitomised by those two fantasias, in E♭ (H. 277) and A major (H. 278), published in Bach's fourth *Kenner und Liebhaber* collection which attracted so much attention in 1783. Both exploit the harmonic deceptions and complexity theorised thirty years earlier by the composer in the *Versuch*, and at the same time they take to an extreme the thematic discontinuities of the musical fantastic. Yet they strikingly call into question the improvisatory spontaneity of invention associated with the free fantasia. Both the E♭ and the A major fantasias are constructed in the tripartite manner of the earlier C minor fantasia (H. 75), with free, unmeasured outer sections framing slower, measured central sections, both of which are placed in remote tonal relationships to the tonic (A minor in the E♭ fantasy, B♭ major in the A major fantasy). The major portion of both fantasias is thoroughly disjointed, for where the outer sections of the C minor fantasia consist largely of continuous passaggi and instrumental recitative textures, in H. 277 and 278 a succession of fragments, an alternation of seemingly unconnected ideas and quick modulations, predominates. However, not only are these fragments sewn together by subtle voice-leading connections and veiled unifying devices (the descending scale that underlies much of H. 278, for example), but an overarching sense of consistency, of a sort, is achieved by the wholesale reprise after the middle sections in both pieces of the material that came before. The reprise effect is subverted by a disorientating reorganisation of the thematic fragments and their reappearance in strange new keys; nevertheless, the fact of the systematic repetition distinguishes these pieces from utterly spontaneous utterances. As Carl Friedrich Cramer noted approvingly, this is not 'merely fantasy in the wild', for these are artificial, indeed artful,

---

[27] Burney, *Present State*, II, 267.

Figure 2.2   C. P. E. Bach, Free fantasia in C minor, H. 75/iii, *18 Probestücke* (1753)

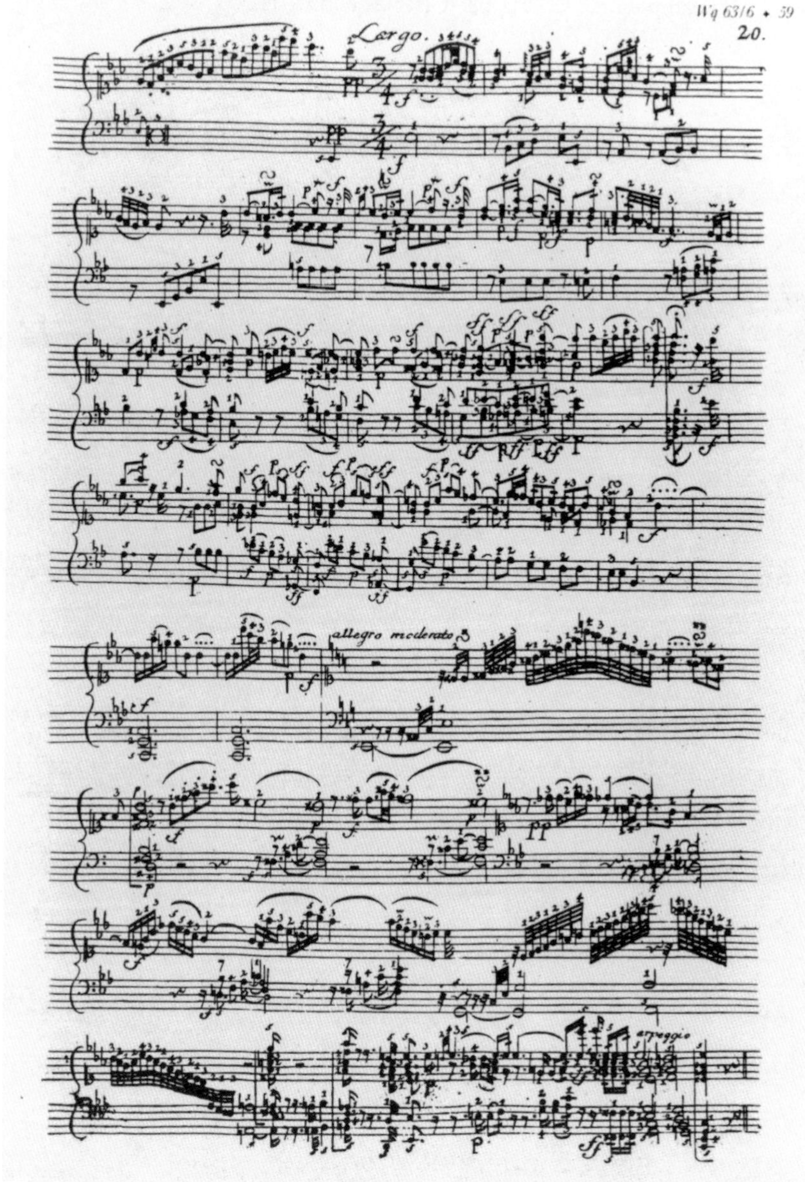
Wq 63/6 + 59
20.
Largo.
allegro moderato
arpeggio

Example 2.4   C. P. E. Bach, Fantasia in E♭, H. 277, *Kenner and Liebhaber* IV (1783)

Example 2.4 (*cont.*)

wildernesses,[28] as an outline of the E♭ fantasy, H. 277 indicates (see also example 2.4):

Allegro	Key areas touched on and departed from
a arpeggios, passaggi	E♭
b semiquaver passagework in octaves	c–b♭
c arioso	b♭–(e♭)
d triplets	B
e free arpeggios	C–G
a arpeggios, passaggi	G–E–a
Poco adagio, 4/4, arioso	a (unstable)
Allegro	
a arpeggios, passaggi	unstable (circle of 5ths)–B♭
c arioso	e♭–(a♭)
d triplets	E
e free arpeggios	E♭ (unstable . . .)
b semiquaver passagework in octaves	g–E♭
a arpeggios, passaggi	E♭ (reprise of opening)

[28] Cramer, review of 'Claviersonaten und freye Phantasien, nebst einigen Rondos fürs Fortepiano, für Kenner und Liebhaber, componirt von Carl Philipp Emanuel Bach, Vierte Sammlung . . .', in Cramer, *Magazin der Musik* 1/2 (7 December 1783), 1254.

Example 2.5   C. P. E. Bach, Fantasia in E♭, H. 277, *Kenner und Liebhaber* IV (1783), end of piece

This fantasia ends as it began, but it goes much further in its open-endedness than the fantasia in B♭ discussed in chapter 1. Not only does the fantasia conclude with a reprise of the opening material, but the ending of that beginning is itself inconclusive, a rapid rising arpeggio from the tonic note in the bass (E♭) to a short staccato iteration of the third degree (G), followed by a crotchet rest. Ambiguous in itself as an ending, the passage is doubly misleading when it occurs at the end of the piece, exactly duplicating what came earlier (example 2.5); given the unpredictable course of the fantasia and despite the reaffirmation of the tonic in this reprise, the listener is unable to be quite sure that the final silence is not simply the articulating caesura before another return of the passagio figure (b) or any other of the fantasia's fragments, habitually separated as they are by rests. A parallel for this playful open-endedness is to be found in the Rondo in C minor (H. 283) from the fifth *Kenner und Liebhaber* collection (composed in 1784, published in 1785), which ends on the fifth degree, g^2, at the top of the ascending arpeggio that constitutes the opening figure of the rondo refrain (example 2.6). Given the pattern of repetition within the rondo structure, this final measure sounds, for a tantalising instance, like simply another return of the refrain, a prolongation of the rondo game. The invitation to the listener to listen on is only revoked when the performer makes it physically clear that the piece is over, even if, in rhetorical terms, it may hardly be said to have ended.[29]

The fantasia in E♭, then, is left strangely open-ended, as the unmistakable closing, or 'enclosing' effect of the reprise is counteracted by the overt absence of an actual 'conclusion'. Although this ending is unusual for Bach's fantasias, its ambiguity is characteristic. More usual is the use of a firm V–I cadence, often in sudden block chords, to provide a clear, if abrupt, ending (as in the C minor (H. 75) and G minor (H. 225) fantasies, and the B♭ fantasia (H. 289)), or an extended succession of arpeggiated chords to perform the same function (as in the A major fantasy

---

[29] Cramer comments on the abruptness of this ending, that 'Beym Schluß fängt der Baß seine Klage pizzicato wieder an, es wird aber durch eine Pause und durch das Final plötzlich der Mund gestopft'. Review of 'Claviersonaten und freye Phantasien . . . Fünfte Sammlung', 871.

Example 2.6   C. P. E. Bach, Rondo in C minor, H. 283, *Kenner und Liebhaber* V (1785), bars 1–2 and 108–9

(H. 278) from this same collection). But even these emphatic cadences relate in an arbitrary way to what has come before, with the result that they give the impression of arbitrariness themselves. It is as if they were artificially imposed from without, and are not true endings at all; given Bach's almost obsessive resistance to closure, their effect is more that of an abruptly slammed door than a graceful and well-prepared exit. Likewise, the arpeggiated openings of many of the fantasias give the impression of starting *in medias res*. The boundaries of the fantasias themselves are blurred.

The harmony in both fantasias of the fourth collection is extremely unstable throughout, sinuous, chromatic, constantly modulating, with little predictability except the expectation of constant change and the surprisingly smooth arrival at remote harmonic locales; likewise there is a paucity of thematic logic connecting fragment to fragment in this music of fleeting gestures and sudden contrasts.[30] Even the repetitions serve less as small climaxes of reinterpretation arising from earlier action than as odd flashes of recognition leading to new juxtapositions – they are like fresh views on a landscape previously glimpsed from a different direction. Ironically, the disjointed, quasi-symmetrical reprise effect in both fantasias of the fourth *Kenner und Liebhaber* collection contributes to the sense of dislocation inherent in the fantasia. A sense of formal order is hinted at by the repetitions, but continual interruptions and intricate changes of texture ensure that the overall pattern eludes the listener.

---

[30] But Cramer singled out such juxtapositions for praise, noting the suddenness of the transition back from the Poco Adagio to the Allegro in the E♭ fantasia: instead of concluding with a cadence the 'exquisite, languishing melancholy' of the Adagio is brusquely interrupted by the 'dazzling Allegro section' that follows it 'so abruptly'. Review of 'Claviersonaten und freye Phantasien . . . Vierte Sammlung', 1254.

III

C. P. E. Bach's improvisations at the clavichord and fortepiano contributed not a little to his status as North Germany's greatest musical *Originalgenie*. Burney's famous description of such a performance, in which as Bach became animated and possessed 'drops of effervescence distilled from his countenance', borrowed the vocabulary of contemporary theories of genius, as the entranced musician generated a sweat that seemed almost to be a condensation of inspiration itself. Burney's rapturous account was matched in tone and emphasis by that of Reichardt, who described how for hours the musician 'could be absorbed in his ideas and lose himself in a sea of modulation'; in this state 'his soul appeared to be wholly absent, his eyes swam as if in a sweet dream, the under-lip hung down over the chin, face and body suspended almost lifeless over the clavichord'.[31] In both descriptions the fantasia is generated in a dreamlike, absent state in which the body of the performer is transcended. Fixed and motionless, the artist goes beyond himself in a kind of ecstasy while the listener, sublimely transported, is impelled to hot tears. C. F. D. Schubart, too, described his own improvisation as taking place in a state of heightened, abstracted inspiration: 'I fantasised with passionate creativity', he writes, explaining that 'I could play to myself in this fire – the principal trait of the musical genius – in such a way that everything around me faded, and I lived only in the music, which my imagination created'.[32] As an expression of genius not only does the fantasia license the performer to break out of the normal constraints of musical rule, just as he transgresses the limits of the body, but it carries with it something close to an imperative to retreat from rational control.[33]

But Burney's claim that the irrationality of Bach's works was simply an illusion was not merely an exercise in appeasement. Contemporary theories of genius posited a tight integration of the wild and the free within imagination itself, and the fantasia necessarily confronted this not always harmonious union. The trance of the fantasist seems akin to the blurred mental state of reverie, in which the imagination hovers between various sensations, 'plunged in a thousand confused but delicious

---

[31] J. F. Reichardt, 'Noch ein Bruchstück aus Johann Friedrich Reichardt's Autobiographie: Sein erster Aufenthalt in Hamburg', *AmZ* 16/2 (1815), col. 28.

[32] C. F. D. Schubart, *Gesammelte Schriften und Schicksale*, 8 vols. in 4 (Stuttgart: Scheible, 1839; reprint edn, Hildesheim: Olms, 1973), I, 50.

[33] For general information on the concept of genius in North Germany see M. H. Abrams, *The Mirror and the Lamp: Romantic Theory and the Critical Tradition* (London, Oxford and New York: Oxford University Press, 1953), especially 187–213; and Jochen Schmidt, *Die Geschichte des Genie-Gedankens 1750–1954*, 2 vols. (Darmstadt: Wissenschaftliche Buchgesellschaft, 1985), I.

reveries without having any particularly determined or constant object in [view]', as Rousseau would have it in the fifth of his *Reveries of a Solitary Wanderer* (1782). But this lingering, suspended state contrasted with the sharp, directed mental activity described by Alexander Gerard in his *Essay on Genius* (1774). A great mind did not succumb to 'useless musings, or endless reveries' that 'hurry a man over large fields, without any settled aim'. True genius, rather, 'pursues a fixt direction'.[34] In Diderot's *Encylopédie* the man of genius is one 'struck' by everything, suddenly, immediately. Similarly, in the *Allgemeine Theorie der schönen Künste* (1771–4) Johann Georg Sulzer described genius as sharply focussed – not mysteriously dark, but brilliantly lit:

Genius normally implies a particular ability to focus imaginative concepts with sharpness, or, as the case demands, to highlight those of particular importance. The clear light of full day shines in the soul of the man of genius and illuminates every object as a brilliantly lit close-up image, one that can easily be scanned and every detail of which can be made out clearly.[35]

Inspiration is figured here as literal enlightenment, the illumination of the hidden secrets of the soul.

The theory of inspiration on which genius depends turned on this paradox. Sulzer's account echoes much of the contemporary discourse of fantasy criticism – indeed, using similar language and imagery, philosophical notions of inspiration slipped easily into the discourse of musical fantasia. Sulzer suggested a two-fold version of inspiration.[36] The first induces the dream-like state described by Reichardt in which 'The soul immediately becomes all emotion; it is aware of nothing but itself and everything within itself. All images of things apart from it fall into darkness; it sinks into a dream which in large measure inhibits the effects of the intellect but proportionately increases the vigour of the emotions.' The effect of such inspiration is paradoxically a kind of obscurity – its brilliant internal light casts the external world into shadow. This inspiration leads to the intense expression and heightened emotion conveyed by the fantasist (or improviser), 'the vigour and power of expression, the sweet eloquence in gentle emotions; the savage, astonishing or deeply moving expression of vehement passions; the great variety of tender or powerful images; the variegated lights and

---

[34] Alexander Gerard, *An Essay on Genius* (London, 1774), 58. Cited in Barbara Maria Stafford, *Voyage into Substance: Art, Science, Nature, and the Illustrated Travel Account, 1760–1840* (Cambridge, MA: MIT Press, 1984), 402.

[35] J. G. Sulzer, *Allgemeine Theorie der schönen Künste*, 2nd edn (Leipzig, 1792–4), s.v. 'Genie'. Translation taken from le Huray and Day, eds., *Music and Aesthetics*, 127–8.

[36] Sulzer's model reflects Baumgarten's distinction between the powers of sense and reason, in which a lower kind of inspiration that affects principally the emotions is paralleled by a higher one which works largely on the mind. For a summary of Baumgarten's aesthetics see Hosler, *Changing Aesthetic Views*, 94–7.

shades of emotion'. The second degree of inspiration is, by contrast, one of clarity and sharp definition, characterised by intense concentration and an exaggerated power of perception. Here the mind visualises everything 'with the greatest clarity . . . The spirit concentrates all its powers, ignores all other objects and endeavours only to perceive clearly' (131–2). But on a higher level the two separate modes may be united, as the sensual and the rational come together in inspiration that is dream-like yet intense, and clearly separated from the realm of the physical. In this state,

as in a dream at night, when all distraction suddenly ceases, the image that we have seen veiled while awake stands before our eyes as clear as the broadest daylight, so, in the sweet dream of inspiration, the artist sees the desired object before his vision, he hears sounds when all is silent, and feels a body which is real only in his imagination.[37]

Ghostly yet tactile, the vivid hallucination conjured by inspiration is intensely real.

Sulzer's description of the imagination or fantasy as a dream, both vague and irrational, yet simultaneously vivid and striking, was a recurring one in the contemporary discourse on genius, one often reconfigured as a landscape – a dark, virgin territory which is explored and illuminated by genius.[38] This idea, of considerable importance for the reception of the free fantasia, was central to Edward Young's *Conjectures on Original Composition* (1759), a seminal text for the conception of genius in North Germany.[39] Not only do landscapes provide the main figuration for Young's aesthetic theory, but the essay itself is presented as a landscape garden, the type of landscape in which the natural and the artificial most subtly and provocatively interact. The author compares the reader to the wanderer in such a garden who is confronted at odd moments by the thought-provoking inscriptions of carefully placed monuments:

[37] Sulzer, *Allgemeine Theorie*, s.v. 'Begeisterung', in le Huray and Day, eds., *Music and Aesthetics*, 131–3.

[38] Jean Paul described genius in his *Vorschule der Aesthetik* (1804) as 'in more than one sense a sleep-walker; in his clear dream he is capable of more than in waking, and in darkness does he mount every height of reality'. Cited in Abrams, *The Mirror and the Lamp*, 212.

[39] Although it attracted little attention in England, Young's essay was translated twice into German within two years of its original publication. Abrams attributes the popularity of this text in Germany to its emphatic call for originality and independence, striking a chord in young German writers seeking to break away from their confined native tradition long subject to foreign rules and models. In addition, Abrams suggests, 'German thought was much more receptive than English to Young's suggestions that a great work of literature grows out of the impenetrable depths of the mind of genius.' See Abrams, *The Mirror and the Lamp*, 201–2.

A serious Thought standing single among many of a lighter nature will some-times strike the careless Wanderer after Amusement only, with useful Awe: as monumental Marbles scattered in a wide Pleasure-Garden (and such there are) will call to Recollection those who would never have sought it in a Church-yard-walk of mournful Yews.[40]

Natural imagery is at the heart of Young's conception of genius as spon-taneous growth: 'An *Original* may be said to be of a *vegetable* nature; it rises spontaneously from the vital root of Genius; it *grows*, it is not *made*.'[41] Digression, too, has a special significance within this theory, and crucial ramifications for criticism of the fantasia, for it functions as one of the prerogatives of originality, and thus of genius. Originality consti-tutes diversion from tradition, veering off the straight road through the landscape: 'All Eminence, and Distinction, lies out of the beaten road; Excursion and Deviation, are necessary to find it; and the more remote your Path from the Highway, the more reputable.'[42] Similarly, William Duff used the image of the errant traveller in his *Essay on Original Genius* (1767): 'To explore unbeaten tracks, and make new discoveries in the regions of Science; to invent the designs, and perfect the productions of Art, is the province of Genius alone.'[43] But while deviation characterises the imagination which, 'perpetually attempting to soar', has a tendency to 'deviate into the mazes of error', genius's object is to illuminate those serpentine tracks, turning them from potential dangers into objects for the exercise and display of its brilliant powers.[44]

IV

In December 1783 a substantial review of C. P. E. Bach's fourth collec-tion *für Kenner und Liebhaber* appeared in the widely read *Magazin der Musik*, edited by Carl Friedrich Cramer, professor of Greek and Oriental languages at the University of Kiel and an enthusiastic supporter of C. P. E. Bach. This complex essay amounts to a lengthy disquisition on the music of C. P. E. Bach, and an extraordinary manifesto for a new musical aesthetic. Citing the two fantasias included in the collection as the quin-tessence of Bach's art, Cramer adduced this genre, in all its wonder and irregularity, to debunk the notion that instrumental music must have a clear semantic content and represent a logical sequence of passions. In their place, he urged a new appreciation of irregularity, digression, the abrupt, fragmentary and surprising. Taking his metaphor from the

---

[40] Edward Young, *Conjectures on Original Composition in a Letter to the Author of Sir Charles Grandison* (Dublin, 1759), 4. Cited in Ken Frieden, 'The Eighteenth-Century Introjection of Genius', in *Poets of Sensibility and the Sublime*, ed. Harold Bloom (New York: Chelsea House, 1986), 62.   [41] Young, *Conjectures*, 8.   [42] Ibid., 14.

[43] William Duff, *An Essay on Original Genius* (London, 1767), 5.

[44] Ibid., 9–10. See also Frieden, 'Introjection of Genius', 64.

visual arts, Cramer called for an entirely new way of looking at the fantasia, downplaying the enthusiasm and emotional excess that formed such a nimbus around the genre and assigning it to the connoisseur rather than the amateur. Fantasies, he writes, are 'precious studies by the great artist for artists' ('kostbare Studia des großen Künstlers für Künstler'), and 'in this genre overall one must not look for sensual and intellectual pleasure simultaneously'.[45] This music engages its audience on a new level, according to Cramer, working less to move the passions of a passive listener than to arouse the curiosity of an active one.

Refuting the views of the Lessing/Forkel camp, which held that a successful musical discourse is one that avoids too much variety and affective change, Cramer dismissed strictures against free-ranging affects as out of date, out of touch with practice, and irrelevant for Bach's music in general. The notion that the musician is unable to make his emotional chiaroscuro coherent, and that sudden transitions are reprehensible, is the mark of 'small-mindedness and narrowness of spirit' ('Kleinkreisigkeit und Eingeschränktheit des Geistes'), dry philosophising that has little to do with actual music. Just let those critics look at the two newest fantasias by Bach, he challenges, as well as his other music, for evidence to the contrary:

Here and in innumerable other places in Bach's practice one finds the most absolute contradiction of their adopted maxims, and I advise them that they had better dismiss all such examples from their minds if they wish to maintain their standing [as critics] . . .[46]

Cramer points directly to characteristics of 'instrumental music of the non-descriptive variety' that had been considered flaws – precisely those 'abstract' qualities that placed the free fantasia outside the usual paradigms for musical coherence (in either the sense of clear rhetorical content, or the related one of formal ordering). He calls for a re-evaluation of music that is not obviously imitative or descriptive but that instead commands a kaleidoscope of changing affects; these 'precious studies' consist of a 'succession of sounds that do not correspond to specific feelings or ideas', and 'even sometimes hold no specific attraction for the ear'; they are 'an assortment of abrupt ideas, thoughts, capriccios', indeed, 'free outbursts of poetico-musical inspiration, of which one can say as Hamlet of Polonius: "Though this is madness, yet there's method in it."' The musical fantastic is Shakespearean in its irregularity and scope, and a listener with insight into the aesthetic underlying Shakespearean drama would understand the disjunctions and abstractions of such music as the poetic work of original genius, both freely

---

[45] Cramer, review of 'Claviersonaten und freye Phantasien . . . Vierte Sammlung', 1250.
[46] Ibid., 1254–5.

emitted like the utterance of a madman, yet subtly and supremely artful; such a listener would find it 'most fascinating listening, and all the more so the greater his familiarity with the secret rules of art and the deeper his penetration into its inner sanctum'.[47]

Cramer goes on to characterise the fantastic music of original genius:

> At every step the most diverse prospects are opened up to the enlightened listener [Denker]. The novelty of so many frequently quite heterogeneous and yet always [harmonically] correctly and artistically interconnected ideas, their unexpectedness and constant surprises, given the absence of any clear theme which might register with the listener and generate expectations, the boldness of the modulations, the harmonic digressions and returns, the inexhaustible fecundity of transitions and turns of phrase, the multiplicity of the individual figures which combine to make up the whole, and the brilliant fingerwork which affords even the most inexperienced listener at least the pleasure of astonishment at hearing technical difficulties overcome: all these things suggest major and significant angles from which to view such works of art, such studies as are appreciated by only a few and are intelligible to only a few, and on which a man such as Bach bases no small part of his fame.[48]

Cramer gestures overtly towards the contemporary discourse of original genius and an English aesthetic context for his thought, but his praise is particularly striking in its use of visual references to account for the experience of music, as well as its forward-looking appeal to the concept of pieces of music as works of art. Cramer focusses on the absence of clearly directed melodies, the lack of obvious beauty, on roughness of texture, abruptness, the risk of getting lost in the many digressions, and a rich diversity which is nevertheless intelligibly connected into a whole. It is an extraordinary manifesto for the status of the fantasia, and 'abstract' instrumental music more generally.

But Cramer's appeal to visual media is not confined to that of painting, the framed artefact hanging on a wall; in calling for new angles from which to view such works, Cramer ranges beyond the two-dimensional surface of the painting to a three-dimensional one, unfolding in time, for, at the heart of his claim that fantasias must be seen anew, in all their multiplicity and diversity, is not just an echo of the visual qualities of the landscape garden but a direct reference to the technical discourse of the new aesthetic of *Gartenkunst* itself, the fine art so recently theorised in the magisterial five-volume *Theorie der Gartenkunst* (1779–85) by Cramer's colleague at the University of Kiel, C. C. L. Hirschfeld. In this music 'at every step the most diverse vistas [Aussichten] are opened up to the intelligent listener' ('Denn für den Denker eröfnen sich hier bey jedem Schritte die mannigfaltigsten Aussichten').

---

[47] Ibid., 1250–1; translation based on H. G. Ottenberg, *C. P. E. Bach*, trans. Philip J. Whitmore (Oxford: Oxford University Press, 1987), 170–1.　　[48] Ibid.

Cramer's use of the word *Aussichten* should not be seen as casual or commonplace. The word entered the language in the eighteenth century,[49] and that the concept of *Aussichten* was still new in the 1770s and constituted a vital signifier in Cramer's writing is underscored in the essay on *Gartenkunst* in Sulzer's *Allgemeine Theorie*; there, *Aussichten* are explained in a footnote, guiding readers into the German version of this discourse with the rather loose translation to the French *Points de vue*, better understood as that essential term of English picturesque jargon, 'Prospects'. The multiple individual beauties of the landscape garden which, as Sulzer explains, come together in the garden plan, present themselves to the eye of the viewer through a series of prospects, glimpses framed perhaps by trees or ruins, usually focussed by a distant 'eyecatcher', a building or folly designed to organise the view. In such landscapes 'the whole countryside is divided into all sorts of scenes, and winding paths that have been cleared through thickets lead to diverse prospects [Aussichten], which attract the eye by means of a building or some other distinguishing object'. *Aussichten* in Sulzer's essay encompass both the strategic placement that frames a particular view (the 'viewpoint'), and the view itself, a new perspective on a temple or monument glimpsed from a different angle at an earlier turn in the path, or a more extensive vista encompassing one of the carefully constructed scenes of the landscape garden (figure 2.3).[50]

The experience of the picturesque garden is characteristically one of *'going down* into, of *being in* and *moving through'*.[51] It is an intimate experience where one scene follows another, apparently unsubordinated though actually related by clever juxtaposition. As in Cramer's account of the 'diverse vistas' of the musical fantasia opening up to the listener 'at every step', so the eye of the viewer in the picturesque garden is governed by his or her foot as it follows a curving, even digressive, road. William Chambers noted the charms of the circuitous route which 'discovers at every step a new arrangement' just as Lord Kames, praising the freedom of such 'pleasure grounds' in his *Elements of Criticism* (1762, translated into German in 1771), emphasised the importance of the indirect route through them in language that echoed Chambers and prefigured Cramer:

A straight road is the most agreeable, because it shortens the journey. But in an embellished field, a straight walk has an air of formality and confinement; and at any rate is less agreeable than a winding or waving walk; for in surveying the beauties of an ornamented field, we love to roam from place to place at freedom. Winding walks have another advantage: at every step they open new views. In

---

[49] Jacob and Wilhelm Grimm, *Deutsches Wörterbuch*, 33 vols. (Leipzig: S. Hirzel, 1854; reprint edn Munich: Deutscher Taschenbuch Verlag, 1984), I, 72, s.v. 'Aussicht'.

[50] Sulzer, *Allgemeine Theorie*, s.v. 'Gartenkunst'.

[51] Ronald Paulson, *Emblem and Expression: Meaning in English Art of the Eighteenth Century* (Cambridge, MA: Harvard University Press, 1975), 22.

Figure 2.3   Imaginary landscape, 'A planted hill, with a temple at its summit'. C. C. L. Hirschfeld, *Theorie der Gartenkunst*, vol. IV (1782)

short, the walks in a pleasure ground ought not to have any appearance of a road: my intention is not to make a journey, but to feast my eye on the beauties of art and nature.[52]

In the free fantasia events do not necessarily relate to one another in a logical sequence; the fantastic style challenges the listener to experience the piece from moment to moment without a teleological sense of its overall pattern. Upon studying the piece the plan may be clear, but the immediate topography of this wilderness of the imagination can

[52] Henry Home, Lord Kames, *Elements of Criticism*, 3 vols. (Edinburgh, 1762), II, 397.

seem almost impassable as, in the course of the journey through the piece, the listener encounters severe and unexpected disruptions. In his book *Musical Form and Musical Performance* (1968) Edward Cone distinguishes between *synoptic comprehension* which is 'our realization of the form of what we have perceived' and *immediate apprehension*, which is our response to a direct contact.[53] The free fantasia problematises the distinction between the two modes of perception. If the listener is in danger of getting lost the piece does indeed risk incoherence, but the fantasia's irregularity and spontaneity require a kind of listening that allows for illogical sequence, for a digressive narrative mode and one that is perceived by immersion rather than overview.

That the idea of the *Aussicht* had particularly rich implications for this type of experience of art is conveyed by another of Cramer's contemporaries, Jacob M. Reinhold Lenz, who compared the function of the *Aussicht* as an important point of focus, articulation, and climax in garden art to Catharsis in drama: 'there are two types of garden, one which one can survey completely at the first glance, the other in which one proceeds little by little from one change to another, as in Nature', writes Lenz:

So there are also two types of drama . . . the one presents everything all at once and interconnected and is therefore easier to survey; with the other one must clamber up and around as in Nature. Now if the roughness of the place is not worth the trouble, then the drama is bad, but if the things that one sees and hears are worth the effort of a little exertion of the imagination, in order to follow the poet in the course of the events he presents, then one can say that the drama is good. And when the prospect [Aussicht] which he opens out at the end of the path is of the kind that our whole soul rejoices over it and succumbs to a thrill of delight having not previously noticed it, then the drama is perfect.[54]

V

The essay on *Gartenkunst* in Sulzer's *Allgemeine Theorie* constituted a highly influential introduction for German readers in the 1770s to the new aesthetic. The first essay of its kind to appear in a German text (alongside the many translations into German of English books on the subject which began to appear in the early 1770s), it established both the leading role of English theory and practice in this area, and, most significantly, made the foundational claim in Germany for the status of *Gartenkunst* as a fine art. Borrowing from William Chambers' *Dissertation on Oriental Gardening* (1772), Sulzer described how the new landscape

---

[53] Edward T. Cone, *Musical Form and Musical Performance* (New York: Norton, 1968), 88–9.

[54] Jacob Michael Reinhold Lenz, *Werke und Schriften*, vol. I, ed. Britta Titel and Hellmut Haug (Stuttgart: Goverts, 1966), 466. First appeared in Summer/Autumn 1774. Cited in Siegmar Gerndt, *Idealisierte Natur: Die literarische Kontroverse um den Landschaftsgarten des 18. und frühen 19. Jahrhunderts in Deutschland* (Stuttgart: J. B. Metzler, 1981), 109.

garden aimed for a constant play of variety and contrast in an alternation of 'smiling', 'terrifying' and 'enchanted' or 'romantic' scenes. Such quick-changing contrasts must be carefully staged, yet their planning concealed: 'In a garden the open and the closed, the ordered or regular and the wild, the light and the dark, must be united in a pleasant alternation.' Most importantly, and perhaps most novel, was the way that such gardens made a unified whole out of the great multiplicity of nature herself, so that 'when everything beautiful is brought together there, the whole must be arranged in such a way that the ordering plan must not be easily perceived'. The garden architect (Sulzer's term) must avoid everything the conventional architect strives for – symmetry, rule, straight lines – and imitate the irregularity and imperfection of nature herself; indeed, the garden architect is perhaps the greatest artist of all, who must possess a thorough knowledge of plants, trees, seasons and natural history in addition to a genius for invention, and the usual aesthetic education, understanding and judgement required of any artist.[55]

The landscapes of genius, then, were less abstract and imaginary than they might have appeared, for they found their realization in the landscape garden itself. Where the theory of *Originalgenie* celebrated spontaneity and irregularity in works of art, alongside the refinement and brilliance of their artistry, so the landscape garden aesthetic advocated a naturalness whose success was precisely predicated on the sophistication that had created it, an aesthetic of the natural that took nature herself as its principal material and that emphatically laid claim to the status of a fine art. The landscape garden offered the perfect model for a theory of original genius, especially one bound up with the idea of the recovery of a national culture, like that articulated in Germany, which extrapolated the notion of the native from that of the natural. Indeed, the potency of the discourse of *Gartenkunst* within contemporary German cultural critique was well illustrated by Justus Möser's seminal polemic 'Über die deutsche Sprache und Literatur' (1781), a rebuttal to Frederick II's francophile 'De la Littérature Allemande'. Bemoaning German infatuation since the Middle Ages with Latinate culture, with 'dwarf trees and spaliered trees and all sorts of beautiful cripples' which could only be kept alive in the German climate with great difficulty, Möser advocated 'improving' on indigenous species in place of the importation and transplantation of the foreign.[56] The finest models for such improvement were, of course, not to be found in Roman lands, but

---

[55] Sulzer, *Allgemeine Theorie*, s.v. 'Gartenkunst'.

[56] Justus Möser, 'Über die deutsche Sprache und Literatur', first published in *Westphälische Beyträge zum Nutzen und Vergnügen* (Osnabrück, 1781). Cited in Gerndt, *Idealisierte Natur*, 107. My discussion here takes Gerndt's chapter 'Garten der Freiheit: Die formalästhetischen und sozialpolitischen Hintergründe des Landschaftsgartens', 106–28, as its starting point.

instead in England, with its greatest indigenous product, and, along with the garden, cultural export, Shakespeare. Art dictated by the many conventions of so-called 'good taste', and ruled by the contrived unities of French classical aesthetics was marked by 'uniformity and poverty'; German art should instead take a 'path to multiplicity . . . even though it can lead us to unruly wildness'. Evidence of the incontrovertible and universally recognised success of multiplicity was to be found, Möser claimed, in the triumphal sweep into continental Europe of the English landscape garden.[57]

Not content with generalities, Möser referred to one of the best known of recent artistic productions in Northern Germany, that controversial yet highly praised example of audacious juxtaposition, the famous double-choir *Heilig* (H. 778) of C. P. E. Bach. 'It remains an incontestable truth', Möser declared,

> that a thousand diverse elements tending towards unity have a greater effect than a unity in which only five are collected; and that a double-choir *Heilig* from Bach is something entirely other than the most beautiful aria, however lovely this may sound.[58]

As a choir of angels alternates with the choir of the peoples (nations) in the *Heilig*, the gulf separating the heavenly from the earthly realms is represented by extraordinary harmonic disjunctions. The angels enter in E major, after the concluding G major of the introduction, and end their first statement in C♯ major; the people then enter in D major; the angels' reply begins directly in B major and ends in F♯ major; the people enter again, now in G major; the angels' third statement begins in F minor and ends in B major. Both choirs then come together in a final statement in C major (example 2.7). The instant effect of this great variety of apparently unrelated harmonies, which drew so much fascinated attention and praise from Bach's contemporaries, is to baffle the ear, yet each disjunction can be illustrated in terms of the fantastic ellipses explained by Bach in the *Versuch*, each bearing an underlying, if absent, logic. Indeed, the harmonic disjunctions and 'multiplicities' of this piece would in turn be adduced by Bach himself in the late additions he made to his own chapter on the musical procedures of the fantastic.[59]

---

[57] Gerndt, 'Garten der Freiheit', 109.   [58] Ibid.

[59] See the paragraph added to the revised edition of the second part of the *Versuch*, published by Schwickert in 1797 (in the Breitkopf facsimile of the *Versuch*, appendix, pp. 15–16). This paragraph, and the unconventional harmonic procedures of the *Heilig*, are discussed at length in Richard Kramer, 'The New Modulation of the 1770s: C. P. E. Bach in Theory, Criticism and Practice', *Journal of the American Musicological Society* 38/3 (Fall 1985), 551–92. See also David Ferris, 'C. P. E. Bach's Paragraph on Modulation: A Defense of Improvisational Style', unpublished paper given at the annual meeting of the American Musicological Society, Baltimore 1996.

Example 2.7   C. P. E. Bach, *Heilig mit zwey Chören und einer Ariette zur Einleitung*, H. 778, bars 47–83, reduction

In citing modern German music to support his claim for the aesthetic cogency of the English landscape garden, Möser made possible further explorations of the common ground between the two arts. In 1782, a year before the publication of Cramer's essay on Bach, J. F. Reichardt, writing in his *Musikalisches Kunstmagazin* (1782), relied on Möser to advocate a new direction in contemporary music. Not only did Möser's characterisation of the difference between French and

A View of the South Side of the Ruins at Kew.

Figure 2.4   Ruins and distant temple at Kew Gardens, William Chambers, *Plans, Elevations, and Sections of the Garden at Kew* (1763)

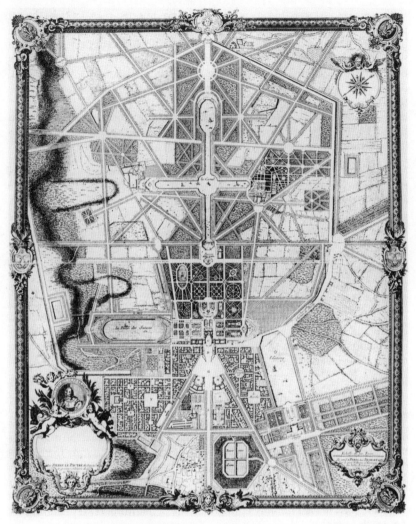

Figure 2.5   Plan of the formal gardens by Le Notre at Versailles

English taste in gardens give an accessible and vivid account of a new aesthetic, but his example could be cited by Reichardt in order to demonstrate that music delighting in irregularity and diversity was neither anomalous nor incoherent, but rather, by analogy with *Gartenkunst*, artful, aesthetically valuable, and up to date. Quoting from Möser, Reichardt explained again to his readers what it was about the English garden that appealed to German taste, in music as well as the other arts. Compare, he writes, an English with a French garden (figures 2.4 and 2.5):

In the former, just as in Shakespeare's plays, we find temples, grottoes, hermitages, thickets, gigantic rocks, grave mounds, ruins, rocky caves, woods, meadows, pastures, and endless diversity, intermingled as in God's creation; in the latter, on the contrary, beautiful straight paths, trimmed hedges, grandly beautiful fruit trees arranged in pairs or artfully bowed, flowerbeds arranged in the shape of flowers, pavilions in the finest taste – and everything is so regularly organised, that by going back and forth one can draw all the divisions with a few lines, and with every step encounters uniformity, which these trifling beauties bring together into a whole. The English gardener wants rather to merge into wildness, than be confined with the French one in *berceaux* and arbours.[60]

Reichardt himself was well versed in the aesthetic of the English garden, as he advertised to his readers in many passages in his *Briefe eines aufmerksamen Reisenden die Musik betreffend* (1774, 1776). Contemporary landscape aesthetics inform his topographical descriptions and colour his critical opinions. At Potsdam he admired the improvements recently made to the Sanssouci park, describing them in language that touches on virtually every aspect of current English landscape critique:

The prospect [Aussicht] from this beautiful building is splendid and of the utmost variety. The king has very successfully increased by means of art the great diversity which nature had already laid out in the region. On a somewhat distant hill, which is covered with young birches, he has had ruins [of buildings] built in the style of Roman antiquity, which stand out excellently against smiling nature, and elevate it.[61]

Reichardt's account of the park displays his familiarity with the landscape garden's fashionable problematisation of the distinction between art and nature:

one is told not so much that there is a great deal of art in it, as that the most beautiful nature holds sway there. Art has rendered the service to nature to bring the unconstrained order and beauty that nature usually observes only in a great expanse into the smaller confines of the park. Then, however, after having arranged everything in the best way, she made the cleverest and finest choice and concealed herself humbly under the cloak of nature, and now continues to remain hidden.[62]

In Hamburg with its advanced garden culture, saturated with English influence, C. P. E. Bach was Reichardt's guide on a tour of the city's sights.[63] Reichardt recounts how Bach showed him the finest walks and

---

[60] Möser, 'Schrift über die deutsche Sprache und Litteratur', quoted in C. F. Reichardt, *Musikalisches Kunstmagazin* 1/1 (Berlin, 1782), 48.

[61] Reichardt, *Briefe eines aufmerksamen Reisenden die Musik betreffend*, 2 vols. (Frankfurt, 1774), I, 177–8, footnote.   [62] Ibid., 176–7, footnote.

[63] Ibid., II, 9. On the impact of the English on culture in eighteenth-century Hamburg, see Brian Douglas Stewart, 'Georg Philipp Telemann in Hamburg: Social and Cultural Background and its Musical Expression' (Ph.D. diss., Stanford University, 1985), especially pp. 76–81. See also Buttlar, *Der Landschaftsgarten*, 166–71.

the most beautiful prospects – 'die allerschönsten Aussichten'. Reichardt uses the term *Aussicht* with casual confidence, displaying his insider's knowledge of a new piece of cultural currency and advertising his familiarity with the parlance of that most recent art, *Gartenkunst*.

Carl Friedrich Cramer's hint that the evocative contrasts and surprises of Bach's fantasias, the 'perpetual shifting of [their] scenes', can be compared to a landscape garden suggests an aesthetic resonance between garden and fantasy that encompasses the ambiguous distinction between natural instinct and contrived artifice, as well as the more complex concatenation of ideas surrounding abstraction, disjunction and discontinuity in visual and musical art. And Cramer was not alone in mapping the free fantasia, epitome of musical genius, onto the landscape garden. That such a garden, with its ode-like illusory disorder, should provide a persuasive model for the fantasia, albeit a later and more debased version of the genre, was explicitly stated by Carl Czerny as late as the 1830s:

If a well-written composition can be compared with a noble architectural edifice in which symmetry must predominate, then a fantasy well done is akin to a beautiful English garden, seemingly irregular, and full of surprising variety, but executed rationally, meaningfully, and according to plan.[64]

As we have seen, Cramer's criticism of Charles Horn's clumsily handled harmony compared well-managed harmonic digressions to sidesteps into 'hidden romantic regions'. It is as if the successful fantasia's harmonic extravagances and digressions, combined with sudden contrasts and surprisingly various textures, lure the listener into the wild part of an English garden, a 'region of romance and fantasy' like the wilderness at Dovedale described by Thomas Whately, in his *Observations on Modern Gardening* (1770):

It seems indeed, a fitter haunt for more ideal beings; the whole has the air of enchantment; the perpetual shifting of the scenes; the quick transitions, the total changes; then the forms all around, grotesque as chance can cast, wild as nature can produce, and various as imagination can invent . . . the dark caverns; the illuminated recesses; the fleating shadows, and the gleams of light glancing on the sides, or trembling on the stream; and the loneliness and the stillness of the place, all crouding together on the mind, almost realize the ideas which naturally present themselves in this region of romance and fancy.[65]

And indeed, a description of the free fantasia contemporaneous with Cramer's draws a direct comparison between the two. In the diary of

[64] Carl Czerny, *Systematische Anleitung zum Fantasieren auf dem Pianoforte*, Op. 200 [1836]; translated as *A Systematic Introduction to Improvisation on the Pianoforte*, by Alice L. Mitchell (New York: Longman, 1983), 2.

[65] Thomas Whately, *Observations on Modern Gardening* (Dublin, 1770, German trans. Leipzig, 1771), 115.

Joseph Anton Sambuga, tutor to Crown Prince Ludwig of Bavaria, written in the 1780s, there is an account of the experience both of listening to and of making a free fantasia that equates it directly with the experience of a landscape garden:

The *free fantasy* – seemed to me like a pleasant garden, where one comes upon flowers of every kind, shrubberies, wildernesses, waterfalls, desolate places, and one finds everywhere the true imitation of nature or nature herself. One admired the man who produces [free fantasy] in this wonderful way, something the highest art can achieve. The man who knows how to give life to his feelings through tones, and who is never forsaken by his friend Music; he finds himself in a flower-covered garden, by huge, grey mountains, surging seas or by softly purling brooks. He seems to me to be like a thinker, who descends from the pleasant hill, where nature appears to him friendly and smiling, to the deep valleys and ravines and nourishes his spirit with the shuddering fright of the shadows, the rushing streams, the overhanging pieces of rock and out of it all creates great ideas, which he expresses in tones.[66]

If the fantasia aesthetic is that of the landscape garden, the startling effects of contrast that characterise it, of ellipsis, digression and disruption, are as central to it, and as much its subject as the affective response such fantasising is designed to arouse. Composed fantasias act as a commentary on the spontaneous outbursts of artistic creation that Burney described as 'those fleeting sounds as are generated in the wild moments of enthusiasm', a framed and artistic representation of them. Improvisation itself, of course, when performed for an audience, is not necessarily the same thing as the 'wild moments of enthusiasm' that might characterise the jottings of a composer at work – for improvisation is a learnt, and in some sense learned art. The contradiction is apparent throughout Bach's discussion in the *Versuch*: in improvisation, he stresses, the performer is allowed the utmost freedom, yet must have a thorough understanding of harmony and some of the rules of construction; 'strange and profuse' modulations are encouraged, yet these must not be excessively used lest 'natural relationships will become hopelessly buried beneath them'. The strange must not be too strange, the wild not too wild, for some artistic decorum must be observed. The landscape garden aesthetic allows for a re-evaluation of the fantasia that focusses precisely on the startling and disruptive elements which have baffled its critics; the strange complexities of this music appear not simply less bewildering, but fascinating in their own right when fantasia is viewed, and heard, as musical picturesque.

---

[66] Cited in Karl Emil von Schafhäutl, *Abt Georg Joseph Vogler: Sein Leben, Charakter und Musikalisches System* (Augsburg, 1888; reprint edn, Hildesheim: Olms, 1979), 90.

3

The picturesque sketch and the interpretation of instrumental music

I'll make a TOUR – and then I'll WRITE it . . .
I'll ride and write, and sketch and paint,
And thus create a real mint;
I'll prose it here, I'll verse if there,
And picturesque it ev'rywhere . . .
I'll make this flat a shaggy ridge,
And o'er the water throw a bridge:
I'll do as other sketchers do –
Put anything into the view . . .
Thus, though from truth I haply err,
The scene preserves its character . . .
He ne'er will as an artist shine,
Who copies Nature line by line:
Who'er from nature takes a view,
Must copy and improve it too. William Combe, *The Tour of Dr. Syntax*
in search of the Picturesque (1812)

The very visions of fancy . . . foil description, and every attempt at
artificial colouring. William Gilpin, 'Essay on Picturesque Travel' (1792)

Touring Scotland in 1773, Bishop Thomas Percy attempted to describe
the scene before him. Struggling to avoid the continual sameness of
travel writing vocabulary, he wrote in his notebook Observanda on 8
August that

> the immense Group of stupendous Mountains beyond to the North, rising up
> in gigantic scenery beyond one another, form a succession of Picturesque won-
> derfully great, astonishing & ~~picturesque~~ fine ~~Picturesque~~ beyond all descrip-
> tion, & to which no language can do justice.[1]

Attending the fashionable appreciation of picturesque landscapes – picturesque, that is, in the sense of landscapes with particular 'painterly'

---

[1] Cited in Malcolm Andrews, *The Search for the Picturesque: Landscape Aesthetics and
Tourism in Britain, 1760–1800* (Aldershot: Scolar Press, 1989), 76.

qualities – was the imperative of getting the scene down on paper as a verbal or visual sketch, a souvenir for later reflection or model for future improvement into a fully formed picture. This picturesque framing of nature combined accurate observation and transcription with fanciful elaboration and manipulation, a paradoxical kind of nature appreciation so popular that it had become clichéd even in the 1770s, as demonstrated by the way that persistent word 'picturesque' threatened to sabotage Bishop Percy's attempts at originality. At the turn of the century Jane Austen, as critical of the fashionable banalities of the picturesque as she was of the excesses of sensibility, would recount Catherine Morland's education in the picturesque in *Northanger Abbey*, a lesson in the modish art of framing nature:

They were viewing the country with the eyes of persons accustomed to drawing, and decided on its capability of being formed into pictures, with all the eagerness of real taste . . . It seemed as if a good view were no longer to be taken from the top of a high hill, and that a clear blue sky was no longer proof of a fine day.

Catherine, regarding the landscape as a pictorial composition, is alerted to the importance of low viewpoints and of cloudy skies. Austen's comment on the whole endeavour is a precisely ironical one, and the picturesque emerges as an exercise in disregarding reality, an aesthetic appreciation of an imaginary vision distanced from the actual scene at hand:

He talked of foregrounds, distances, and second distances; side screens and perspectives; lights and shades; and Catherine was so hopeful a scholar, that when they gained the top of Beechen Cliff, she voluntarily rejected the whole city of Bath, as unworthy to make part of a landscape.[2]

Tours of areas of natural beauty became increasingly popular in the second half of the eighteenth century, following the example of William Gilpin, the author of numerous *Picturesque Tours* and so-called 'father of the picturesque' whose own tours, undertaken between 1769 and 1776, were published from 1782 on. The picturesque viewpoint was essential for a proper appreciation of landscape, and tourists stressed the freshness and originality of their experience; one enthusiast declared: 'I follow no written guide, lest I should enter too much into other people's ideas, and not give nature scope to my own: I shall do the best I can, frequently writing upon the spot from whence the object strikes me.'[3]

---

[2] Jane Austen, *Northanger Abbey* (London: Collins, 1953), 91–2. Cited in Martin Price, 'The Picturesque Moment', in *From Sensibility to Romanticism: Essays Presented to Frederick A. Pottle*, ed. Frederick W. Hilles and Harold Bloom (New York: Oxford University Press, 1965), 266.

[3] Joseph Budworth, *A Fortnight's Ramble to the Lakes* (1788), 2–3. Cited in Andrews, *Search for the Picturesque*, 80.

The framing of the sublime landscape for consumption by the picturesque traveller was aided by the Claude glass, a device for picturesque
viewing which contains a small convex mirror on dark foil and gathers
the whole scene into a tiny picture, its colours slightly darkened. The
glass both reflects the landscape presented to it, yet simultaneously
modifies it, presenting an already-framed image, one whose tinting
evokes the yellowed glow of an Old Master. Characteristic of the medi-
ated experience of nature that typifies the picturesque, the user of the
mirror and admirer of the landscape must turn her back to the scene in
order to catch its controlled reflection. It is a strange conflation of the
natural with the artificial, the real with the illusory.[4] William Gilpin
noted that as he used the mirror while travelling in his carriage, 'a succession of highly coloured pictures is continually gliding before the
eye'. Fragmentary and vivid, the glass presents images that are like 'the
visions of the imagination' and 'the brilliant landscapes of a dream':

Forms, and colours, in brightest array, fleet before us; and if the transient glance
of a good composition happen to unite with them, we should give any price to
fix, and appropriate the scene.[5]

There was an inherent difficulty in fixing and notating form, and imposing it on such visions. How was one to capture the experience of the
sublime, describing, circumscribing, framing, containing it?

Gilpin's image of the natural world presented to the perceiver as a brilliant dream landscape echoed that of contemporary discourse on musical
fantasy. Indeed, Daniel Gottlob Türk suggested that the contorted and
blurred relation improvisations bore to 'normal' musical discourse was
like that of a dream to reality. 'We often dream through actual experienced
events in a few minutes', he wrote in his *Klavierschule* (1789), 'which make
an impression upon us by their most lively sensations, but are without
any coherence or clear consciousness.'[6] Stressing that the value of the free
fantasia lay precisely in the fact that it was a kind of natural outpouring,
not the product of premeditation or something subsequently improved
by artifice, Türk insisted on the vague and fragmented nature of the
genre, the spontaneous performance all the more vivid and memorable
for its resistance to notation. Likewise Johann Friedrich Unger, the Berlin
mathematician and fantasy enthusiast described improvisations as necessarily the outcome of an almost supernatural somnambulant state, in

---

[4] See Andrews, *Search for the Picturesque*, and also John Dixon Hunt, *Gardens and the
Picturesque: Studies in the History of Landscape Architecture* (Cambridge, MA: MIT Press,
1992), chapter 6, 'Picturesque Mirrors and the Ruins of the Past'.

[5] William Gilpin, *Remarks on Forest Scenery, and other Woodland Views . . .*, 2 vols. (London:
R. Blamire, 1791), II, 225. Andrews, *Search for the Picturesque*, 70.

[6] Daniel Gottlob Türk, *Klavierschule, oder, Anweisung zum Klavierspielen für Lehrer and
Lernende* (Leipzig, 1789), 312.

fundamental contradiction to ordinary consciousness – the consciousness needed to write them down:

the ideas of a musical genius are often able to reach the highest degree of beauty as soon as he finds himself in a state of mind that might seem supernatural, however easily recognised and often encountered it may be . . . And many of the most powerful musical geniuses never handle their instrument more excitingly than when they gradually withdraw their mind from it completely, and concentrate on quite another object. However, they subside into something more dull as soon as their occupation once again becomes conscious.[7]

All too often dreams disappear and are forgotten, and it was this transience, the fantasia's escape from memory, that particularly troubled enthusiasts of the genre. The continual process of simultaneous creation and disappearance in the fantasia's performance highlighted the shifting distinction between the improvised and the notated fantasia. The vanished fantasy performances (the improvisations) maintained a spectral presence in texted, 'composed' fantasias, but, as contemporary commentators were quick to point out, these may misrepresent the enterprise of fantasia. The genre questions the locus of the musical work, asking whether it resides in the notated piece or in its performance – in its 'congealed written state' or 'the fluid state [that] signifies', to borrow Adorno's formulation,[8] and it is perhaps this liminality that has contributed to the marginalisation of the free fantasia in modern histories of late eighteenth-century music.

The difficulty, for those who saw the fantasia as the highest form of musical art and revelled in its poetic instability, lay in fixing a music that is ephemeral – in setting it down on paper for study, repeat performance, or as the foundation for a composition – without robbing it of its unique freedom. It was a problem shared with the visual arts, and in the article on the fantasia in his *Allgemeine Theorie der schönen Künste* (1771–4) Sulzer compared fantasias to sketches in describing the intensity and brilliance of such improvisations as are invented in the 'fire of inspiration'; even while he praised their instantaneity, he lamented their impermanence:

The fantasias of great masters, particularly those which are played from a certain profusion of feeling and in the fire of enthusiasm, are often, like the first sketches of a sketcher, works of exceptional power and beauty, which could not be achieved in a calm state of mind.

---

[7] J. F. Unger, *Entwurf einer Maschine wodurch alles was auf dem Clavier gespielt wird, sich von selber in Noten setzt* . . . (Braunschweig, 1774). Quoted in Peter Schleuning, 'Die Fantasiermaschine: Ein Beitrag zur Geschichte der Stilwende um 1750', *Archiv für Musikwissenschaft* 27 (1970), 200.

[8] Theodor W. Adorno, *Quasi una Fantasia*, trans. Rodney Livingstone (London: Verso, 1992), 296.

It would consequently be an important matter if one had a means to write down the fantasias of great masters.[9]

Fascination with the fantasia's ephemerality lies at the heart of Sulzer's comparison between the fantasia and the sketch, and it is a comparison that carries broad implications for the interpretation of both the gaps and digressions of the fantasia itself, and of the role of the score in representing music.

In an attempt to preserve fantasias from their instantaneous absence (the genre's hallmark) a machine had been constructed that purported to be able to make exact transcriptions of improvisations.[10] The Fantasy Machine was exhibited in 1753 at the Royal Academy of Sciences in Berlin, and was described even decades later by writers such as Sulzer, Forkel, Hiller and Koch who were obsessed with the idea that this machine might be able to effect an instant transformation of performance into text, thus bypassing the potential distortions of memory and self-criticism.[11] Even as late as 1837, Carl Czerny wistfully mentioned the possibility of such a machine, looking for a way 'immediately to commit to paper such improvisations as are made in propitious moments'.[12] An account published in 1770 described the ability of the Fantasy Machine somehow to preserve music that is as fragile as a soap bubble, and attests to contemporary fascination with the mysterious impermanence of the improvised performance:

[This is] indeed an important invention for music, which can imperceptibly, without the artist troubling himself about it, bring to the paper many a musical thought, a beautiful sudden idea and a wonderful piece that a quick-witted harpsichordist improvises, and can therefore, so to speak, catch in mid-air and hold tight the most beautiful pieces of music, which otherwise vanish before the ears as they are being made, more quickly than beautifully coloured bubbles before the eyes.[13]

[9] J. G. Sulzer, *Allgemeine Theorie der schönen Künste*, 2nd edn (Leipzig, 1792–4), s.v. 'Fantasiren; Fantasie'.

[10] For a detailed account of the machine, see Schleuning, 'Die Fantasiermaschine'.

[11] See Sulzer, *Allgemeine Theorie*, s.v. 'Fantasiren; Fantasie'; Forkel, 'Erzählung der merkwürdigen Erfindungen, die Musik betreffend', *Musikalischer Almanach für Deutschland*, 4 vols. (1782–4, 1789), I (1782), 26–7; Forkel's account echoes Burney's in *The Present State of Music in Germany, the Netherlands and the United Provinces*, 2nd edn, 2 vols. (London, 1775), II, 213–16; and Heinrich Christoph Koch, *Musikalisches Lexicon* (Offenbach am Main, 1802), cols. 1076–7. s.v. 'Notenschreib-Maschine'.

[12] Carl Czerny, *School of Practical Composition*, Op. 600, 3 vols. (1839), trans. John Bishop (London: Cocks, 1848), I, 82. Bishop, apparently unaware, like Czerny, of earlier attempts at such a machine, adds a footnote citing a recent French invention of a 'Pianograph' that could transcribe such improvisations.

[13] J. von Stählin, 'Nachrichten von der Musik in Rußland', in *Beilage zum neuveränderten Rußland*, ed. J. J. Haigold, vol. II (Riga, 1770), reprinted in J. A. Hiller, *Wöchentliche Nachrichten und Anmerkungen die Musik betreffend* 4/25 (1770), 194–8.

The Rev. John Creed, who had conceived of a plan for such a machine and presented it to the Royal Society in London in 1747, had encapsulated the paradox of the project's aim to fix the free by claiming that with the device the 'most transient Graces' could be 'mathematically delineated'.[14] Likewise, the enthusiasm of Charles Burney for the Fantasy Machine testified to the appeal of such a project for his contemporaries, for 'to fix such fleeting sounds as are generated in the wild moments of enthusiasm . . . would be giving permanence to ideas which reflection can never find, nor memory retain'.[15]

J. F. Unger, the inventor of the German version of the Fantasy Machine, claimed that the system could be set up cheaply and quickly in any keyboard instrument and could transcribe onto paper any musical fantasia at the instant of its creation. Claiming to have had the idea since 1745, Unger presented a formal proposal in Latin to the Berlin Academy in 1753, along with a version of the machine built by Johann Hohlfeld. The essay itself was eventually translated into German and published in 1774, and in it Unger mused more generally on the problem of translating spontaneous musical inventions into texts, for the composer forgets what he has played as he tries to write it down, and the more often he tries to repeat the process, 'the more unlike itself the whole work becomes'. In the act of transcription, the composer 'loses the brilliant ideas which are wont to be the more fiery, the more they are animated by a spontaneous impulse'.[16] Unger's anxiety over the weakening of creative inventions in the process of their conversion into composed pieces prefigured Sulzer's comparison of the fantasia with the impulsive sketch. But this was not just a transcription machine; rather, it was conceived both to record improvisation and to aid invention – ideas could be sketched out with it, to be refined later into careful composition, but, entangling musical performance and composition, the ultimate composition was figured here as the most free and spontaneous improvisation.

The Fantasy Machine was widely commented upon and was tried out by several well-known musicians, including Scheibe and Marpurg and perhaps also Bach, in 1753, the publication year of Bach's *Versuch*.[17] But despite Sulzer's claim that it could accurately transcribe everything that was played on it, even the smallest ornament,[18] the consensus appears to have been that the machine was not a success. Although the notes of the improvisations played on it may have been accurately transcribed, the Fantasy Machine failed to record the nuances of performance: it could not

---

[14] Creed's plans were published in the *Philosophical Transactions of the Royal Society for the Year 1747* 44/2 (London, 1748), 445–50 and Table 1. Cited in Schleuning, 'Die Fantasiermaschine', 196.   [15] Burney, *Present State of Music* (London, 1773), 214.

[16] Unger, *Entwurf einer Maschine*, 4.

[17] Burney cited the opinions of a 'great performer', who tried the machine, perhaps referring to Bach himself.   [18] Sulzer, *Allgemeine Theorie*, s.v. 'Fantasiren; Fantasie'.

reproduce dynamics, and when played with a soft touch it failed to transcribe anything; retranscription into musical notation was very difficult (although Sulzer enthusiastically asserted that it did not take long to become good at this), and above all, as Scheibe and Marpurg concurred, an intelligible rendering of a free fantasia was impossible. In short, the machine could produce only pale imitations of free improvisation, from which all fantastic elements had been erased. As critics noted, the failure of the Fantasy Machine highlighted the dubious relation between the note-text of a fantasia and its performance – a disjunction which Carl Friedrich Cramer hinted at in his comments on the two fantasias published in C. P. E. Bach's fifth collection for *Kenner und Liebhaber* (1785):

Those who haven't heard the Kapellmeister [Bach] for themselves can get *some idea* of [his improvisation] from these Fantasias, although this idea always remains deficient, if one compares them to the real performance of the improviser, which, if it were fully notated, few, perhaps none, could play properly.[19]

Not only would these printed pieces lack a crucial element of the free and accidental present in Bach's actual performance, but those performances themselves (the improvisations) could never be rendered exactly on the printed page. Indeed, the free fantasia hinted at an unbreachable rift between performance and score.

The composed fantasia, as the imitation of an improvisation, may be considered tautological, even fraudulent. But borrowing Sulzer's comparison between the fantasia and the sketch, Heinrich Christoph Koch suggested that to 'write' a fantasia was not simply to create a counterfeit; instead, the process of composition itself could in fact be just such a spontaneous and transgressive performance, an improvisation with pen and paper rather than musical instrument:

One also gives the name *fantasia* to pieces actually composed, in which the composer binds himself neither to a definite form nor to a totally clearly connected order of ideas etc.; since the Ideal brought forth by Genius loses nothing of its first liveliness through the further working-out towards a more strictly ordered whole, these pieces very often contain far more prominent and striking traits than a piece composed according to forms and the other necessary characteristics of a perfected whole. It is a similar case with sketches in painting, where likewise through the execution and completed depiction of the painting many of the finer traits of the Ideal that are still present in the sketch get lost.[20]

In this case, the brilliant spark of inspiration is retained in the casual roughness of the (composed) result, its looseness of syntax, freedom of form and sketch-like immediacy.

---

[19] Review of 'Claviersonaten und freye Phantasien . . . Fünfte Sammlung', C. F. Cramer, *Magazin der Musik* 2/2 (5 August 1786), 871–2.
[20] Koch, *Musikalisches Lexicon*, cols. 554–5, s.v. 'Fantasie'.

The sketch provided a vital tool for the picturesque traveller, the means with which to record immediate responses to scenes of natural splendour and beauty. William Gilpin codified a theory of sketching landscape and appreciating the picturesque in his *Three Essays* (1792) – 'On Picturesque Beauty', 'On Picturesque Travel' and 'On Sketching Landscape'. For Gilpin, sketches made at the scene provided a means of recording an immediate reaction, more truthful to nature than a drawing composed in calm reflection, for 'they are not the offspring of theory; but are taken warm from the scenes of nature, as they arise'.[21] The sketch has the qualities of an improvisation, a closer identity to the original ideas of the artist than a work produced in a more careful and studied fashion:

It is his first conception; which is commonly the strongest, and the most brilliant . . . And in these happy moments, when the enthusiasm of his art is upon him, he often produces from the glow of his imagination, with a few bold strokes, such wonderful effusions of genius as the more sober, and correct productions of his pencil cannot equal.[22]

But even this supposedly unmediated art was problematic, for sketches made on the spot, in the heat of the moment, did in fact require artful adjustments. Gilpin suggested the need for a continual combination of instinct and reflection, immediate truth to the first impression combined with subsequent alterations to the sketch thus produced. And if the sketch was to be more than a simple personal souvenir and was instead to be publicly exhibited, it had to be worked up into something more complete, for although the scene 'familiar to our recollection, may be suggested by a few rough strokes', in order to communicate the image to a viewer who has not seen the original, 'there should be some *composition* in your sketch – a degree of *correctness, and expression* in the outline – and some *effect of light*' (see figures 3. 1a and b).[23]

Both Sulzer and Koch noted how the improvisation and the painter's sketch alike preserve an identity closer to the original ideas of the artist than a work produced in a more careful and studied fashion. The sketch is like the performed (that is, improvised) fantasia but, unlike the fantasia, it needs no recording machine. The fleeting temporality of its performance precludes completion, and its very 'sketchiness' allows a free range to the imagination of the viewer who can enter into and fill out the work itself. Indeed, while sketches were seen as the most truthful representation of the imagination of the artist, they were understood to invite the viewer to use his/her own imagination in supplying the details.

---

[21] William Gilpin, *Observations on the River Wye, and Several Parts of South Wales, etc., relative chiefly to Picturesque Beauty; made in the Summer of the Year 1770* (London, 1782), 2.

[22] Gilpin, 'On the Art of Sketching Landscape', in *Three essays: – on Picturesque Beauty; on Picturesque Travel; and, on Sketching Landscape: to which is added a Poem, on Landscape Painting* (London, 1792), 61–2.   [23] Ibid., 66.

Gilpin suggested that the rough sketch of a master 'has sometimes an astonishing effect on the mind; giving the imagination an opening into all those glowing ideas, which inspired the artist; and which the imagination *only* can translate'.[24] In his fourteenth Discourse, delivered at the Royal Academy of Art on 10 December 1788, Sir Joshua Reynolds noted that 'from a slight, underdetermined drawing, where the ideas of the composition and character are . . . only just touched upon, the imagination supplies more than the painter himself, probably, could produce'. But danger lurked in the ambiguity of the sketch, its promiscuous invitation to the viewer's imagination. Reynolds continued with a caution: 'We cannot . . . recommend an undeterminate manner or vague ideas of any kind, in a complete and finished picture . . . Science and Learning must not be sacrificed and given up for an uncertain and doubtful beauty . . .'[25] Another contemporary warning went further:

Useful as sketches are, artists, certainly young ones, must use them with sobriety, in order not to accustom themselves to the *mistaken and fantastic*. The artist must protect himself from the seduction of the thousand vague and irrational ideas which *sketches* suggest to him. He must examine with great rigour his libertine ideas at the moment that he establishes his composition.[26]

The fear of over-indulgence in fantasy at the expense of reason, and its concomitant quasi-erotic effect on the body, is as tangible here as it is in contemporary critiques of the musical fantasia.

That Sulzer and others in the 1770s and 1780s should have continued to be interested in a curious machine of the 1750s (which was destroyed by fire only a few years after its invention and exhibition) reflects both the increasing prominence of the fantasia in these decades, and the active critical debate on these issues as it was expressed in the literature on sketching. In 1785 the landscape painter Alexander Cozens published a scheme for drawing landscapes, one familiar to Gilpin, entitled *A New Method of Assisting the Invention in Drawing Original Compositions of Landscape*. Cozens' *Method*, which directly addressed the evanescent productions of an artist's fantasy, had gained considerable notoriety in both Germany and England, and both it and the earlier *Essay* are listed in the bibliography appended to the article on 'Landschaft' in Sulzer's *Allgemeine Theorie* (revised and enlarged edition of 1786). Cozens had

---

[24] Ibid., 50.

[25] Joshua Reynolds, Discourse XIV (1788), in *Discourses*, ed. Pat Rogers (London: Penguin, 1992), 225–6.

[26] Francesco Miliza, *Dizionario delle belle arti del disegno* (1797), s.v. 'Schizzo'. Reprinted in the article 'Esquisse, esquisser' in the *Dictionnaire des arts . . .* of Watelet and Levesque (Paris, 1792). Cited in Jean-Claude Lebensztejn, *L'Art de la Tache* (Montélimar: Editions du Limon, 1990), 122–3.

Figure 3.1   A 'beautiful' and 'picturesque' version of the same underlying landscape form, William Gilpin, 'On the Art of Sketching Landscape' (1792)

been teaching his blotting method since the early 1750s at Eton and Christ's Hospital, and numbers of English artists after him used his technique whose aim paralleled that of the fantasy machine of the same decade. Yet despite Cozens' position as drawing master to the royal children, as well as many aristocrats (including the incorrigibly exotic William Beckford), his system was widely ridiculed, and he himself was dismissed by some wags as 'Blotmaster-general to the Town'.[27]

Cozens' method was designed, like the Fantasy Machine, to preserve spontaneity and truth in recording the ideas of the artist – for a great composition, 'how perfect soever in conception, grows faint and dies away before the hand of the artist can fix it upon the paper or canvas'. Cozens promised an 'instantaneous method of bringing forth the conception of an ideal subject fully to the view (though in the crudest manner)'. His system was based on the use of blots which, like musical improvisations, make a virtue of accident while being by no means entirely accidental. The blot is a 'production of chance, with a small degree of design'. It provides a freely expressive way of creating an outline of the artist's idea, one which can then be worked up into a more conventional drawing or painting; the blot is not simply a random confusion, for the process is governed by a controlling idea (see figures 3.2 and 3.3). Blotting, Cozens claims, is 'the speediest and the surest means of fixing a rude whole of the most transient and complicated image of any subject in the painter's mind'. Yet, given that a single blot may serve a number of finished paintings, the blot functions not only as a recording device but also as an aid to invention, a type of sketch that, in its indeterminacy, stimulates the imagination of the viewer.[28] Clearly, however, Cozens' own mounting and signing of some of his blots suggests their self-sufficiency as works of art, like the apparently random and sketchy improvisations of great musicians.

Cozens' blots were as much machines of invention as of transcription or translation, and in this they paralleled both the fantasy machine and improvisation in general. Both Johann Friedrich Reichardt and Karl Ludwig Junker, for example, suggested that a composer wishing to evoke a particular affect should first concentrate on a literary or pictorial representation of the affect in question, and then improvise at length

---

[27] For more on Cozens, and his son, John Robert, see Kim Sloan, *Alexander and John Robert Cozens – The Poetry of Landscape* (New Haven and London: Yale University Press, 1952); see also Lebensztejn, *L'Art de la Tache*; and E. H. Gombrich, *Art and Illusion: A Study in the Psychology of Pictorial Representation* (Princeton, NJ: Princeton University Press, 1989), 181–91.

[28] Alexander Cozens, *A New Method of Assisting the Invention in Drawing Original Composition* (London, 1785), 3, 2, 10. Cozens suggested that a number of different people could use the same blot as the basis for their own compositions (useful, no doubt, in the classroom).

in order to develop suitable musical ideas.[29] According to Koch, improvisation could facilitate invention by setting loose the imagination and letting inspiration take over: 'This improvisation . . . can very often be a means by which the composer arouses the activity of his genius or puts himself into that state known as inspiration.'[30] Likewise Haydn, in the last years of his life, explained his compositional process to Griesinger as a tripartite one of *phantasieren, componieren* and *setzen*: 'I sat down [at the keyboard] and began to fantasize, according to whether my mood was sad or happy, serious or playful. Once I had seized an idea, my entire effort went toward elaborating and sustaining it according to the rules of art.'[31] Improvisation constitutes the initial free search for ideas, in the course of which a main idea is generated, and is subsequently elaborated into a composition.

Cozens' *Method* was an enlarged version of an earlier *Essay to Facilitate the Invention of Landskip* published anonymously in London in 1759; in another obscure English pamphlet of the 1750s a system of blots analogous to Cozens' method appeared together with the fantasy machine as methods of musical invention in a satirical attack on modern music by the organist and Oxford professor of music William Hayes. Hayes' (anonymous) treatise on *The Art of Composing Music by a Method entirely New, suited to the meanest Capacity* (1751) ridicules its putative author, one Barnabas Gunn, organist and postmaster at Birmingham, but it also makes a broad swipe at the unruliness of contemporary music in general, lamenting the demise of the old 'manly' style of Handel, and the popularity of effeminate new Italian music – represented here as the product of lax, improvisatory compositional method. Gunn, presented as a gung-ho admirer of the new music, recounts the sorry progress of his own musical education. Having gone to a learned Dr P. (Pepusch, presumably), the young genius found himself struggling under the constraints of the Doctor's rules, which were 'too abstruse, too dry, and too full of Labour, for one of my volatile Disposition . . . '. Such 'Principles of Harmony' proved to be merely 'so many Clogs to a sprightly Genius', and, deciding to rely on his own brilliant imagination, 'Gunn' reports that he 'resolved to give them up entirely . . . finding my own unerring

---

[29] Quoted in Bellamy Hosler, *Changing Aesthetic Views of Instrumental Music in 18th-Century Germany* (Ann Arbor, MI: UMI Research Press, 1981), 170.

[30] Koch, *Musikalisches Lexicon*, col. 778, s.v. 'Improvisieren'.

[31] Georg August Griesinger, *Biographische Notizen über Joseph Haydn* (Leipzig: Breitkopf and Härtel, 1810), 78, cited in Mark Evan Bonds, *Wordless Rhetoric: Musical Form and the Metaphor of the Oration* (Cambridge, MA: Harvard University Press, 1991), 116. See also Hollace Ann Schafer, '"A Wisely Ordered Phantasie": Joseph Haydn's Creative Process from the Sketches and Drafts for Instrumental Music' (Ph.D. diss., Brandeis University, 1987); and Elaine Sisman, 'After the Heroic Style: Fantasia and the "Characteristic" Sonatas of 1809', *Beethoven Forum* 6 (1998), 67–96.

Figure 3.2 Blot sketch, Alexander Cozens, *A New Method of Assisting the Invention in Drawing Original Compositions of Landscape* (1785)

Figure 3.3 Blot sketch, Alexander Cozens, *A New Method of Assisting the Invention in Drawing Original Compositions of Landscape* (1785)

Fancy to produce infinitely more charming Effects'.[32] The intrepid would-be composer looks for alternatives to the old strict rules of composition, a system that will allow him the indulgence of his fantasy, and that will enable anyone, even five-year-olds, to compose as well as he – a rebuff to the elitist critics who have snubbed him in the past. One of these alternatives, an apparently easy solution to the problem of composing in the new style, is the Fantasy Machine:

I then took into Consideration a Scheme proposed to the Royal Society for writing down Music played extempore on a Harpsichord, or any such instrument, by means of Pencils being fixed to the underside of the Keys, and a Barrel, or Roller, to turn round, having Lines ready ruled upon it, to receive the Marks which the Pencils would make thereon; and the Proportions of the Notes to be calculated according to the different Lengths of the Strokes.

Unfortunately, however, some degree of talent is necessary even for this aid to random composition: the machine 'might have done; but then it was necessary to be a musician (at least a Performer) before you could be a Composer; for which reason I laid that aside'.[33]

At last the perfect tool for composition in the new style presents itself: the Spruzzarino. The narrator describes how, visiting a local bookbinder's shop, and noticing how the binder decorates the books using an ink-pot and brush 'to sprinkle the Edges of the Leaves, and (with some Variation) the Outside of the Covers', he realised its potential in a flash of inspiration. He rushed home and took his own ink and brush 'which for the future I shall beg leave to call a Spruzzarino; not by that vulgar Name a Brush any longer'.[34] The instructions for composition 'In the New Style' with the Spruzzarino are as follows:

Take a Gallipot, put therein Ink of what Colour you please; lay a Sheet of ruled Paper on your Harpsichord or Table; then dip the Spruzzarino into the Gallipot; when you take it out again shake off the superfluous Liquid; then take the fibrous or hairy Part betwixt the Fore-finger and Thumb of your Left-hand, pressing them close together, and hold it to the Lines and Spaces you intend to sprinkle; then draw the Fore-finger of your Right-hand gently over the Ends thereof, and you will see a Multiplicity of Spots on the Paper; this repeat as often as you have Occasion, still beginning where you left off. This done . . . take your Pen and proceed to the placing the Cliffs or Keys at the Beginning, marking the Bars, and forming the Spots into Crotchets, Quavers, etc., as your Fancy shall prompt you, first the Treble, then the Bass; observing a proportionable Quantity in the latter to suit with the former; this done, season it with Flats and Sharps to your taste.[35]

---

[32] [William Hayes], *The Art of Composing Music by a Method entirely New, suited to the meanest Capacity* (London, 1751), 15. For a short account of the article and the dispute between Hayes and Gunn, see Otto Erich Deutsch, 'Ink-Pot and Squirt-Gun, or "The Art of Composing Music in the New Style"', *The Musical Times* 93 (1952), 401–3.

[33] Hayes, *Art of Composing Music*, 23.   [34] Ibid., 25.   [35] Ibid., 29–30.

This random spattering at the promptings of fancy was the nonsense that Cozens was accused of promoting in his *Method*, its results differing only in degree from the chaotic patterns of the fantasy machine's emissions. Hayes presents fantastic improvisation as the inventive root of modern instrumental music, and attacks that new music as rambling and incomprehensible.

One year later, Charles Avison published his *Essay on Musical Expression* (1752) and he too complained of 'vague and unmeaning' pieces of new Italian instrumental music, with their 'deluge of unbounded Extravaganzi' and tedious modulation. Modern instrumental music, according to Hayes, mistakenly valued a kind of inept virtuosity; broken, discontinuous and fantastical, it was the work of composers not unlike Barnabas Gunn 'without abilities':

the Subject or Air is no sooner led off, than it is immediately deserted, for the sake of some strange unexpected Flights, which have neither Connection with each other, nor the least Tendency to any Design whatever. This kind of random Work is admirably calculated for those who *compose* without *Abilities*, or *hear* without *Discernment*; and therefore we need not wonder, that so large a share of the music that hath of late appeared, should fall under this Denomination.[36]

Music such as this was marred by excessive 'flights' of the imagination, strange, unexpected digressions, and unconnected ideas. This view was not confined to a certain circle of mid-century musical conservatives in England: when the German translation of Avison's book appeared twenty-six years later in 1778 it was given a lengthy review in the *Musikalisch-kritische Bibliothek* (1778–9) by Johann Nikolaus Forkel, who concurred emphatically that 'everyone who truly understands the state of our modern music must be in complete agreement with the author here'.[37]

One important aspect of Avison's book which received detailed attention from Forkel was its lengthy section on the analogies between music and painting, one which attempted to deal with the definitive character of instrumental music. Indeed, much of the aesthetic of the new music was explained here in terms of painting, especially the manipulation of musical contrasts. Avison described a 'chiaroscuro' of consonance and dissonance (in moderation, of course) as a fundamental ingredient of good composition:

[36] Charles Avison, *Essay on Musical Expression*, 2nd edn (London, 1753; reprint edn, New York: Broude Bros., 1967), 31, 37.
[37] 'Karl Avison's Versuch über den musikalischen Ausdruck. Aus dem Englischen übersetzt . . .', *Musikalisch-kritische Bibliothek*, ed. Johann Nikolaus Forkel, 3 vols. (Gotha, 1778–9), II, 153.

As a proper mixture of light and shade, chiaroscuro, is necessary in painting, so the judicious Mixture of Concords and Discords is equally essential to a musical composition: As shades are necessary to relieve the Eye, which is soon tired and disgusted with a level glare of Light, so Discords are necessary to relieve the Ear, which is otherwise immediately satiated with a continued, and unvaried Strain of Harmony.[38]

In the chapter on 'Musical Colouration' in his *Ideen zu einer Aesthetik der Tonkunst*, C. F. D. Schubart praised Avison's demonstration that the musician, like the painter, uses outline, coloration, chiaroscuro, mezzotint and perspective, and indeed considerable interest in the analogies and connections between music and painting was expressed in the many articles which appeared in German music journals between the 1750s and the 1780s.[39] A particularly striking example of the effort to analyse the congruence between music and painting is provided by the 'Beitrag zu einem musikalischen Wörterbuch', published by Hiller, which gives equivalents in music for terms used in painting. The author of the lexicon, signed 'T. S.', points to the need for new musical terminology on the grounds of the close relationship between the terms of painting and those of music. Accordingly, the lexicon gives musical redefinitions for such terms as *Auslöschen* (to erase), *Retuschieren* (to retouch, touch up), *Linie* (line), *Malen* (to paint), *Licht* (light), *Schatten* (shade) and *Zeichnung* (drawing, sketch). The definitions themselves are somewhat strained, but the attempt, and Hiller's reprinting of the dictionary, demonstrate the contemporary fascination with the issue.[40]

---

[38] Avison, *Essay on Musical Expression*, 23. Norris Stephens notes in his article 'Charles Avison' in *The New Grove* that, by his own admission, Avison's essay was not entirely his own work but that of a 'junto' that included the poet and landscape gardener William Mason and possibly his fellow poet Thomas Grey. Mason, whose famous and influential poem *The English Garden* appeared in 1772, was a friend of William Gilpin, and was responsible for the publication of Gilpin's *Picturesque Tours*. He is also cited familiarly by Uvedale Price as the source for a comparison between the necessity for contrast in both landscape and music.

[39] See especially Hiller's *Wöchentliche Nachrichten die Musik betreffend* (Leipzig, 1766–70) and Cramer's *Magazin der Musik* (Hamburg, 1783–7). These include the 'Beantwortung der Frage: Was finden sich zwischen der Musik und der Mahlerey für Aehnlichkeiten?' in Hiller's journal, translated from the *Mercure de France* (August 1768), and the essay 'Ob Mahlerey oder Tonkunst eine größere Wirkung gewähre?' which appeared in the *Magazin der Musik* in 1787.

[40] Musical pictorialism (*musikalische Mahlerey*) was also the subject of much debate in the context of more general links between music and painting. Such 'musical painting' was generally regarded with suspicion, as tasteless and easily clichéd. The seminal text on the subject was Johann Jakob Engel's *Über die musikalische Mahlerey* (Berlin, 1780), reprinted with two appendices – the articles 'Mahlen' and 'Gemähld' from Sulzer's *Allgemeine Theorie*, and Section 26 of Lessing's *Hamburgische Dramaturgie* – in Cramer's *Magazin der Musik* 1/2 (10 November 1783), 1139–98.

Though the metaphor has by now achieved the invisibility of cliché, for Schubart and his contemporaries the notion of 'musical colours', used especially to describe dynamic contrast, was a fashionable and rather new figure; Reichardt self-consciously used the analogy to describe how a crescendo or diminuendo, 'if I may so express myself, passes through all the shades of a light or dark colour',[41] and many of his contemporaries characterised the replacement of the old terraced dynamics with crescendi and diminuendi as a breakthrough from performance in black and white to full colour. Echoing many of his contemporaries, J. J. Quantz likewise encouraged his pupils to 'proceed as in painting', 'where so-called mezze tinte . . . by which the dark is imperceptibly joined to the light, are applied to express light and shadow'.[42] Not only did such concern with musical colour exemplify contemporary attempts to find parallels between the arts, just one of many such carefully drawn analogies between music and painting, but it was long lived. In 1801 Thomas Busby's *Complete Dictionary of Music* defined musical contrast in explicitly painterly terms, as the chiaroscuro of dynamic change:

Contrast in music is that opposition and relief produced by the difference of style in the several movements of a composition; or the chiara oscura of the several passages in the same movement: the alternate crescendos and diminuendos, pianos and fortes, employed by the composer, to awaken the attention, and interest the feelings of his audience.[43]

Likewise, Busby cited the play of light and shade achieved by various contrasts as essential to good musical composition in his definition of 'Effects', which 'by that happy contrast of instrumental tones, and timely relief of fullness and tenuity' give 'light and shade', and moreover create a 'picturesque impression' that delights the ear and interests the feelings.[44]

---

[41] J. F. Reichardt, *Briefe eines aufmerksamen Reisenden die Musik betreffend*, 2 vols. (Frankfurt, 1774), I, 11. The invention of this nuance was popularly ascribed to Nicolò Jommelli, responsible for 'the precise determination of musical colours, and certainly the all-important Crescendo and Diminuendo', whose gradual increase and decrease in intensity had the power to draw listeners out of their seats; Schubart wrote that 'When he introduced this expression into an opera in Naples for the first time, all the people in the stalls and balconies stood up, and astonishment shone from wide eyes. People experienced the magic of this new Orpheus, and from that time on he was considered to be the foremost composer in the world.' C. F. D. Schubart, *Ideen zu einer Ästhetik der Tonkunst*, ed. Ludwig Schubart (Vienna: Degen, 1806; reprint edn, Hildesheim: Olms, 1973), 46–8.

[42] J. J. Quantz, *Versuch einer Anleitung die Flöte traversiere zu spielen* (Berlin, 1752; reprint of 3rd edn [1789] Kassel: Bärenreiter, 1953), 145; trans. Edward R. Reilly as *On Playing the Flute* (New York: Schirmer, 1985), 172.

[43] Thomas Busby, *A Complete Dictionary of Music* (London, 1801), 68, s.v. 'Contrast'.

[44] Ibid., 93–4, s.v. 'Effect'.

In his review of the *Essay on Musical Expression*, Forkel listed the extensive parallels between music and painting explored by Avison and tentatively agreed that 'Design' (*Zeichnung*) and colour in painting might correspond to melody and harmony in music, that both music and painting were united in their primary concern with 'Expression' (*Ausdruck*) and that a clever mixture of consonance and dissonance in music might be seen to parallel light and shade in painting. But Forkel questioned Avison's more ambitious idea that the various degrees of distance in painting – foreground, middle ground and background ('off-skip') may be compared with the different parts in music – bass, tenor and descant – for 'whereas all the parts of a picture are fixed and lasting', this analogy fails to take into consideration 'the successio temporis on which listening to a piece of music depends'. To take into account the temporal dimension is to cast doubt on the whole project of a comparison between painting and music, for, as Forkel explains, music is dynamic, unfolding in time, whereas a painting remains static and is perceived all at once. Likewise, a painting does not change with time, it is permanent, whereas music is temporary and ephemeral. Thus, Forkel concludes, 'it is easy to determine where the limits of our comparisons lie'.[45]

Of course the visual art that incorporated a temporal dimension, landscape gardening, was itself theorised as a form of painting. Horace Walpole, who coined the term 'landscape gardener', noted how 'an open country is but a canvass on which a landscape might be designed'. It was the task of the gardener to make imaginative projections onto such a canvas, to 'realise' its compositional/formal potential, so that in the 'improved' countryside of the landscape park, 'every journey is made through a succession of pictures'.[46] Unlike the painting, the landscape garden is experienced gradually in time, rather than apprehended all at once, and, crucially, it is constantly and ineluctably changing; the landscape garden quickly escapes the artist's control, inevitably transformed by the effects of weather, ageing or use – effects which, in properly conceived plans, are incorporated into its original design. Indeed, it is this that contributes to the crucial instability of the picturesque, which Martin Price has characterised as an uneasy mode that wavers between the sketch and the ruin:

The picturesque in general recommends the rough or rugged, the crumbling form, the complex or difficult harmony. It seeks a tension between the disorderly or irrelevant and the perfected form. Its favourite scenes are those in

---

[45] Forkel, 'Karl Avison's Versuch', 151.

[46] Horace Walpole, *On Modern Gardening*, first published with the 4th edn of Walpole's *Anecdotes of Modern Painting* (London, 1771; reprint edn, London: Brentham Press, 1975), 68, 43.

which form emerges only with study, or is at the point of dissolution. It turns to the sketch which precedes formal perfection, and the ruin, which succeeds it.[47]

In the *Critique of Judgement* (1790) Immanuel Kant classified gardening as a kind of landscape painting which 'takes its form bodily from nature (the trees, shrubs, grasses and flowers taken, originally at least, from wood and field)', but one characterised by its abstractions and openness to interpretation, for 'the arrangement which it makes is not conditioned by any concept of the object or of its end (as is the case in sculpture), but by the mere free play of the imagination in the act of contemplation. Hence it bears a degree of resemblance to simple aesthetic painting that has no definite theme (but by means of light and shade makes a pleasing composition of atmosphere, land, and water).'[48] Kant's notion of landscape painting as 'simple aesthetic painting', that is, painting without the kind of subject a history painting or portrait might be based on, mirrors contemporary judgement of music without words as lacking clear semantic content. Instrumental music, like landscape painting and the landscape garden, relies for its effect on 'light and shade', the 'abstract' manipulation of contrasts.[49] Indeed, Kant compares the two, classifying both 'what in music are called fantasias (without a theme), and, indeed, all music that is not set to words', as 'free beauties', which, like the designs on wallpaper, 'have no intrinsic meaning; they represent nothing – no Object under a definite concept'; but just as with the landscape garden, the imagination is all the more free to be 'at play in the contemplation of the outward form'.[50] The critique of modern instrumental music in Germany and England was in many ways a complaint against its more fantastic elements and given the overlapping concerns of contemporary writers on the fantasia and on landscape, it is perhaps not surprising that a common analogy for the abstractions of such music was provided by landscape painting. Prefiguring Kant's notion of this art as abstract, the article 'Ausdruck in der Musik' in Sulzer's *Allgemeine Theorie* compared instrumental music to the indeterminate, if beautiful patterns in the sky at sunset:

[47] Martin Price, 'The Picturesque Moment', in *From Sensibility to Romanticism: Essays Presented to Frederick A. Pottle*, ed Frederick W. Hilles and Harold Bloom (New York: Oxford University Press, 1965), 277.

[48] Immanuel Kant, *The Critique of Judgement* (1790), trans. James Creed Meredith (Oxford: Clarendon Press, 1952), 187, footnote.

[49] The changing status of landscape painting during the course of the eighteenth century mirrored that of instrumental music. What began as topographical record became a medium for expressing emotional response to natural scenery. At the end of his life, William Gilpin stated explicitly what much of his earlier work had implied: that if the landscape painter can create images 'analogous to the various feelings, and sensations of the mind' then 'where would be the harm of saying, that landscape, like history painting hath its ethics!' Andrews, *Search for the Picturesque*, 37–8.

[50] Kant, *Critique of Judgement*, 72–3.

A composition that merely fills the imagination with a sequence of harmonious sounds, without touching the heart, is like a sky beautifully painted by the setting sun. The attractive kaleidoscope of colours pleases us; but the heart is not involved by the cloudscape.[51]

For Georg Joseph Vogler, however, music without words could not only make sense, but be rich in meaning. Reconfiguring Sulzer's image, Vogler compared the ambiguous character of instrumental pieces such as symphonies to 'arbitrary' landscape paintings which, though imaginary, could correspond to an actual scene, in a conflation of the real and the imaginary something like that suggested by Alexander Cozens' blot method:

Symphonies, instrumental pieces which are subordinated to no particular pantomimic expression, without words, can, moreover, be meaningful. Their course must be original, their flight the flight of eagles – trifling pleasantries and vulgar diversion do not belong there. Even though their discourse is ambiguous, their traits are as captivating as one would expect of good drawing masters, as open to all images, as soft wax in the hand of a modeller. Such instrumental symphonies, which apply such various shades of colours, are like an arbitrary landscape painting, which without the knowledge of its creator may come close to a real landscape, or a spontaneously done sketch of an old man, that perhaps actually matches an unseen original.[52]

In such pieces, the imagination of the perceiver, finding shapes in the cloudscape, is spurred to construct forms out of apparently formless matter, as wax in the hands of a sculptor.

Conjuring coherent shapes from amorphous masses was the principle at work behind Cozens' blot method, and indeed, in presenting his blots as ambiguous creations designed to allow multiple interpretations, Cozens cast his whole project as an exercise for the imagination of the viewer. Further, the epigram from Shakespeare with which Cozens introduced the essay likened the *Method* itself to a freely fantastical game of seeing shapes in clouds:

> Sometime we see a Cloud that's dragonish,
> A Vapour sometime like a Bear, or Lion,
> A tower'd Citadel, a pendant Rock,
> A forked Mountain, or Promontory,
> With Trees upon't, that nod unto the World,
> And mock our Eyes with Air.[53]

---

[51] Sulzer, *Allgemeine Theorie*, s.v. 'Ausdruck in der Musik'. Translation based on le Huray and Day, *Music and Aesthetics*, 124.

[52] G. J. Vogler, 'Thätige Geschmacks-Bildung für die Beurtheiler der Tonstücken', *Betrachtungen der Mannheimer Tonschule*, 4 vols. (Mannheim, 1780; reprint edn, Hildesheim: Olms, 1973), I, 290; p. 284 in the reprint due to wrong pagination in original.   [53] Shakespeare, *Anthony and Cleopatra*, Act IV, Scene xiv.

And in fact the *Method* contained an extended series of cloud studies, at first glance rather out of place among its concluding examples of blots (see figure 3.4). The openness of clouds to interpretation is like that of sketches, or music without words – or 'incomplete' fantasias. As William Gilpin noted, the sketch that has not been 'worked up' into something more complete is open to multiple readings, as the spontaneity of its invention and execution necessarily incurs a risky (or rich) lack of closure. While seeing shapes in clouds might signal a pathological delirium, clouds also offered a heightened reality, where the spectacle of fantastic metamorphoses was played out in the theatre of the imagination.[54]

The blurred and blotted business of the performance and interpretation of musical fantasies coalesced, in the second half of the eighteenth century, around C. P. E. Bach's fantasia in C minor, H. 75, the concluding *Probestück* from the *Versuch* (1753), the piece that provided the touchstone for subsequent contributions to the genre, as well as for critical discussion of musical fantasy well into the nineteenth century. In 1763 the poet Heinrich Wilhelm von Gerstenberg made an experimental 'analysis' of this famous fantasia, this quintessential clavichord piece providing him, he claimed, with the most obscure, yet paradoxically the clearest example of musical expression; out of its complex mosaic of precisely ordered *Bebungen*, and sudden dynamic changes, Gerstenberg had crystallised two dramatic verbal texts, both of which are meditations on suicide: one is a freely adapted version of Hamlet's monologue 'To be or not to be' ('Sein oder nicht sein'), the other imagines Socrates about to drink the fatal hemlock (see figure 3.5).[55] In Gerstenberg's interpretation the fantasia's discourse is dark, intimate and portentous of death; as the voice rises out of the opening C minor harmony to embark on a strange rhapsody that ghosts the determinedly unmelodic body of the fantasy, this 'most obscure of instrumental pieces' is cast not as the 'arbitrary' conveyor of pleasing effects, but rather as the impassioned vehicle for the tragic meditations of great men (less landscape than history painting). Perhaps not coincidentally, Cozens' epigram to the *New Method*, taken from *Anthony and Cleopatra*, addresses similar subject matter: considering suicide, Anthony imagines himself to be as ephemeral as cloud patterns, now a visible form, soon to disappear.

[54] For a brief survey of attitudes towards seeing images in the clouds, see Lebensztejn, *L'Art de la Tache*, 95–100; and Gombrich, *Art and Illusion*, 181–202.

[55] Gerstenberg's experiment is documented in detail in Eugene Helm, 'The "Hamlet" Fantasy and the Literary Element in C. P. E. Bach's Music', *Musical Quarterly* 58 (1972), 277–96. See also Friedrich Chrysander, 'Eine Klavier-Phantasie von Karl Philipp Emanuel Bach mit nachträglich von Gerstenberg eingefügten Gesangsmelodien zu zwei verschiedenen Texten', *Vierteljahrsschrift für Musikwissenschaft* 7 (1891).

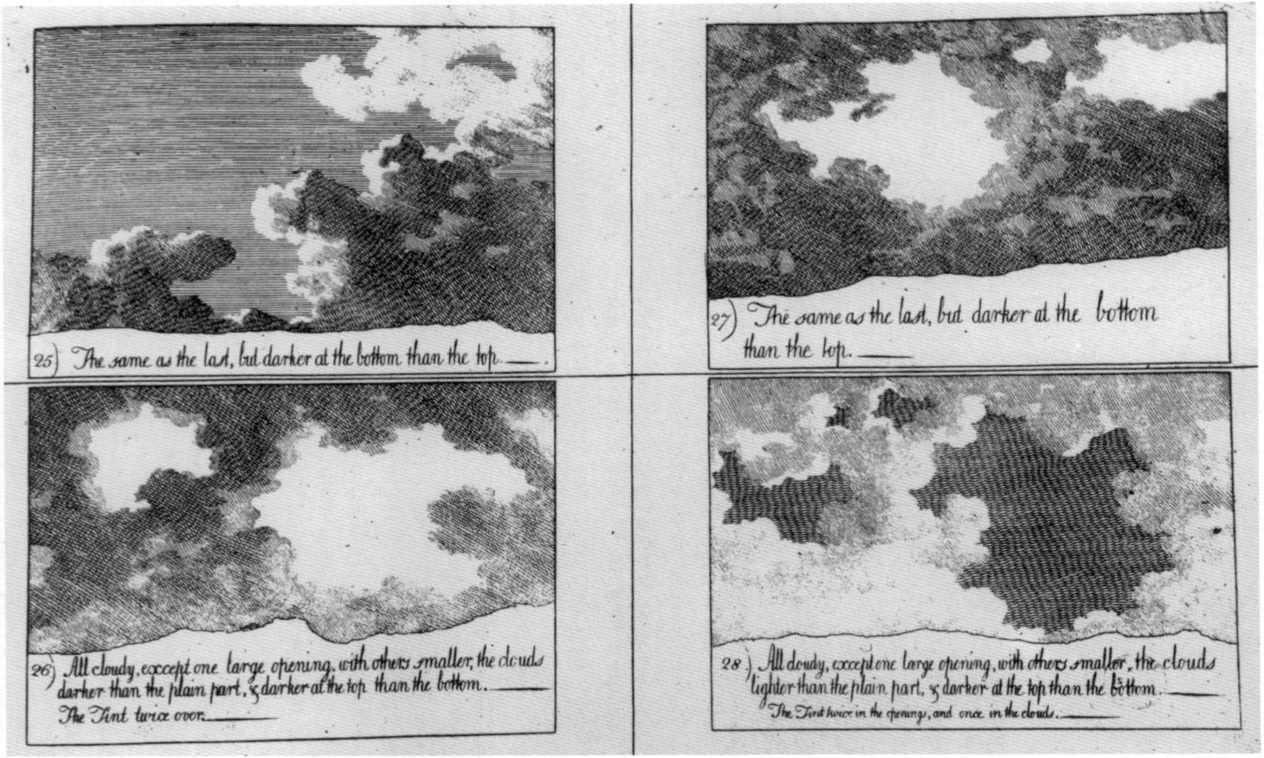

25) The same as the last, but darker at the bottom than the top. ——

26) All cloudy, except one large opening, with others smaller, the clouds darker than the plain part, & darker at the top than the bottom. ——
The Tint twice over. ——

27) The same as the last, but darker at the bottom than the top. ——

28) All cloudy, except one large opening, with others smaller, the clouds lighter than the plain part, & darker at the top than the bottom. ——
The Tint twice in the opening, and once in the clouds. ——

Figure 3.4   Cloud studies, Alexander Cozens, *A New Method of Assisting the Invention in Drawing Original Compositions of Landscape* (1785)

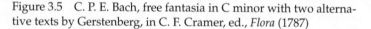

Figure 3.5   C. P. E. Bach, free fantasia in C minor with two alternative texts by Gerstenberg, in C. F. Cramer, ed., *Flora* (1787)

Gerstenberg's project subsequently became the subject of a long essay by Carl Friedrich Cramer published in 1787, which describes a fascinating process of musical interpretation. Cramer's essay addresses not only the fantasia, but more generally the hermeneutic potential and problems of the newly ascendant instrumental music; Gerstenberg's experiment, he claimed, posed the question 'whether pure instrumental music in which an artist had expressed only the dark passionate conceptions that lay in his soul might also be susceptible to a clear definite analysis'.[56] It perhaps seems ironical that the argument Cramer presents here for the value of 'absolute' music should derive from the festooning of the fantasia with two verbal texts, but Cramer rationalises this aspect of the project: he apologises for the addition of constraining and overly specific words to the free fantasia, the most open and freely instrumental of genres, and argues instead for what the texts represent of the fantasia's hermeneutic possibilities on a more thematic level. They provide examples for a notion similar to that expressed by Friedrich Schlegel a

---

[56] C. F. Cramer, announcement for 'Flora. Eine Sammlung Compositionen für das Clavier und den Gesang', in Cramer, *Magazin der Musik* 2/2 (22 June 1787), 1359; translation based on Helm, 'The "Hamlet" Fantasy', 287.

few years later in the *Athenaeum* fragments: 'Some find it strange and
foolish when musicians speak of the thoughts in their compositions . . .
but . . . must not pure instrumental music itself create a text of its own?'[57]
The idea is encapsulated in a single image: 'Out of all the flights and
leaps', Cramer writes,

never coercible by meter or rhythm and moving through every region of modulation, of these cloud formations, [the critic's] plastic genius lifts out here a
nose and there an eye, like the Lesbian Tragelaph, and assembles for you such
a shape of deep emotion, that certainly might not be equally clear to everybody,
but will reward the wise, if he takes the trouble to – *study* – it. – – and *one* shape
is not enough![58]

Cramer figures the fantasy as a multivalent cloudscape, and the work
of the interpreter as that of discovering shapes in clouds. Having
explained that this fantasia is the expression of 'the unfettered flight of
Bach's sublime imagination', Cramer describes how Gerstenberg has
engaged in an idiosyncratic fantasy performance of his own, giving
'unrestrained flight' to his own sublime imagination.

Cramer presents the constant shifts and changes of the fantasia not as
empty ravings but as a fabulous cloudscape full of potential meanings.
Indeed, he emphasises the multiplicity of possible interpretations – 'one
shape is not enough'. Not only does the analogy with seeing shapes in
clouds focus on the activity of the listener in 'performing' his own work
of fantasy, it allows for the discovery of multiple meanings in this indeterminate instrumental music, without compromising the essential
freedom of the fantasia by imposing a rigid interpretative framework on
it. Cramer figures the spontaneous, performative fantasia as meaningful, not in terms of the formal coherence advocated by Forkel, but in a
new way in which, as the imagination of the artist works with as little
mediation as possible to produce a shifting and transitory soundscape,
the resultant gaps allow the listener to perform her own imaginative
work of interpretation: just as Bach often gives the listener time to
reinterpret and reconfigure at the moments of most extreme digression,
it is precisely the irregularities, disappearances and absences of the fantastic itself that allow a dialogic engagement between performer and listener.[59]

---

[57] Cited in Carl Dahlhaus, *The Idea of Absolute Music*, trans. Roger Lustig (Chicago and
London: University of Chicago Press, 1989), 107.

[58] Cramer, announcement for 'Flora', 1359–60.

[59] In his review of Bach's fourth *Kenner und Liebhaber* collection Cramer advocated a more
specifically pictorial listening; having noted that Bach might do well 'to assist us with
simply a small explanation' of the fantasies, 'so that we might be able perhaps to enter
into some definite feelings', he reports that the eccentricities of the Fantasia in A major
(H. 278) from that collection had been explained by Bach as the product of a particularly bad bout of gout – the fantasia was a 'fantasia in tormentis'. Likewise, in the

It is ironically appropriate, then, that Cramer's interpretation of the fantasia as a shifting cloudscape has itself disappeared from the recent critical literature on the genre. In his detailed commentary on this key fantasia text, Eugene Helm omitted the paragraph I have quoted above from his translation of Cramer's essay, its absence signalled by an ellipsis. Perhaps the omission may be due to the difficulty and, at first sight, obscurity of the passage's bizarre reference to clouds; perhaps it has something to do with the odd body parts, here a nose, there an eye, of the unknown 'Lesbian Tragelaph'. Perhaps the allusion to Lesbos baffled the critic and tempted him to suppress the passage altogether. But this strange creature is central to Cramer's interpretation of a new kind of music, for the Tragelaph is a figure of classical mythology, half stag and half goat, which functions in classical philosophy as a standard metaphor for the unreal.[60] Amalgamating his classical allusions, Cramer situates this polymorphous monster on the isle of Lesbos, presumably thus referring to the 'Lesbian rule' mentioned by Aristotle in the Nichomachean Ethics, a flexible measuring stick that can be made to conform to any shape. 'All things are not determined by law', Aristotle writes,

[indeed] about some things it is impossible to lay down a law, so that a decree is needed. For when the thing is indefinite the rule also is indefinite, like the lead rule used in making the Lesbian moulding; the rule adapts itself to the shape of the stone and is not rigid, and so too the decree is adapted to the facts.[61]

In Cramer's formulation, then, the fantasia, neither straight, fixed, nor predetermined, is to be celebrated for its richly varied and brilliantly shifting topography, one which the listener is expected to confront without fixed aesthetic assumptions. Far from being empty and incoherent, it is, like the sketch or indeed the landscape itself, music rich with its own forms, however unstable they may be.

The fantasia demands a kind of listening that indulges a free-ranging imagination, with its promise of intense emotions, morbid reflections and, not least, libidinous updraughts – it promises the sublime but threatens chaos. While the issue of indeterminacy was central to the contemporary debate over the fantasia, fantasy characteristics themselves were constantly described, both positively and negatively as

Sonata in G major (H. 273) Cramer hears the 'sweet joy of an innocent maiden sitting by a brook in the haze of a summer evening'. Review of 'Claviersonaten und freye Phantasien . . . vierte Sammlung', in C. F. Cramer, *Magazin der Musik* 1/2 (7 December 1783), 1243.

[60] See Giovanna Sillitti, *Tragelaphos: Storia di una metafora e di una problema* (Naples: Bibliopolis, 1981).

[61] Aristotle, *Nichomachean Ethics*, 1137b 30, trans. W. D. Ross, *The Complete Works of Aristotle: The Revised Oxford Translation*, ed. Jonathan Barnes (Princeton, NJ: Princeton University Press, 1984), 1796.

intrinsic elements of contemporary instrumental music. If the free fantasia could be meaningful despite its apparent incoherence, then so too could 'abstract' instrumental music. Extrapolating from Cramer's interpretation of Bach's C minor fantasia, the way in which the fantasia enacts musical meaning may be taken as a model for other kinds of instrumental music in this period. Where late twentieth-century analytical techniques emphasise formal coherence and downplay surface discontinuities, Cramer valued the contingent and disruptive as opportunities for imaginative play by the listener. Indeed, Cramer advocates a fantastical listening which establishes individually constructed meaning precisely through a creative intervention on the part of the listener. Resituating the fantasia within a broader, more picturesque, conception of the eighteenth-century musical imagination offers the present-day performer and listener the opportunity for a new and lively engagement with this music which, in its resistance to notation and its intrinsic instability might offer us – as it offered educated listeners of the period – an unruly and rewarding way to hear anew even the more 'ordered' masterpieces of the late eighteenth-century canon.

4

Haydn's humour, Bach's fantasy

Writing, when properly managed . . . is but a different name for
conversation; As no one, who knows what he is about in good
company, would venture to talk all; – so no author, who understands
the just boundaries of decorum and good-breeding, would presume
to think all: The truest respect which you can pay to the reader's
understanding, is to halve this matter amicably, and leave him
something to imagine, in his turn, as well as yourself.

Laurence Sterne, *The Life and Opinions of Tristram
Shandy, Gentleman* (London, 1760–7)

I

The picturesque was the visual and verbal language of the new tourism,
presenting nature as culture, culture as nature; in late eighteenth-
century England landscape gardens represented and commodified
English cultural supremacy for the foreign visitor. England's landscaped parks were as definitive as its idiosyncratic literary productions,
epitomised by Shakespeare and Laurence Sterne, and a crucial part of
any tour of the country's sights. That the diary kept by the Austrian
noble Count Carl von Zinzendorf, which provides such a vital source of
information on musical life in Vienna and in the Eszterháza circle,
should offer a particularly rich insight into the status of the English
garden as an icon of tourism may seem unlikely; yet Zinzendorf visited
the British Isles in 1768 and, travelling around the country between
February and November of that year, he visited all the important
gardens and a good number of the lesser ones, diligently writing up his
visits as he went. Over the course of his stay, Zinzendorf visited forty-
four different parks and gardens, and his trip culminated in the summer
months in what amounted to a two-month long garden tour, by which
time he was well versed in the semiotics of this art form.[1]

---

[1] See Géza Hajós, 'The Gardens of the British Isles in the Diary of the Austrian Count Karl
von Zinzendorf in the year 1768', *Journal of Garden History* 9/1 (1989), 40–7.
Zinzendorf's diary entry for 11 August refers to 'Gilpin Tome II p. 184 sequ.' and is
indicative of the widespread appeal, and usefulness, of Gilpin's *Observations*; presumably this note to himself was added later, as Gilpin's volumes had not begun to appear
in print in 1768.

At Lord Hamilton's park at Painshill in early May, despite the typically abysmal English weather, he admired the mixture of trees, the
skilful design of the route through the park, the grotto, and especially
the variety of 'points de vue', some of them produced naturally by the
undulating terrain, and some achieved by artful manipulation of the
scenery:

There are very beautiful views into the distance [and] others equally admirable,
of the different parts of the park. From a Gothic Temple one sees at first a large
artificial lake crossed by numerous bridges, all beautifully shaped. Further
away one notices a hermitage in the middle of the trees, and a somewhat elevated tower which yields a beautiful view. Despite the rain, which was considerable, we proceeded through this vast park, we passed a bridge and arrived at
the grotto under which a trickle of water passes. This grotto is made entirely of
crystals so realistic that one would swear that it is natural . . . We arrived near
the Belvedere; this is the tall tower which we had already seen in passing yes-
terday; the rain stopped us from going up and from going on to a hermitage
where we are told there is yet another enchanting view. Returning to the house,
we came upon a sort of thatched cottage, which is almost face-to-face with the
Gothic Temple, only the canal between the two; there one has yet another delicious view, over the temple, the canal, and the distant countryside.[2]

Later that month Zinzendorf admired the 'very picturesque' ('très pit-
toresque') landscape through which the Thames flowed at Horace
Walpole's Gothic extravaganza, Strawberry Hill; by early August he
was in Yorkshire, and his taste turning to the rougher and wilder aspects
of landscape. At Cocken, near Durham, he described the park's five-
mile circuit which passed through woods and between menacing rocks,
descending to a murmuring river, obscurity alternating with brightness,
glimpses of ancient ruins giving way to expansive, yet carefully framed,
views of the countryside: 'You are sometimes in the wood, alongside a
stream, in a narrow valley with a small trickle of water, then suddenly
you see the river reappear, forming near you a beautiful, tranquil sheet
of water, and further off a vaulting cascade between the wooded hillsides, and precisely at the place where the two hillsides seem to meet
there appears between the two the church spire of Chester in the Street.'[3]
Zinzendorf visited Stourhead in Wiltshire and was shown the grottoes,
the hermitage, the temples, and all the varied artifices of this elaborate
park by Sir Henry Hoare himself; at the famous gardens of Stowe in
Buckinghamshire, guided around the circuit by the proprietor Richard
Temple, Lord Cobham, Zinzendorf remarked on the Palladian Bridge
and the Stone Bridge, the Elysian Fields and the Shepherds Cove, the
temple to Venus, the temple to Bacchus, the Greek temple, the temple of
British Worthies, the temple of Ancient Virtue, the Rotunda, and the

[2] Ibid., 43.   [3] Ibid., 44.

Egyptian Pyramid, climbing eagerly to the tops of the buildings to take in the immense variety of views. His trip had educated him to be an enthusiastic student of landscape appreciation.

For the remainder of the century garden tourism continued to increase in popularity for continental visitors to England, and twenty-three years later Zinzendorf's fellow countryman and acquaintance Joseph Haydn joined their ranks. In 1791 Haydn described in his note-book the 'beautiful English gardens' and 'glorious view' at Oatlands in Surrey, a park whose grotto Zinzendorf had particularly admired; Haydn too, staying there as the guest of the Duke of York, was impressed by the 'most remarkable grotto which cost £25,000 Sterling, and which was 11 years in the building'.[4] (Could Haydn have got this right? this was surely more likely to have been the sum, and duration of construction, for the whole garden.) One of the most famous foreigners in the country in the 1790s, Haydn received generous hospitality on his visits to the country estates of the English upper classes (he stayed, for example, for five weeks in the summer of 1791 at Roxford in Hertfordshire, the country house of the banker Nathaniel Brassey); he would certainly have been exposed to the aesthetics and discourse of the picturesque, not just as a hot issue of contemporary debate, but also in its practical relevance to his hosts, those upper-middle-class and aris-tocratic landowners who so eagerly and conspicuously spent vast sums of money creating and maintaining magnificent landscape gardens which they took pride in showing to their visitors.

While Haydn admired the gardens of the English elite, his London audiences were captivated by the picturesque qualities of his music, which he claimed to have created after he had conscientiously set about 'studying the taste of the English'.[5] The London critics, delighted by the manipulation of surprise and drama, the fantastic and unexpected, in Haydn's new symphonies, enthused over their mixture of styles, the variety of their musical topography. As the critic for *The Times* wrote of the Symphony in D major, no. 93 (the first of Haydn's second London season, performed in February 1792),

Such a combination of excellence was contained in every movement, as inspired all the performers as well as the audience with enthusiastic ardour. Novelty of ideas, agreeable caprice, and whim, combined with all Haydn's sublime and

---

[4] H. C. Robbins Landon, *Haydn: Chronicle and Works*, 5 vols. (Bloomington and London: Indiana University Press, 1976–80), vol. III, *Haydn in England 1791–1795*, 109.

[5] See David P. Schroeder, *Haydn and the Enlightenment: The Late Symphonies and their Audience* (Oxford: Clarendon Press, 1990), 96; and A. Peter Brown, 'The Sublime, the Beautiful and the Ornamental: English Aesthetic Currents and Haydn's London Symphonies', in *Studies in Music History, Presented to H. C. Robbins Landon on his Seventieth Birthday*, ed. Otto Biba and David Wyn Jones (London: Thames and Hudson, 1996), 44–71.

wonted grandeur, gave additional consequence to the soul and feelings of every individual present.[6]

In addition to sublime grandeur, it was a humorous quality based on novelty and wit that caught the public's attention. Charles Burney had already hinted at the picturesqueness of such qualities in Haydn's more humorous music in his *History*, citing, in addition to allegros that are 'exhilarating' and adagios that are 'pathetic' and 'sublime', movements 'that are sportive *folatres*, and even grotesque, for the sake of variety, but they are only the entremets or rather intermezzi between the serious business of his other movements'.[7]

It is not hard to see how the famous surprises and jokes of both the first and second symphonies composed for, and performed at, that second season, were heard as musical instances of the picturesque. The second movement, Largo cantabile, of no. 93, for instance, opens as a lilting, if somewhat falteringly 'beautiful' melody for solo string quartet, yet the first period is hardly completed before it lurches into the tonic minor at bar 17, with a fortissimo trumpets-and-drums tutti whose double dots and trills verge on an archaic parody of the opening theme, a pseudo-Handelian travesty (example 4.1);[8] poking fun at the proclivities of some members of his audience, Haydn shows himself well attuned to contemporary musico-aesthetic debate (the Ancients v. the Moderns). But satirical humour turns disruptive, even frankly rude. As the texture becomes increasingly fragmented and begins to wind down as if to a halt (bars 72–9), it is interrupted and galvanised back into action by a shocking fortissimo bassoon blast (bar 80); not only comical, this is an archetypal picturesque moment – disruptive, eccentric and unjustified, both shocking and hilarious (example 4.2). It was effects of this sort that Uvedale Price warned against when he claimed that modern listeners may need excessive stimulation in order to be aroused to wonder, a sign of a jaded and degraded taste. 'Effects' as an end in themselves, Price suggested, are meaningful only in their function of arousing attention, as antidotes to boredom.[9] And yet the picturesque's

---

[6] *The Times*, 20 February 1792, quoted in Simon McVeigh, *Concert Life in London from Mozart to Haydn* (Cambridge: Cambridge University Press, 1993), 159. See also Roger Barnett Larsson, 'The Beautiful, the Sublime and the Picturesque in Eighteenth-Century Musical Thought in Britain' (Ph.D. diss., SUNY Buffalo, 1980), 157.

[7] Charles Burney, *A General History of Music*, 4 vols. (London, 1776–89), II, 960; quoted in Larsson, 'The Beautiful, the Sublime and the Picturesque', 157.

[8] See Brown, 'The Sublime, the Beautiful and the Ornamental', 46.

[9] Price wrote that 'Many people seem to have a sort of callous over their organs of sight, as others over those of hearing; and as the callous hearers feel nothing in music but kettle-drums and trombones, so the callous seers can only be moved by strong oppositions of black and white, or by fiery red.' Price, 'On the Picturesque', *Essays on the Picturesque, As Compared with the Sublime and the Beautiful; and, on the Use of Studying Pictures, for the Purpose of Improving Real Landscape*, 3 vols. (London, 1810), I, 129.

Example 4.1   Haydn, Symphony no. 93, ii, Largo cantabile, bars 9–22

focus on stimulation, on the roughness and irregularity produced by the ornamentation of smooth surfaces, relies precisely on such devices – they are the source of the 'almost perverse cultivation of surprise' that lies at the heart of this aesthetic.[10]

[10] Angus Fletcher, *Allegory: The Theory of a Symbolic Mode* (Ithaca, NY: Cornell University Press, 1964), 257.

Example 4.2   Haydn, Symphony no. 93, ii, Largo cantabile, bars
71–81

The unforgettable 'surprise' of Symphony no. 94, in which a sudden
fortissimo shout violently disrupts the sweetest and most gentle lyricism of the slow movement, works as a similar, if even more intense,
evocation of the 'effects' of the picturesque. This is surely not, as some
modern commentators have suggested, an example of the musical
sublime, for while, in the abstract, the fortissimo shock appears to
conform to Edmund Burke's description of sublimity in sound as
having to do with 'a sudden beginning, or sudden cessation of sound of

any considerable force', the conspicuous collapse into the absurd rules out any possibility of the sublime: rather than transporting the listener beyond him or herself the instant fortissimo only draws attention to the conscious act of listening, both privately and, more devastatingly, collectively, and becomes a quintessential example of the picturesque manipulation of effect.[11] The commentary that appeared in the *Oracle* of 24 March 1792 suggested as much in a description that is picturesque both in the colloquial sense and in its appreciation of a humorous incongruity: 'the surprise might be not unaptly likened', wrote the reviewer, 'to the situation of a beautiful Shepherdess who, lulled to slumber by the murmur of a distant Waterfall, starts alarmed by the unexpected firing of a fowling-piece'.[12] Such a puncturing of an illusion of pastoral beauty by a violent interruption is portrayed as comic, if not verging on the lewd.

There is perhaps a faint allusion to the sublime, but flanked by the beautiful and later the recherché, the variations of the slow movement of Symphony no. 94 constitute a picturesque patchwork of effects. The third variation crashes in with the most extreme of contrasting affects, a lumbering *Minore* fortissimo replete with trumpets and drums and heavy off-beat accents, and an ostentatiously Baroque excursion in the second half of the couplet. The rest of the movement serves to enhance this effect of exaggerated posturing, though in somewhat less extreme guise – in the fourth variation, *Maggiore*, oboes and flutes sound out a version of the theme with dainty repeated notes and delicate ornaments that verge on a parody of nursery-rhyme primness. It is as if the composer were hovering on the knife-edge of exaggeration that Uvedale Price cautioned against when he suggested that a composer who has 'too great [a] fondness of discords and extraneous modulations' is in danger of smothering 'a sweet and simple air beneath a load even of the richest harmony', like an architect who, 'from a false notion of the picturesque' mistakenly tries to improve a simple building with 'a profusion of ornaments'.[13] A slippage of this sort similarly undermines what might have been a turn towards the sublime in the Finale of Symphony no. 94: as the end approaches, an ominous timpani crescendo (beginning in bar 226) ushers in a sudden crashing modulation from G to E♭ (bar 234) that evokes a distanced, perhaps parodic, or even 'picturesqued' representation of sublimity, so well controlled and framed is it by the jovial contredanse within which it is set (example 4.3).[14]

---

[11] Brown and other commentators have suggested that the 'surprise' here may be read as an instance of the musical sublime.   [12] Landon, *Haydn Chronicle*, III, 150.

[13] Price, 'On the Picturesque', 108.

[14] Brown interprets this as a 'dramatic turn from the country dance to the terror of the sublime'.

Example 4.3   Haydn, Symphony no. 94, iv, Allegro di molto, bars
226–44

Uvedale Price ascribed to the picturesque not only variety and
sudden changes, but 'marked character', a quality that when applied to
music brings together both the abstract 'picturesque' and its more colloquial counterpart, the 'pictorial'. The poet and prolific letter-writer
Anna Seward heard what she understood as the musical picturesque in
a vividness of effects that, in their intensity, could conjure up visual
images. 'The real source of the picturesque', Seward wrote, 'and the
stimulative effects of musical sounds, result from the judicious inter-

mixture of discords, hurrying and clashing in descriptive or in animating harshness.'[15] It was this sort of animation that especially caught the attention of the audience at the first performance of Haydn's famous 'Military' Symphony (no. 100). The symphony presents a catalogue of picturesque conceits, from its strange harmonic detours, sudden pauses, exaggerated contrasts, odd effects of colour, 'stimulating' dynamic changes and games with form. But it was the second movement in particular that took London by storm. The *Morning Chronicle* announced that

> Encore! encore! encore! resounded from every seat: the Ladies themselves could not forbear. It is the advancing to battle; and the march of men, the sounding of the charge, the thundering of the onset, the clash of arms, the groans of the wounded, and what may well be called the hellish roar of war increased to a climax of horrid sublimity![16]

It is certainly an impressive movement, and yet the notion of such music as the actual representation of 'horrid' war, combined with the enthusiasm of the ladies, introduces an element of the absurd and suggests a bathetic mode; this music plays on an instability that works less to arouse the unarguable wonder of the sublime, than to intimate the picturesque, if not its alter-ego the grotesque. The effect is created not simply by the raucous Turkish instruments in the second and last movements, but by the extravagant and entertaining use of orchestral colour and timbral contrasts; individual voices or sections of the orchestra, especially winds in alternation with strings, create a brilliant kaleidoscope of 'marked character' that threatens to disintegrate into caricature. In combination with Haydn's sublime gestures and moments of enchanting beauty, this music's sense of humorous posturing, of toying with incongruity and casting doubt on sincerity found a receptive audience in Haydn's London listeners.

II

In England, in the decades around 1800, a specific theory of the musical picturesque was articulated not only in the works of Uvedale Price, but also, more cogently, in the lectures of the Oxford professor of music, William Crotch, who associated this style in particular with the wit and humour of C. P. E. Bach and Haydn. As contemporary theorists asserted, the picturesque slips easily between the sublime and the comic: according to Price, while the sublime 'never descends to anything light or

---

[15] Seward to Dr Darwin, 29 May 1789, in Anna Seward, *Letters Written between the Years 1784 and 1807*, ed. A. Constable, 6 vols. (Edinburgh, 1811), II, 265. As quoted in Larsson, 'The Beautiful, the Sublime and the Picturesque', 178.

[16] *Morning Chronicle*, 9 April 1794, in Landon, *Haydn Chronicle*, III, 247.

playful', the picturesque 'is equally adapted to the grandest and to the gayest scenery'.[17] Picturesque intricacy and fancifulness signalled a self-conscious interest in play, and the picturesque's mixture of high and low, its games with light and shade, its delighted awareness of the ambiguous tension between artifice and accident, were infused with a ludic quirkiness. Arguing on the basis of modern instrumental music and that of Haydn in particular, Crotch asserted that the picturesque in music was fundamentally humorous and playful, a low style by contrast with the bracing challenge of the sublime and the gentle pacification of the beautiful; rather than elevating its listener, the 'wit and humour' of the musical picturesque would inspire 'amusement and delight'. In his *Substance of Several Lectures on Music* – printed in 1831 but based on a series of lectures given at Oxford and in London between 1800 and 1804[18] – Crotch borrowed extensively from Price's writings on the picturesque, but proposed the term 'ornamental' as a substitute for 'picturesque', perhaps in response to Price's notion that the conjunction of the decidedly visual 'picturesque' with music might be thought untenable.

Crotch traced the origins of this style to the keyboard works of Domenico Scarlatti, who had

struck out in that more ornamental, humorous, or witty style, which gave birth to most of the eccentricities and novelties of modern piano-forte music. To insure originality he set the rules of composition . . . at defiance. In his works . . . all is calculated to amuse and surprise, to create a smile if not a laugh.[19]

Not that Crotch particularly approved of this, but at least, he added rather stuffily, Scarlatti's pieces were free from the 'one great fault of the modern school' in that 'they are not too long'. His use of the term 'ornamental' is taken from Sir Joshua Reynolds who, in his famous series of *Discourses on Art*, distinguished between the Grand (which subsumes

---

[17] Price, *An Essay on the Picturesque, As Compared with the Sublime and the Beautiful; and, on the Use of Studying Pictures, for the Purpouse of Improving Real Landscape* (London, 1794), 80–1.

[18] A number of the ideas contained in the lectures appeared earlier in the *Specimens of Various Styles of Music referred to in A Course of Lectures read at Oxford and London,* 3 vols. (*c.* 1808–15). Crotch's work is discussed at some length in Larsson, 'The Beautiful, the Sublime and the Picturesque'; see also Brown, 'The Sublime, the Beautiful and the Ornamental'; and Tilden A. Russell, '"Über das Komische in der Musik": The Schütze–Stein Controversy', *Journal of Musicology* 4/1 (1985–6), 70–90.

[19] William Crotch, *Substance of Several Lectures on Music, Read in the University of Oxford and in the Metropolis* (London: Longman, Rees, Orme, Brown and Green, 1831), 129–30. Scarlatti's preface to the *Essercizi per gravicembalo* (London, 1738) hinted at an intent both humorous and didactic: 'Whether you be Dilettante or Professor, in these Compositions do not expect any profound Learning, but rather an ingenious jesting with Art, to accommodate you to the mastery of the Harpsichord.' Translated by Ralph Kirkpatrick in his *Domenico Scarlatti*, rev. edn (Princeton, NJ: Princeton University Press, 1983), 102.

both sublime and beautiful) and the Ornamental styles in painting. Crotch's substitution is significant, for, following Reynolds, it relegates the picturesque to the bottom of the aesthetic hierarchy. For Price, the sublime, beautiful and picturesque were distinct but equal in terms of value; for Crotch, however, the picturesque or ornamental is inferior to the beautiful, which, in its turn, takes its place below the sublime. The particular relevance of the picturesque, or ornamental, to the fantastical and transgressive elements in contemporary instrumental music emerges from the remarkable cluster of adjectives used by Reynolds, and his source, the sixteenth-century theorist Giorgio Vasari, to describe the 'Ornamental' style of sixteenth-century Venetian painting: painters such as Veronese and Tintoretto, Reynolds writes, used 'capricious composition', and 'violent and affected contrasts'. Reynolds quotes Vasari on Tintoretto:

'Of all the extraordinary geniuses that have practised the art of painting, for wild, capricious, extravagant, and fantastical inventions, for furious impetuosity and boldness in the execution of his work, there is none like Tintoret[to]; his strange whimsies are even beyond extravagance, and his works seem to be produced rather by chance, than in consequence of any previous design, as if he wanted to convince the world that art was a trifle, and of the most easy attainment.'[20]

Following Reynolds, Crotch opines that 'the undue prevalence of the ornamental style is a sure indication of the decline and decay of any art'. Moreover, in music it belongs particularly to instrumental genres whose ascendance, he states, is the sign of eroding standards of taste and the degeneracy of modern music.[21]

Crotch's lectures undertake to coax the student away from the easy attractions of the 'low' picturesque style of modern music towards the more demanding, acquired tastes of the sublime or beautiful music of earlier times (a typically English antiquarian project), educating the indiscriminate consumer of modern ornamental music who 'may find his imagination fired by powerful effects, strong contrasts, and sudden transitions', but who will otherwise miss the 'delicate refinements of taste'.[22] Like many of his English contemporaries, Crotch was conservative in his musical tastes and considered the long-dead Handel the paragon of musical excellence. His project, in general terms, was not so different from Forkel's efforts to educate the taste of the musical amateur in Germany, but given the wide currency of the sublime, beautiful and picturesque in late eighteenth-century British aesthetic debate, it is perhaps to be expected that Crotch, sooner than a continental writer, would attempt this demonstration.

---

[20] Quoted in Reynolds, 'Discourse IV' (1771), *Discourses on Art,* ed. Pat Rogers (London: Penguin, 1992), 125–6, 127.   [21] Crotch, *Substance,* 66.   [22] Ibid., 15, 19.

Crotch claimed not to be an opponent of modern music as such; rather his essay is a diatribe against faddish taste, a protest against novelty, and the 'absurd and mischievous opinion', commonly held, that music is 'continually improving from every invention, innovation, and addition'. The love of the new fired the contemporary enthusiasm for fantasias, for spontaneous performances by virtuosi were admired as the ultimate in novelty. The London of the 1790s which responded with such excitement to the latest works of Haydn was a society fascinated with, and greedily drinking in, anything new. Crotch particularly associated this behaviour with women, remarking that the obsession with novelty was 'displayed in the daily practice of our young females [purchasers of keyboard music] who, on entering a music shop, simply enquire if any thing new is published'.[23]

But the self-consciously erudite Crotch was a more modern critic than he was perhaps aware, for at the climax to his work his text reveals itself to be curiously infected by the discourse of landscape theory and its current fashions. He reaches Handel, whom he considers the apex of musical achievement, and invites the reader to stand back and reflect for a moment:

Having guided the steps of the student to this lofty summit, let him contemplate the prospect and enjoy the enlargement of his views. He must surely now regard as beneath him the scenery which he once most admired, but which is, by comparison, so limited and humble. He may not, perhaps, choose to dwell on this eminence, and in every direction he may easily descend; but it is hoped he will frequently revisit these higher walks, which raise him far above all earthly and common sounds, and in their stead give him sublime and sacred strains.[24]

It is surely ironical that in contrasting the sublime heights of the old Handelian style with the ornamental or picturesque lower paths of the modern style, Crotch shows an impeccable understanding of the picturesque experience, one that rejects the too-obvious large-scale overview and relishes the complexities of a succession of partially obscured and often unexpected vistas that the lower path through the landscape offers.

Uvedale Price had described picturesque music as capricious and irregular, possessing 'a certain wildness' in which 'sudden and quickly varying emotions of the soul are exposed'. Referring closely to Price's picturesque, Crotch summarised the ornamental style in the Preface to his *Specimens* as 'playfulness of melody, broken and varied measure, intricacy of harmony and modulation, and a perpetual endeavour to excite surprise in the mind of the auditor'.[25] Crotch's example of this

---

[23] Ibid., 72. On the taste for novelty among the English public, see also Simon McVeigh, *Concert Life in London from Mozart to Haydn* (Cambridge: Cambridge University Press, 1993), esp. 64–101.   [24] Crotch, *Substance*, 127.   [25] Crotch, *Specimens*, I, 1–2.

style, the Sonata in D (K. 21, published in the *Essercizi* of 1738) by Domenico Scarlatti, is hardly representative of modern instrumental music in the 1790s, but its inclusion here is consonant with the particular popularity of Scarlatti in English music criticism of the second half of the eighteenth century. The piece is, though, playful and surprising, and while it does not exactly explore unconventional modulation, it has its share of piquant chromaticism and modal mixture; above all, it is a flamboyant exercise in keyboard virtuosity, with its perverse leaps and difficult, and totally arbitrary, handcrossings.

In addition to Scarlatti Crotch's commentary discusses that other renowned composer of keyboard music, so often linked with Scarlatti in English criticism, C. P. E. Bach. Bach's works, according to Crotch, abounded in 'chromatic passages, new harmonies and bold modulations', and although these were at first 'regarded as extravagant' they had since been not only tolerated but had become 'objects of universal imitation'.[26] The 'Specimen' Crotch chooses in this case is the fantasia in C major, H. 291 from the sixth *Kenner und Liebhaber* collection (1787). This, Bach's last published fantasia, is thoroughly playful and witty, and is, perhaps paradoxically, a model of control, indulging in almost none of the wild ravings associated with the improvisations of genius. The fantasia is barred throughout, with the exception of the final cadenza, and its large-scale organisation reflects the formal structure of a rondo. Its five sections correspond to rondo refrain and couplets, A B A C A, and on the small scale the refrain sections themselves form miniature monothematic rondos.[27] The three 'refrains' are full of tricks to catch the listener out, jokes derived from a constant play with the rondo-like principal subject through fragmentation of the thematic material, frequent interruptions, sudden stops, and games with periodicity and rhythm. These are juxtaposed with two incongruous slow sections which could not be more different from the rondo theme, all the more surprising for the contrast their serious and serene beauty makes with the prevailing drollery.

Wit and humour in this fantasia are spun out of the roguish frolickings of its principal subject (bars 1–12, example 4.4). The theme, a fast contredanse tune organised in two asymmetrical phrases (2+2 answered by 2+6), is made up of four cells: a semiquaver upbeat motif which outlines the tonic triad; a group of four quavers reiterating the fifth scale degree, and followed by a dotted neighbour-note decoration of the same degree; a pair of staccato crotchets on the dominant, with an added lower voice in sixths; and a descending quaver scale, also in sixths. These elements,

---

[26] Crotch, *Specimens*, III, ii.
[27] The piece is discussed in Leonard Ratner, *Classic Music: Expression, Form and Style* (New York: Schirmer, 1980), 310.

Example 4.4   C. P. E. Bach, Fantasia in C, H. 291, *Kenner und Liebhaber* VI (1787), bars 1–48

taken apart, extended, truncated, recombined, in a great variety of per-mutations and combinations, provide all the material for the 'refrain' sections of the fantasia. The repeated quavers remain undisturbed in all but one statement, and act as the signal for the actual restatements of the theme among all its fragmentations, yet already in the first section (bars 30–6) a humorous hesitating effect is created by the isolation of this figure, blankly repeating in ever-diminishing fragments under which

Example 4.5   C. P. E. Bach, Fantasia in C, H. 291, *Kenner und Liebhaber* VI (1787), bars 87–110

the left hand triads creep slowly upwards (example 4.4). Forward motion is recovered only with the descending scale of the second half of the theme, a figure which is itself the source for plenty of tricks – in its variable length it constantly defeats the listener's expectations, arriving at the cadence apparently at random. In the second 'refrain' an extended version of the scale figure metamorphoses into a duet with a variation of the first part of the subject at bar 98, and then, as if it has overshot the mark, overlaps with the next entry of the subject proper, in D minor, at bar 106, the only entry of the subject in the whole piece which is not separated from what has gone before (example 4.5).

Extension is one recurring device, truncation another. Bits are chopped off and chopped up, start in one direction, stop suddenly, begin again in another. At bar 13 (example 4.4) an interpolated fragment tricks the listener by sounding like what should be there, and turning out not to be – a pianissimo statement of the theme in the dominant disappears into an upward arpeggio in the third bar, followed by silence; yet it is then recast as an interpolated pre-echo by the real dominant entry of the subject an octave lower and forte. Phrases are short and frequently isolated by

Example 4.6   C. P. E. Bach, Fantasia in C, H. 291, *Kenner und Liebhaber* VI (1787), bars 49–53

Example 4.7   C. P. E. Bach, Fantasia in C, H. 291, *Kenner und Liebhaber* VI (1787), bars 125–33

caesuras. In the second refrain, the statement of the subject in the tonic, beginning in bar 87, is abruptly cut off by rests which impudently preserve the length of the phrase they have interrupted, so that the suddenly muted theme may continue unimpeded in the listener's imagination (example 4.5). While straightforward diatonic key relationships prevail on the large scale, the games are played out over strange and surprising leaps directly into new keys without preparation.

But in its incorporation of extreme mood changes this fantasia moves beyond the merely comical and light-hearted. The two intervening slow sections are clearly set apart from the rest, both structurally and in terms of style and affect. The first, Andante, modulates from B♭ major to E minor. It is pathetic and rhetorical, and its three-part texture provides a fuller sonority after the light, two-part texture of the preceding refrain section (example 4.6), though not as lush as the Larghetto to come. The Larghetto sostenuto is even more incongruous, with the low tessitura and full pulsating chords of its opening bars and elegiac eight-bar theme (example 4.7), standing as a sentimental ruin in the midst of its animated and capricious surroundings. The Larghetto modulates from G major to C♯ major before coming to rest on a diminished seventh on D♯ in bar 152, reconfigured (the D♯ respelled as E♭) as a diminished chord on A with a dominant function leading not to E minor (as had been expected) but to B♭ major.

The two slow sections in this fantasia maintain a seemingly unbridgeable distance from the rondo-like refrains, and, by contrast with many of C. P. E. Bach's other fantasias, there is no intrusion of material from either

Example 4.8   C. P. E. Bach, Fantasia in C, H. 291, *Kenner und Liebhaber* VI (1787), bars 207–end

of these into the faster contrasting sections. Indeed, the extended and unrelated melancholy in the midst of the rondo context comes across almost as a parody of the principle of contrast, an ironising of the quintessential characteristic of fantasia. Moreover, the unlikely supremacy of the introverted over the extroverted is paradoxically affirmed in this apparently jovial piece by the unlikely and unsettling ending, in which, with a sudden shift to an A♭ chord (♭VI) at bar 215, and a cadenza, a conventional, if colourful, cadential formula is exaggerated and extended in order to derail the prevailing liveliness, leading to the subdued, piano descent of the final cadence (example 4.8). This negation of the brilliant rondo effect throws much greater emphasis, in retrospect, on the two slow sections, transforming the piece from a low-comic romp into a more complex exploration of mood change and high-comic sentiment.

The C major fantasia, H. 291 combines the expressive range and humorous unpredictability of the fantasia with the patterned wit of the rondo. For Crotch, it was proof that C. P. E. Bach was the 'father of modern music', and that Haydn, the third member of his ornamental triumvirate alongside Bach and Scarlatti, was 'more indebted [to him] than to any other composer',[28] – and Haydn, in Crotch's theory, represented the apotheosis of the ornamental style. Despite his reservations about this style, Crotch praised Haydn for his 'invention, playfulness, variety, and instrumental effects',[29] and he singled out the symphonies

---

[28] Crotch, *Substance*, 134. Crotch's example of the combination of sublime, beautiful and ornamental, in which the ornamental predominates, is the second movement, Allegretto, of Haydn's Symphony no. 82 ('The Bear', 1786); this Allegretto variation movement seems an unlikely choice, and is certainly not the most obvious example of the picturesque, despite the generally light and playful affect of its principal theme and contrasting central section.   [29] Crotch, *Specimens*, III, ii.

in particular for their 'variety, novelty, brilliancy, and gaiety of style';[30] indeed, in citing Scarlatti, C. P. E. Bach and Haydn, all three of whom were undisputed classics in England by 1805, Crotch could not plausibly dismiss the modern, 'ornamental' style.[31] Re-emphasising the by then common linkage of Haydn and C. P. E. Bach, Crotch traced the 'ornamental' lineage between the two by pointing to a quintessential example of musical humour, the 'last movement of [Haydn's] first sinfonia composed for Salomon's concert' which, he claimed, was 'copied' from C. P. E. Bach's C major fantasia, H. 291.

It was presumably the finale of Symphony no. 97 (1792) that Crotch had in mind (though this was the last symphony performed in Haydn's second season in London), for this piece accords perfectly with Crotch's 'ornamental' style. It is a scintillating C major sonata-rondo whose lively contredanse theme carries echoes of the Bach fantasia subject, most especially in the upbeat semiquavers, and the descending scale and cadence figure that constitute the second half of the theme (example 4.9), and the repeated-note figure that closes the initial binary statement of the rondo refrain (bars 41–50, example 4.10). The potential for the repeated-note figure to hesitate, stutter and peter out, rather than emphatically to close a paragraph, or to lead confidently back into the refrain, is exploited to wonderfully humorous effect. In the coda this figure pushes on to a statement of the refrain that loses direction in a suspended, drawn-out cadence to the relative minor (A minor) at bars 240–60, twice restarts piano after an odd pizzicato in the strings, each time in a different key, before eventually crashing into the driving descending scale, tutti, in the tonic (bar 270, example 4.11); more drastically still, it genuinely appears to bring matters to a halt at bars 303–12 (example 4.12). A different kind of surprise, relying both on structural ambiguity and abrupt dynamic and tonal contrast, is effected at bar 121 with the sudden fortissimo about-face to the tonic minor in the midst of the rondo refrain itself (example 4.13); the carefree refrain metamorphoses into an extensive *Sturm und Drang* development section from which it has trouble extricating itself, even after the unexpected caesura at bar 156 and the tentative introduction of the repeated-note closing theme; far from leading to the close of the episode, this simply provides opportunity for continued development, taking the harmony even further into the dark, flat side, with a sudden detour to C♭ to destabilise the prevailing E♭ harmony (example 4.14). All these jokes, the ambiguous returns of the theme, leaps into unexpected

---

[30] Crotch, *Substance*, 143.

[31] The conjunction of Domenico Scarlatti with C. P. E. Bach is not peculiar to the English context, despite the fact that Scarlatti appears to have been canonised earlier in England than elsewhere. In Germany, G. J. Vogler had referred to Scarlatti's 'bizarre, complex, raving fantasias' as comparable to Bach's overly complex and irregular style. See above, p. 35.

Example 4.9   Haydn, Symphony no. 97, iv, Presto assai, bars 1–16

keys, gradual windings-down and gearings-up, stops and starts, work to create both brilliant amusement and aesthetic distance – it is a piece whose self-aware humour highlights the process of listening itself.

III

The musical picturesque is fantastical and humorous; it creates its effects through the incongruous or seemingly inappropriate insertion, transgressions of decorum which excite surprise and wonder. It may be understood in terms of Mary Douglas' definition of the joke – a 'play upon

Example 4.10   Haydn, Symphony no. 97, iv, Presto assai, bars 36–50

form' which 'brings into relation disparate elements in such a way that the accepted pattern is challenged by the appearance of another which in some way was hidden in the first'.[32] It is a play both on internal form and on the external patterns of social decorum within which it is framed. Humour shares with fantasy its transgressive impulses: 'The fantastic is always a

[32] Mary Douglas, *Implicit Meanings: Essays in Anthropology* (London: Routledge, 1975), 96. Cited in Janet Levy, '"Something Mechanical Encrusted on the Living": A Source of Musical Wit and Humour', in *Convention in 18th- and 19th-Century Music: Essays in Honor of Leonard Ratner*, ed. Wye J. Allenbrook, Janet M. Levy and William P. Mahrt (Stuyvesant, NY: Pendragon Press, 1992), 225–56.

Example 4.11   Haydn, Symphony no. 97, iv, Presto assai, bars 240–79

(*continued*)

break in the acknowledged order, an irruption of the inadmissible within the changeless everyday legality.'[33] Indeed, to the reviewer for the *Hamburgischer unpartheyischer Correspondent*, Bach's fantasy procedures, as demonstrated in the C major fantasia, H. 284 (*Kenner und Liebhaber* V, 1785), were a miniature charade of social impropriety. He commented that for the

---

[33] Roger Caillois, *Au Cœur du Fantastique*, quoted in Tzvetan Todorov, *The Fantastic: A Structural Approach to a Literary Genre*, trans. Richard Howard (Ithaca, NY: Cornell University Press, 1975), 26.

Example 4.11 (*cont.*)

most part this piece, his favourite fantasia ('unsere Lieblingsfantasie'), 'holds itself suitably within the bounds of decorum', yet it also manages to indulge in several 'sideways leaps' ('Die . . . Fantasie . . . hält sich noch ziemlich in den Schranken der Sittsamkeit, obgleich auch einige Seitensprünge gemacht werden').[34] *Seitensprünge* were associated with the tricks of contemporary writers who 'make all sorts of humorous

---

[34] *Hamburg unpartheyischer Correspondent* (3 December 1785). Reprinted in Ernst Suchalla, ed., *Carl Philipp Emanuel Bach: Briefe und Dokumente, Kritische Gesamtausgabe*, 2 vols. (Göttingen: Vandenhoeck & Ruprecht, 1994), II, 1105–7.

Example 4.12   Haydn, Symphony no. 97, iv, Presto assai, bars 303–12

Example 4.13   Haydn, Symphony no. 97, iv, Presto assai, bars 119–29

Example 4.14   Haydn, Symphony no. 97, iv, Presto assai, bars
155–71

digressions' ('allerhand launige Seitensprünge machen'), or with those
brilliant conversationalists who 'don't keep strictly to the subject, but
unexpectedly and wittily turn towards topics lying off to one side' ('der
nicht streng bei der Sache bleibt, sondern sich überraschend und mit Witz
zu abseits liegenden Gegenständen wendet').[35]

[35] Jacob and Wilhelm Grimm, *Deutsches Wörterbuch*, vol. XVI (Munich: Taschenbuch
Verlag, 1984; reprint of 1st edn of 1905), cols. 397–8, 1274–5. The word 'Seitensprünge'

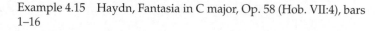

Example 4.15   Haydn, Fantasia in C major, Op. 58 (Hob. VII:4), bars 1–16

Musical humour, like the picturesque, relies as much on games with form as on sudden incongruous effects. In this, too, Crotch could have pointed to the affinity between Haydn and C. P. E. Bach, and to be sure, Haydn's quintessentially picturesque fantasia in C major, Op. 58 (Hob. VII:4) owes not a little to Bach's fantasias, and especially the C major fantasia, H. 291 (example 4.15). In 1788, the year of Bach's death, Haydn had written to Artaria requesting 'the last two Works for keyboard by C. P. Emanuel Bach' (*Kenner und Liebhaber* V and VI);[36] the following year he composed Op. 58, the product, he told Artaria, of 'humorous hours' ('bei launiger Stunde'), which, 'on account of its taste, singularity and particular execution [working out] must be received with all approbation from professional and non-professional alike'[37] – a nod to the connoisseurs and amateurs to whom Bach's collections were addressed. This glittering, extended 3/8 Presto is a brilliant exercise in dynamic surprises, strange chromaticisms, harmonic disjunctions, and formal ambiguity.[38] It relentlessly manipulates the listener, asserting its claim to the genre 'fantasia' in its audacious digressions and games with time and in its free mixture of sonata and rondo conventions; indeed, given

---

also carries connotations of adultery and immoral escapade. Given the specifically gendered eighteenth-century use of *Sittsamkeit* as the term for female modesty and decorum, this free fantasia might perhaps be read as a comic scenario of domestic transgression (which points to themes I will discuss in chapter 5).

[36] 'der letzern 2 Werke für das Clavier von C. P. Emanuel Bach'; letter of 16 February 1788; cited in Peter Schleuning, *Die Freie Fantasie: Ein Beitrag zur Erforschung der klassischen Klaviermusik* (Göppingen: Kümmerle, 1973), 251–2.

[37] 'welches wegen Geschmack, Seltenheit, besonderer Ausarbeitung ganz gewiß von Kennern und Nichtkennern mit allem Beifall muß aufgenommen werden'. Schleuning, *Freie Fantasie*, 320.

[38] See Elaine Sisman, 'Haydn's Solo Keyboard Music', in *Eighteenth-Century Keyboard Music*, ed. Robert Marshall (New York: Schirmer, 1994), 293–5.

Example 4.16   Haydn, Fantasia in C major, Op. 58 (Hob. VII:4), bars
70–94

the generic mixture of fantasia and rondo so brilliantly undertaken by
Bach in the fifth and sixth *Kenner und Liebhaber* collections, Haydn's fantasia points to influence between the two that runs deeper than their
vague correspondences in thematic profile. This piece is in effect an
extended sonata-rondo form, but one in which the structure is veiled by
extensive development and bridge passages, a wayward recapitulation
that swerves off into still further development, and fragmented thematic returns, often in unlikely keys.

After the initial statement of the thematic material, structural articulation is blurred by a determined effort to avoid any real cadences;
indeed the procedures of formal articulation are called into question in
this piece which makes use of frequent caesuras, whose continuations
either constitute shocking changes of direction, tonally and texturally
(as at bar 87, with its sudden full-force plunge from the delicate decorated horn calls on V of G to stormy arpeggios in B♭, example 4.16) or
introduce a creeping insinuation of new movement, as in the slow
ascent from the long held E in the bass at bars 113–16, up the chromatic
scale in bars 116–23 back to the theme in the tonic (example 4.17). This
long bass-note, tonally ambiguous, even disorientating, and a suspension of action and direction, foreshadows the more radical version of the

Example 4.17   Haydn, Fantasia in C major, Op. 58 (Hob. VII:4), bars
112–25

Example 4.18   Haydn, Fantasia in C major, Op. 58 (Hob. VII:4), bars
188–98

same trick, which occurs twice later in the piece: at bar 192 a rapidly
descending A major arpeggio arrives at the same low E octave, but this
time the sonority is held for as long as it takes for the sound to die away,
a gradual encroachment of silence that utterly disrupts the prevailing
lightning energy and threatens to rip apart the temporal fabric of the
piece. Characteristically, the question posed by the disorientating halt is
given an unpredictable answer as the thread is resumed with a whispered chromatic ascent from E to F, and a new statement of the horn-call
theme, now in the remote key of B♭ major (example 4.18).

Haydn repeats the device later: after eight bars of recapitulation of the
A theme in the tonic at bar 255, he veers off towards C minor, and then
E♭ major, with a figure that threatens to repeat itself ad infinitum, before
an eventual enharmonic modulation from E♭ to B major (bar 295), and an
arpeggiated descent to a low F♯; it is not until this note has completely

127

Example 4.19   Haydn, Fantasia in C major, Op. 58 (Hob. VII:4), bars 283–308

died away that the action is resumed with a slide up to G (example 4.19). Such effects, of course, exploit the colour resources of the instrument, but they also demand a certain dramatic performance; indeed, the whole piece constitutes a tour-de-force of comedic gesture on the part of the pianist, who not only has convincingly to wait out the dying notes, but flamboyantly to perform the almost perverse hand-crossings, the dramatic pauses, the humorous repetitions, the unexpected digressions, the sudden heavy-handed octaves at the end, and the coy tinkling that sets up the final cadence itself. Such a wide repertoire of jokes and gestures, both aural and visual, distorts the listener's experience of an underlying form – the sonata-rondo structure is thoroughly disguised by its surface effects, digressions and interruptions, those striking local articulations that catch the attention and distract it from any large-scale patterning.

Disruptive and surprising effects such as these greatly appealed to Haydn's London public, attuned as it was to a taste for the picturesque; indeed, featuring centrally in Crotch's analysis of the ornamental style, they seem to have played a seminal role in the contemporary formation in England of a concept of the musical picturesque. Uvedale Price had described the picturesque as a playful, even comic, forum for wit; he compared the effect of the picturesque to that of a brilliant conversationalist who inspires rapt attention by making strange but apt juxtapositions from 'singular' yet 'natural' angles, one who is

full of unexpected turns, – of flashes of light: objects the most familiar are placed by him in such singular yet natural points of view, – he strikes out such unthought of agreements and contrasts, – such combinations, so little obvious, yet never forced or affected, that the attention cannot flag; but from the delight of what is passed, we eagerly listen for what is to come. This is the true picturesque.[39]

In adducing witty conversation as a model for the picturesque Price recapitulated a trope of contemporary writing on music which figured the exchange between musical performer and listener in similar terms. In explaining the essential impossibility of teaching improvisation, for example, Daniel Gottlob Türk had compared the combination of preconceived ideas and spontaneous inspiration in cadenzas (which 'should be more like a fantasia which has been fashioned out of an abundance of feeling, than a methodically constructed composition') to the same mixture in good conversation; it is as difficult, Türk wrote in his *Klavierschule*, to prescribe good cadenzas as it is

to teach someone to memorize flashes of wit beforehand. For the former and the latter are partly inspired and partly determined by circumstances and occasion. Through diligent reading and observation of the flashes of wit of others, however, one can awaken and sharpen one's own wit, just as one can keep it in order through the directions of reason.[40]

Wit was unexpected and novel; it surprised and delighted and was figured as a kind of magic trick – a sleight of hand in which surprise resemblances are suddenly revealed, the 'connection, invented or displayed unexpectedly, between incongruous and dissonant objects'.[41] Its striking juxtapositions and contrasts, both revealing and concealing unlikely connections, paralleled the trickery of partial concealment at the centre of the picturesque, and indeed, subtly balancing artifice and natural instinct, ideal wit had been described by Pope as the perfect garden art: 'True Wit is Nature to advantage dress'd / What oft was thought but ne'er so well express'd.'[42]

---

[39] Price, *Essay* (1794), 282–3.

[40] Daniel Gottlob Türk, *Klavierschule, oder, Anweisung zum Klavierspielen für Lehrer und Lernende* (Leipzig, 1789; trans. Raymond H. Haggh as *School of Clavier Playing, or, Instructions in Playing the Clavier for Teachers and Students* (Lincoln: University of Nebraska Press), 302.

[41] William Richardson, *Essays on Shakespeare's Dramatic Character of Sir John Falstaff* (1788), quoted in *Monthly Review* 81 (1789), 55. In Gretchen A. Wheelock, *Haydn's Ingenious Jesting with Art: Contexts of Musical Wit and Humor* (New York: Schirmer, 1992), 24.

[42] Alexander Pope, *Essay on Criticism* (London: W. Lewis, 1711), l. 297. Cited by Reynolds as the definition of the ideal landscape gardening in 'Discourse XIII' (1786), *Discourses*, 295.

While comic effects occupied an anomalous and contested position in German music theory in the eighteenth century, in aesthetic theory more generally the comic came to be understood as a sophisticated, if unstable, mediator between the ridiculous and the sublime. The legitimation of the humorous via the picturesque in the music of Haydn and C. P. E. Bach represented a radical transformation in contemporary musical thought. In North Germany, comic effects in music had been either censured outright or at least disparaged and discouraged for the large part of the century.[43] Sudden disjunctions and extreme mixtures of affect were considered to be a breach in decorum, and instability of tone inappropriate and farcical. Georg Simon Löhlein, in his *Klavier-Schule* (1765, 1782), exhorted performers to take care to maintain the propriety of a piece by sustaining the prevailing affect, for the use in an adagio, for example, of ornaments more suited to an allegro would produce a ridiculous result, 'as if Harlequin in his motley were to play a tragic role'.[44] In 1767 Johann Adam Hiller deployed the same theatrical metaphor in comparing the abrupt interpolations of contrasting material in this style to the antics of Hans Wurst intruding into a piece of serious theatre. Not only were such interruptions rude and destabilising, they were fundamentally incoherent and served only to shatter the aesthetic illusion. Such an 'odd mixture of styles', Hiller complained, of 'the serious and the comic, of the lofty and the vulgar, so often found side by side in the same piece' was as unnatural as it was to laugh and to cry at the same time.[45]

In the *Musikalisches Kunstmagazin* of 1791, Johann Friedrich Reichardt proposed a scenario in which such extravagance might make sense, but one in which nonsense was the point – the depiction of madness. The comic of incongruous mixture intersects with the picturesque in the realm of the irrational, where genius verges on lunacy, a tale told by an idiot perhaps, but one in which 'though this is madness, yet there's method in it', as C. F. Cramer had claimed for the fantasias of Bach's fourth *Kenner und Liebhaber* collection. 'Impulsive recklessness and a tendency towards melancholy', Reichardt wrote,

---

[43] On theories of the musical comic in the late eighteenth century, see Wheelock, *Haydn's Ingenious Jesting with Art*; Mark Evan Bonds, 'Haydn, Laurence Sterne, and the Origins of Musical Irony', *Journal of the American Musicological Society* 44/1 (1991), 57–91; Russell, '"Über das Komische in der Musik"', and 'Minuet, Scherzando, and Scherzo: The Dance Movement in Transition, 1781–1825' (Ph.D. diss., University of North Carolina, Chapel Hill, 1983).

[44] Georg Simon Löhlein, *Klavier-Schule* (4th edn, Leipzig, 1782), 65.

[45] See Hiller's essays in the *Wöchentliche Anmerkungen und Nachrichten die Musik betreffend* 2/2 (13 July 1767), 14; 'Zehnte Fortsetzung des Entwurfs einer musikalischen Bibliothek', 3/14 (3 October 1768), 107; Anhang 3/25 (18 December 1769), 191–3; 'Ueber den musikalischen Ausdruck nach dem Rousseau', 4/3 (15 January 1770), 19.

can possibly exist together in one person, but at least never in this person simultaneously or alternating so quickly with each other that this could be the subject for an immediate work of art. The combination can possibly have a moral truth, but certainly not an aesthetic one – unless it should aim to express a third character, such as madness – and that is what it is in this case, the way in which Ophelia in Hamlet sings songs and dances, and yet entertains thoughts of death, all in one breath.[46]

In the same journal in 1782 Reichardt had voiced the old complaint that a 'most unnatural mixture of juxtaposed affects' was the cause of the 'most unnatural Sonatas, Symphonies, Concertos and other pieces of our new music'. Strikingly, however, he made a significant exception at the end of his diatribe, claiming that such strangenesses or bizarrerie could be effective in special cases and were in fact essential for the expression of the peculiar artistic disposition of two famous composers, C. P. E. Bach and Haydn: 'Only Bach and Haydn require all possible means in order to express their original humour [originelle Laune].'[47] In the exceptional cases of Haydn and Bach such effects were not only necessary tools but could lay claim to the highest aesthetic value.

The humour invoked by the term *Laune* signified something more lofty and introverted than Hans-Wurstian comedy; indeed, contemporary German theory conceived of *Laune* as the 'true root of comic action'.[48] Loosely paralleling the English tripartite aesthetic system, J. G. Sulzer described a three-fold classification of the comic into the low comic, 'which is ridiculous in its absurdity', the middle comic, which is essentially polite wit that 'delights and amuses', and the high comic, that comedy 'which borders on tragedy' and where 'powerful and serious passions come into play'. The *Laune* intrinsic to the high tragic-comic in particular was itself considered peculiarly English; this was a temperament made familiar not only by the protagonists of Laurence Sterne's *Sentimental Journey* and *Tristram Shandy*, but also by the mixture of tone so characteristic of the dramas of Shakespeare. Kant defined *Laune* as 'that talent to put oneself voluntarily in a particular frame of mind in which all things become totally other than normal, even turned upside down, yet judged according to certain principles of reason'.[49] Likewise, for Wieland, a humorous composition was one which was rather more the 'involuntary outpouring of a rich wellspring of wit and humour' than a 'work of reflection and art',[50] a definition which underscored the relation between *Laune*, improvisation and the picturesque. The linkage between *Laune* and fantasia was reinforced by the frequent meaning of *Laune* as 'caprice' and *Launigkeit* as 'capriciousness'.

---

[46] J. F. Reichardt, *Musikalisches Kunstmagazin* 2/2 (Berlin, 1791), 39.

[47] Ibid., 1/1 (Berlin, 1782), 25.

[48] Johann Georg Sulzer, *Allgemeine Theorie der schönen Künste,* 2nd edn (Leipzig, 1792–4), s.v. 'Laune'.   [49] Cited in Grimm, *Deutsches Wörterbuch,* col. 347.   [50] Ibid.

Both Bach and Haydn were regarded as the greatest composers of the high comic, their names linked in the contemporary press for their like-minded capriciousness. C. P. E. Bach tends to be viewed today as eccentric rather than funny, by contrast with the jovial and joking Haydn, but eighteenth-century commentators were not in doubt as to the humour (*Laune*) both shared, whether whimsical and fantastical, or comical and jesting. The serious fools of both Sterne and Shakespeare offered literary analogues to the musical characters and caricatures of Haydn and C. P. E. Bach, as well as theoretical grounding for writers on mixed modes in England and Germany. Haydn was described as 'a musical jester . . . of the high comic', who could even express this kind of humour in his adagios, 'where people should actually weep', and Bach's humour received similar attention. Carl Friedrich Cramer praised the utterly original humour ('der alleroriginellsten Laune') of Haydn's Op. 33 quartets, which were performed in Hamburg on 1 March 1783, by recounting that Bach, 'however distanced in everyday life from the unloving, sternly dismissive judgement of talents inferior to his own' had expressed his most complete satisfaction with these works.[51] More generally, Reichardt reported that Haydn claimed to have learnt the most from the great 'composer and humorist' Bach.[52] The lively debate over the issue of influence between the two in the contemporary press was perhaps best exemplified by the controversial article first published in the *European Magazine* in 1784 and printed in translation by Cramer in 1785, with its claim that Haydn's strangest humorous excesses were deliberate parodies of Bach's *bizarrerie* at their most fantastical (and regressive) – an 'explanation' of Haydn's eccentricities by means of a jibe at Bach: Bach's 'capricious manner, odd breaks, whimsical modulations, and often very childish manner, mixed with an affectation of profound science, are finely hit off and burlesqued', it claimed, by Haydn.[53] Cramer dismissed the allegations as mere 'trumped-up tales', suggesting 'how deeply ashamed must Haydn feel at heart to be extolled by a panegyrist at the expense of a man to whose studies he, I know for certain, himself willingly thanks for a great part of his excellence, and who values him in return without envy and spite'.[54]

---

[51] Review of 'Six Quatuor ou Divertissements . . . von [G. Haydn]', in C. F. Cramer, *Magazin der Musik* 1/1, 260.

[52] J. F. Reichardt, 'Noch ein Bruchstück aus Johann Friedrich Reichardt's Autobiographie', *AmZ* 16/2 (12 January 1814), col. 29.

[53] 'An Account of Joseph Haydn, a Celebrated Composer of Music . . .' *European Magazine, and London Review, for October 1784*, 252–4; reprinted in A. Peter Brown, 'The Earliest English Biography of Haydn', *Musical Quarterly* 59/3 (1973), 339–56. A German translation of the article was published by Cramer in *Magazin der Musik* 2/1 (7 April 1785), 585–94.   [54] Brown, 'Earliest English Biography', 349.

Bach's status as musical humorist was not in question. Reichardt, for one, went so far as to suggest that the love of witty conversation and word games that characterised Bach's social persona were also the source of his idiosyncratic compositional style: in fact, 'if he could be assigned to any particular category as a composer', he opined, 'it would be to that of the humorist'.[55] Some critics wondered whether Bach had not in fact overindulged in the comic and pandered to popular taste in his later music, a criticism directed especially at his inclusion of rondos in the later *Kenner und Liebhaber* volumes. Yet while the rondo represented the most fashionable indulgence in the lightweight, its metamorphosis in Bach's hands into music of fantastic and digressive substance embodied his particular *Laune*, as well as the disruptive effects of the picturesque, so much so that C. F. Cramer cited Bach's rondos as evidence of the heights to which humour could be taken. In an ecstatic elevation to the sublime, Cramer suggested that the Bachian rondo approaches the 'grace of the one and only God'. In fact, he continued, with ecstatic enthusiasm, 'we will surely hear Bachian rondos in the celestial music of the New Jerusalem'.[56] For their part, the reviewers of the *Kenner und Liebhaber* collections for the *Hamburgischer unpartheyischer Correspondent* were unstinting in their praise of these rondos, taking them seriously as the embodiment of the high comic.

The tripartite system learnt from English aesthetics shadowed not only the theory of the comic in Germany, as reflected in Sulzer's essay but aesthetic theory more generally and, around the turn of the nineteenth century, it fed directly into the scheme of musical aesthetics laid out by Friedrich Rochlitz in his essay 'Über den zweckmässigen Gebrauch der Mittel der Tonkunst' (1805–6).[57] Rochlitz's system paralleled those of Uvedale Price and William Crotch in dividing musical styles and genres among categories corresponding to the sublime – *das Erhabene* and *das Grosse*, the beautiful – *das Anmuthige und Liebliche*, and the picturesque – the *Niedlich*, a category that recapitulates Crotch's ornamental style and incorporates the popular, the lively, the charmingly naive, and the comic. The *Niedlich* is to be found especially, Rochlitz explains, in the 'wholly original and humorous' music of Haydn, where it appears most obviously in rondos and 'Scherzi' (minuet movements) from his symphonies and quartets; yet it is also

---

[55] Reichardt, 'Noch ein Bruchstück aus Johann Friedrich Reichardt's Autobiographie', col. 29.

[56] 'Unter die Saitenspiele des neuen Jerusalems gehören gewiß auch bachische Rondeaus.' Review of 'Musikalisches Kunstmagazin von J. F. Reichardt', in C. F. Cramer, *Magazin der Musik* 1/1, 35, footnote.

[57] *AmZ* 8/1 (2 October 1805), cols. 3–10; 8/4 (23 October 1805), cols. 49–59; 8/13 (25 December 1805), cols. 193–201; 8/16 (15 January 1806), cols. 241–9. Rochlitz's essay is briefly summarised by Russell in '"Über das Komische in der Musik"', 75–6.

particularly characteristic of 'solos', presumably sonatas for the keyboard, and, like Crotch, Rochlitz assigns this aesthetic category to popular, amateur taste, especially that of women.

The *Niedlich* is playful and naive, childlike and dainty; it is the most easily appreciated of musical styles, and yet Rochlitz's description transgresses those parameters as it veers towards assigning this category qualities more seriously disruptive than would normally belong to mere light entertainment. While consisting of ingratiating melodies and agile figuration, the *Niedlich*, like the ornamental style, is characterised by quick-changing tempos and metres, a chiaroscuro of shifting dynamic levels, and sudden modulations to distant keys. Further, it might incorporate a peculiar, *pikant* use of instrumental colour, even using instruments 'against their nature', a 'whimsical opposition of heterogeneous voices', odd use of dissonances which are 'approached quickly and as quickly left' and 'surprising returns of themes' which are often subtly and wittily altered.[58]

The space opened up by Rochlitz for a darker and more demanding musical comic in the *Niedlich*, was expanded by one of the most extended of early nineteenth-century German discussions of the humorous in music, the essay 'Ueber das Humoristische oder Launige in der musikalischen Komposition' published by the Kantian philosopher Christian Friedrich Michaelis in the *Allgemeine musikalische Zeitung* in 1807.[59] We might recall Price's awareness of the arbitrariness of his signifier: though objects which are picturesque, being neither beautiful nor sublime, 'deserve a distinct title', it matters little 'whether such a character, or the set of objects belonging to it, is called beautiful, sublime or picturesque, or by any other name or by no name at all'. The musical character Michaelis describes as humorous in this essay is closely allied to Price's picturesque, both in its general mediation between high and low and in its specific attributes. It comes as no surprise to find that what Michaelis describes as high comic should be explicitly situated within the sphere of the free fantasia.

Michaelis describes the humorous or *das Launige* in music as the personal and private expression of an idiosyncratic artistic temperament, privileging a quasi-improvisatory imaginary freedom over conventional rule: 'Music is humorous when the composition displays more the whim [Laune] of the artist than the strict application of an artistic system' (col. 725). Like the eighteenth-century fantasist, Michaelis' musical humorist possesses a mercurial temperament, a strong and original imagination and a quick mind. Humorous music itself consists

[58] Rochlitz, *AmZ* 8/16, cols. 241–9.
[59] *AmZ* 9/46 (12 August 1807), cols. 725–9; translations here are based on that given in Peter le Huray and James Day, eds., *Music and Aesthetics in the Eighteenth and Early Nineteenth Centuries* (Cambridge: Cambridge University Press, 1981), 204–5.

of abrupt transitions, surprise turns and sudden modulations – indeed, Michaelis might almost be quoting from Price's picturesque:

In this case the musical ideas are extremely peculiar and unusual; they do not follow one another as one might expect on the basis of certain conventions, or the natural progressions of harmony and modulation. Instead, they surprise us by their wholly unexpected turns and transitions, through their entirely new and unusually combined figures. (cols. 725–6)

Michaelis classifies the humorous or *Launig* in music as two-fold, encompassing 'scherzo' on the one hand and 'capriccio' on the other. In the *scherzo* the humour is comic and naive ('komisch und naiv'), related to the beautiful and the pleasing; it is more easily comprehensible than the capriccio and appeals especially to the less expert listener. The capriccio, by contrast, is serious and sublime ('ernsthaft und erhaben') and might even tend towards obscurity and incomprehensibility; in it the composer is caught up in the flight of his own imagination and, almost oblivious to the listener, he is like the private, self-absorbed fantasist:

[He] appears to depend too much on the caprice of his mood [den Eigensinn seiner Laune], on the peculiarity of his immediate frame of mind, to be able to aim at a particular end, that of entertaining the listener, and winning his sympathy by means of intelligible regularity. He seems rather to be motivated by an inner impulse to lay bare his immediate soul, to portray the peculiar succession and transformation of his emotions and ideas. (col. 728)

The capriccio, the serious comic, requires a listener who has 'a similar temperament' ('eine analoge Gemüthsstimmung') and who is something of a connoisseur. Michaelis designates this latter type of humour as being 'only for the few, who have enough training and inclination to follow the peculiar paths of the serious humorist' (col. 728). Crucially, Michaelis specifically identifies those idiosyncratic paths as belonging to the realm of fantasia: 'What I understand here by capriccio our composers often entitle fantasia, and particularly free fantasia' (col. 728).

Like Crotch, Michaelis cites humour as integral to modern music, and Haydn, especially in his symphonies and quartets, as the 'greatest master' of the style, which permeates not only the music of Haydn but also that of Mozart, Pleyel, Viotti, Rode, Kreuzer, Clementi and Beethoven; older music, by contrast, was more unrelentingly serious, since composers 'were reluctant to embark on those bold, imaginative essays that transcend the conventional'.[60] Nevertheless Michaelis cites C. P. E. Bach as one of those who 'composed not infrequently in the humorous style' (col. 728). In the absence of a satisfactory term in German music criticism around 1800 equivalent to the English 'picturesque', the concept of the humorous takes on a special significance. In place of the

---

[60] Translation based on le Huray and Day, *Music and Aesthetics*, 205.

too-pictorial *Malerisch*, or somewhat trivialising *Niedlich*, the *Launig*, newly incorporated into German music theory towards the end of the eighteenth century and encompassing both the comic and the tragic, points towards the picturesque.

IV

Michaelis' humorous composer is actively engaged in confounding the listener by pushing to the limits the usual rules of composition. Ideas are syncopated and inverted, voices 'entangled' and manipulated, keys and themes 'audaciously' and 'abruptly' discarded, and just as suddenly resumed, so that 'nothing can be explained in terms of the customary practice of the musical system . . . or natural, regular procedure' (col. 726). Instead, it is as if we have entered a novel in which the narrator 'links together the most heterogeneous elements, and in the peculiar disposition of his temperament gives the most familiar things a new appearance, and without paying attention to the over-restrictive rules of good taste, gives free play to his thoughts with a daring candour' (col. 727). The comparison with the strategies 'of a humorous or comical narrator' ('eines launigen oder humoristischen Erzählers') is neither accidental nor casual; rather, it offers suggestive ways of reading the musical picturesque, both within the individual-orientated cult of sensibility, and the self-conscious ironising of genre represented by the novels of Laurence Sterne and his German counterpart Jean Paul.[61]

The literary discourse of sensibility, made famous by the German translation of Sterne's *A Sentimental Journey* (*Yoricks empfindsame Reise durch Frankreich und Italien*; Hamburg, 1768), is non-linear, prone to digression and fragmented by pervasive punctuating (and puncturing) dashes. This was not confined to novels, but is also to be found in the musical-critical literature of the period. It permeates Johann Friedrich Reichardt's *Briefe eines aufmerksamen Reisenden die Musik betreffend* (1774, 1776), as well as the prefaces to musical publications, especially of song collections addressed to sentimental amateurs. Reichardt introduces an account of his first visit to C. P. E. Bach in Hamburg with a warning worthy of Sterne, exhorting his reader, a fellow Bach enthusiast, to 'expect no order in this letter, but rather give yourself up to the overflowing flood from my brimming heart'.[62] Overcome by a performance of Handel's *Judas Maccabeus*, Reichardt grapples with the limits of language in the face of such emotion:

---

[61] On Sternian irony and musical humour, see Bonds, 'Haydn, Laurence Sterne and the Origins of Musical Irony'.

[62] Reichardt, *Briefe eines aufmerksamen Reisenden die Musik betreffend*, 2 vols. (Frankfurt and Leipzig, 1774–6), II, 7.

had we been able to communicate our emotions to each other through soulful glances and through hot hand clasps, and thus to heighten them, I would wish for nothing more; there is no rapture that I would exchange for that. But how shall I tell you everything that I felt on that happy evening? You know my sensibility; you also know that words fail the highest, most intense emotions.[63]

This letter is an extraordinary paean to brotherly love – or sublimated eroticism – as well as to the passion aroused by music in the sensitive listener, and the failure of words to express much of either. It is also very long, and indicative of its supreme excess is the fact that the reader only finds out which piece Reichardt is describing indirectly after six pages of turbulent emotions have rolled past. This failure of language in the face of heightened emotion was a common topos. A somewhat later anonymous English account of a visit to the famously beautiful Vale of Llangollen in Wales in 1795 describes the disintegration and eventual silencing of verbal expression (though not without a Cole Porteresque exchange): 'we hardly ever spoke! or if we did, it was only between long pauses that involuntarily we cried out sometimes all together, did you ever? – no never – [until] fatigued with our own barren exclamations . . . we all agreed to be *quite silent*'.[64]

The break-down of conventional syntax is marked by the dash – the sign of interruption, or silence, which ruptures the text to heighten the level of inexpressible excitement. Something of this compelling and highly emotional discourse was attempted by the Einbeck organist Christoph Heinrich Hartmann and his collaborator Johann Adrian Junghans, organist at Arnstadt, in the preface to their 1783 publication *Wonneklang und Gesang für Liebhaber*. Johann Nikolaus Forkel ridiculed their overblown style in his *Musikalischer Almanach* (1784), fearing that the 'affected tone' of their preface, which is punctuated almost entirely by exclamation marks and dashes, augured ill for the rest of the work. Forkel gives the reader a taste of the style:

True believers – or unbelievers!
This – this it shall be – the joyful Sound of Delight and Song! – Take it! – Taste it! – – and then judge: – 'stolen Bread tastes ??? . . . !' Judge it how you will! – Neither Praise nor Censure will abduct my Muse from the Borders of the Nature that has become her own.[65]

[63] Ibid., I, 82.

[64] Anon., 'Welch Journal Aug^st 20th 1795', quoted in Malcolm Andrews, *The Search for the Picturesque: Landscape Aesthetics and Tourism in Britain, 1760–1800* (Aldershot: Scolar Press, 1989), 117.

[65] Review of 'Wonneklang und Gesang für Liebhaber – auch Anfanger des Claviers, von Christoph Heinrich Hartmann, Organist zu Einbeck, und Johann Adrian Junghans, Organist zu Arnstadt. Erste Sammlung, Arnstadt und Einbeck, 1783', Forkel, *Musikalischer Almanach für Deutschland*, 4 vols. (1784), III, 21–2.

The dash, or *Gedankenstrich*, that predominates here is the characteristic punctuation mark of the sentimental style, or, as Jean Paul would have it, the characteristic condition of the sentimental man: 'Man is the great dash [Gedankenstrich] in the book of nature.'[66] Such dashes are almost ludicrously manipulated by Sterne, serving to interrupt and fragment the text. They act as fantastic openings for the reader's imagination, as meaningful as the text into which they intrude; through hyphens, dashes and extended asterisks, the non-verbal is represented (made present) in the spaces between words, which may be loud expressions of the unsayable (a censored expletive evoking excruciating pain) or silent enactments of time (the time it takes to read a letter or to whisper a piece of gossip). A concurrent effect of Sterne's use of dashes is to create a typographical texture of such variety that it emphasises the sheer materiality of the book and the artificiality of the reading experience.[67]

In the musical picturesque the *Gedankenstrich* finds its corollary in the peppering of the texture with rests. The sudden moments of silence work to create surprise, to initiate a startling change of direction and to arouse the listener's interest. In his *Dialogue upon the Gardens at Stowe* (1748) William Gilpin compared the effect of the musical pause to that of 'impertinent' (but essential) hedges blocking the view in a landscape garden: 'Did you never experience in a concert vast pleasure when the whole band for a few moments made a full pause? The case is parallel: you have already had a great many fine views, and that you may not be cloyed, this hedge steps in to keep your attention awake.'[68] Such pauses have the effect of momentarily suspending the diachronic trajectory of the piece and allowing an expansion of the synchronic instant, an out-of-time moment which may encompass an extended digression. The prevalence of rests in the music of Haydn and C. P. E. Bach was noted by their contemporaries and theorised in the second decade of the nineteenth century by the Swiss music publisher and writer, Hans Georg Nägeli in his *Vorlesungen über Musik* (1826). 'What is particularly striking in these works', he writes, is that 'these compositions are copiously *cut through by rests*'; in Bach's 'free music' such caesuras function as gaps demanding interpretation, moments in which the listener becomes the

---

[66] Jean Paul, from *Auswahl aus des Teufels Papieren* [1789]; published as motto to *Die Unsichtbare Loge* [1793] in *Werke*, series 1, ed. Norbert Miller, 6 vols. (Munich: Hanser, 1959–63), I.

[67] See Peter J. de Voogd, 'Tristram Shandy as Aesthetic Object', in *Interactions: A Selection of Papers Given at the 2nd International Conference on Word and Image, Universität Zürich, August 27–31, 1991*, ed. Martin Henssen (Basel: Weise, 1993), 383–9; also his 'Laurence Sterne, the Marbled Page, and "the Use of Accidents"', *Word and Image* 1/3 (1985), 279–87.

[68] Gilpin, *A Dialogue upon the Gardens of the Right Honourable The Lord Viscount Cobham, at Stowe in Buckinghamshire* (London, 1748), 11.

principal player. Nägeli suggests that the pause provides a moment of rest for the ear, the emotions and the mind, but, more importantly, it suddenly highlights the act of listening, allowing a momentary reassessment of the music that has passed, combined with an imaginative projection forward to what is to come – a sort of interpretative Augustinian *distentio animae* in which past and future are collapsed onto the present as the basis for new interpretation.[69] Likewise, Karl Herman Bitter, C. P. E. Bach's nineteenth-century biographer, perhaps glossing Nägeli, emphasised the sudden collapse into self-consciousness experienced by the listener at such moments. 'The many pauses to be met with in Bach's music', he writes,

> were an astonishing novelty for his contemporaries. The listener, who usually had to follow polyphonic pieces with attention, in order not to lose the thread of the musical thoughts, was here abruptly thrust out of a richness of melody and harmonic effect before his inner self, his imagination [Phantasie] set free and challenged to go independently further for a moment, until Bach saw fit to resume the interrupted progress of the piece.[70]

As with the surprising obstructions of the picturesque, in the multiple rests of the free style the listener is suddenly confronted with him- or herself, and the imagination is released for a digressive and suspended moment.

The sudden silence, the pause with fermata, so often remarked on by Haydn's London audiences, is intrinsic to the effects of the musical picturesque. Such rests fragment the discourse; they create surprise, even wonder, at the unexpectedness of the interruption and at the unpredictability of the continuation. The aporia forces active listening. But the fermata also acts as the sign for musical fantasy itself; it is the *ad libitum* at a cadenza that invites the performer to take licence and indulge his or her own imagination. In the cadenza the drive of the movement is temporarily suspended, and the tight temporal fabric of the formal organisation is split open by digression. The cadenza takes place in some sense outside the main time of the movement, and is the point at which artistic illusion is broken and the attention of the listener is directed away from the musical discourse and towards the performer.[71] The virtuosic improviser of a cadenza is like the humorous narrator or ambitious gardener who draws attention to himself, playing up his own presence and

---

[69] Hans Georg Nägeli, *Vorlesungen über Musik mit Berücksichtigung der Dilettanten* (Stuttgart and Tübingen, 1826), 138.

[70] Karl Herman Bitter, *Carl Philipp Emanuel Bach und Wilhelm Friedemann Bach und deren Brüder* (Berlin: Wilh. Müller, 1868), 232.

[71] An exception should perhaps be made here for Mozart's later written-out cadenzas (such as that to K. 488), which consist of a discursive reworking of the thematic material of the movement.

parading his artistry, highlighting the artificiality of the work. The virtuoso, like the narrator, flirts with the undoing of aesthetic illusion. Hence eighteenth-century critics' distrust of 'empty' virtuosity, and the particular instability of the fantasia which, while professing heightened powers of expression, gave itself easily to brilliant displays of technique. William Crotch complained that one of the fundamental faults of the musical picturesque was that its virtuosity undermined the serious work of real music with empty bluster, an echo of Reynolds' criticism (via Shakespeare) of the ornamental style in Venetian painting, that it was 'a tale told by an idiot, full of sound and fury, signifying nothing'.[72]

Like the landscape garden, the novels of Sterne and Jean Paul play with the reader's expectations, as the narrator both changes direction without warning, and directly solicits the reader's opinion of his tactics, as if the reader were a character in some meta-narrative.[73] The ambiguous relation between author, narrator and reader in this kind of novel mirrors that of composer, performer and listener, where the roles of composer and performer blur and the act of listening is made conscious and problematic. The reader in a Sterne novel is led less into a story than into the process of writing a story as she is conducted through the labyrinthine workings of the author/narrator's mind. Similarly, in listening to a fantasia which unfolds before the listener in the moment that it is being created, or music which makes a show of indulging the temporary whim of the composer at the expense of the listener, 'we wonder, not what is coming next, but what the author will think of next'.[74] For Sterne, and in his wake Jean Paul, the sentimental experience and its representation are tinged with irony; picturesque music, similarly open-ended, irregular and unpredictable, without set patterns or plots to orientate the listener, gestures beyond the tearful sincerity of *Empfindsamkeit*.

C. P. E. Bach would surely have known Sterne's idiosyncratic sentimental-ironic literary style. Not only was Hamburg the hub of English culture in North Germany, importing both its literature and its garden style, but the height of the Sterne craze in Hamburg coincided with Bach's arrival there in 1768, the publication year of J. J. C. Bode's translation of Sterne's *A Sentimental Journey* (*Yoricks empfindsame Reise durch Frankreich und Italien*). Bach became a member of Bode's intellectual circle, which included the poets Klopstock, Lessing, Claudius, Voss,

---

[72] On the destruction of aesthetic illusion in the context of musical irony, see Bonds' extensive discussion in 'Haydn, Laurence Sterne and the Origins of Musical Irony'. See also Wheelock, *Haydn's Ingenious Jesting with Art*, Part III, 'The Implicated Listener', esp. pp. 203–6.

[73] See John Preston, *The Created Self: The Reader's Role in Eighteenth-Century Fiction* (London: Heinemann, 1970).

[74] Northrop Frye, 'Towards Defining an Age of Sensibility', in *Poets of Sensibility and the Sublime*, ed. Harold Bloom (New York: Chelsea House, 1986), 11–18.

Gerstenberg, the historian Christoph Daniel Ebeling and the philosopher Reimarus. The group met regularly at the house of the mathematician Johann Georg Büsch; many were keen amateur musicians, including Bode who played the cello in the regular music-making at Büsch's house.[75] Bode, with Ebeling, was also the translator of Charles Burney's *Present State of Music in Germany, the Netherlands and the United Provinces*, and was responsible for soliciting from Bach his autobiography for the German translation of the work. Bode was the self-confessed 'prophet and priest' of the Sterne cult in Germany, the principal translator of Sterne's works, who considered himself to have 'a kind of vocation to give in German everything that Sterne has written, or whatever has immediate relation to his writings'; with the rest of his group, he played a crucial role in the reception and dissemination of Sterne's works in Germany, and Bode's twenty-page preface to *Yoricks empfindsame Reise* amounted to a self-styled manifesto for Sterne worship.[76]

Following the huge success of *Yoricks empfindsame Reise*, which the reviewer in the *Hamburger unpartheyischer Correspondent* of 1768 regarded as an unparalleled work of genius with a potentially medicinal effect on melancholics, Bode undertook the translation of the more difficult, and quintessentially English, *Tristram Shandy*. In his preface to *Yoricks empfindsame Reise* Bode had claimed that *Shandy* had already been read by many Germans, but, like Bach debating the comprehensibility of his fantasias to the general public, he wondered 'How many have understood it? One finds people who despise it as the most nonsensical

---

[75] For information on Bach's Hamburg circle see J. F. Reichardt, 'Noch ein Bruchstück aus Johann Friedrich Reichardt's Autobiographie'; Heinrich Miesner, *Philipp Emanuel Bach in Hamburg: Beiträge zu seiner Biographie und zur Musikgeschichte seiner Zeit* (Heide: Holst, 1929; reprint edn, Wiesbaden: Breitkopf und Härtel, 1969); and Hans-Günter Ottenberg, *C. P. E. Bach*, trans. Philip J. Whitmore (Oxford: Oxford University Press, 1987), especially 142–55. During his years in Berlin Bach's friendship circle included Krause, Sulzer, Lessing, Ramler and Gleim. See Darrell M. Berg, 'C. P. E. Bach's Character Pieces and his Friendship Circle', in *C. P. E. Bach Studies*, ed. Stephen L. Clark (Oxford: Oxford University Press, 1988), 1–32.

[76] See Harvey Waterman Thayer, *Laurence Sterne in Germany: A Contribution to the Study of the Literary Relations of England and Germany in the Eighteenth Century* (New York: Columbia University Press, 1905), 67, 40 and passim. Bode acknowledged Lessing's role in the translation project (it was Lessing who had made the crucial suggestion to render 'sentimental' in the title as 'empfindsam'). Lessing, who was in Hamburg from 1767 to 1770 as director of the new National Theatre, was himself a devotee of Sterne, and in 1769 or early 1770 he composed a fake sermon in the manner of Yorick, the title and part of the introduction of which were privately printed by Bode and passed about among the circle of friends as if the whole were in press. See also Roswitha Strommer, 'Die Rezeption der englischen Literatur im Lebensumkreis und zur Zeit Joseph Haydns', in *Joseph Haydn und die Literatur seiner Zeit*, ed. Herbert Zeman (Eisenstadt: Institut für österreichische Kulturgeschichte, 1976), 123–55; and Peter Michelsen, *Laurence Sterne und der deutsche Roman des 18. Jahrhundert*, Palästra vol. CCXXXII (Göttingen, 1962).

twaddle, and cannot comprehend how others, whom they must credit with a good deal of understanding, wit and learning, think quite otherwise of it.'[77] In speaking of those who thought well of it, Bode surely had in mind his Hamburg circle of Sterne enthusiasts – the same group of people who would champion Bach's music against those who considered his more fantastic pieces nonsensical ravings. Not only were the critics who responded most favourably to the musical fantastic deeply immersed in the digressive paths and misty landscapes of the Sterne aesthetic, but it seems inconceivable, given the Sterne-obsession of his friends, that the 'great humorist' Bach, even if he had read none of Sterne's writings, would not have been familiar, at least indirectly, with the idiosyncrasies of Sterne's ironical humour.

Sterne's name, of course, was commonly cited in connection with Haydn. The *Musikalischer Almanach auf das Jahr 1782* compared Haydn as a 'musical jester . . . of the high comic' to 'Yorick'. Triest, in 1801, reflected on the Englishness of Haydn's humour, 'which the German word "Laune" does not capture entirely' and suggested that 'it is from this latter characteristic that his inclination towards comic turns, and their still greater success than serious ones, may be explained'. Triest went on to compare Haydn with Sterne and also Jean Paul:

> If one wanted to look for a parallel here with other famous men, then Joseph Haydn, as regards the fruitfulness of his fantasy, might perhaps be compared with our Jean Paul (excluding, of course, the latter's chaotic ordering, for lucid presentation (*lucidus ordo*) is not among the least of Haydn's merits), and as regards his humour, his peculiar disposition (*vis comica*), with Lor. Sterne.[78]

Jean Paul himself stated that a fitting comparison may be made between Sterne's techniques and those found in a good deal of music, especially Haydn's, emphasising that the similarities lie in the abrupt modulations and sudden changes of dynamic and tempo. Haydn's is an 'annihilating' humour ('vernichtenden Humor') that delights in 'contradictions and impossibilities'.[79] It was precisely this type of humour that came to define the musical picturesque for its English codifiers, a mixed mode comparable to tragicomedy which aspires to 'neither the full tragedy of the sublime nor the serene comedy of the beautiful',[80] but instead

---

[77] Thayer, *Laurence Sterne in Germany*, 34. The translation of Shandy was completed in 1774 and appeared with over 650 names in the subscriber list, including Claudius, Gerstenberg, Gleim, Goethe, Hamann and Herder.

[78] See Bonds, 'Haydn, Laurence Sterne and the Origins of Musical Irony', 62. Translation based on Bonds.

[79] Jean Paul Richter, *Vorschule der Ästhetik* (1804) in *Werke*, series 1, ed. Norbert Miller, 6 vols. (Munich: Carl Hanser, 1963), V, 132; trans. Margaret R. Hale as *Horn of Oberon: Jean Paul Richter's School for Aesthetics* (Detroit: Wayne State University Press, 1973), 93. Also cited by Bonds, 'Haydn, Laurence Sterne and the Origins of Musical Irony', 63.

[80] Martin Price, 'The Picturesque Moment', 277.

relieves and animates the paralysis associated with the sublime, 'loosening those iron bonds with which astonishment chains up its faculties'.[81] The *Launig*, like the picturesque, was sited on the shifting ground between the sublime and the ridiculous, as Jean Paul indicated: to the question 'What . . . is the converse of the ridiculous?' he replies 'Neither the tragic nor the sentimental, as the very expressions "tragicomic" and "sentimental comedy" prove.' Rather, both Sterne and Shakespeare achieved a transcendent, even sublime, humour: 'Shakespeare cultivates his humorous Northern growths to full heights in the midst of the fire of pathos as well as in the frost of comedy. Indeed, a Sterne changes Shakespeare's simple succession of the pathetic and the comic into a *simultanaeum* of the two.'[82] German writing on music at the turn of the nineteenth century, echoing the work of Crotch and Price, points to the role of the picturesque as an essential mediator in the integration of the comic into late eighteenth- and early nineteenth-century musical aesthetics.[83] Indeed, the picturesque elevated the comic to new heights, with important ramifications for the reception of German instrumental music towards the end of the eighteenth century. It was precisely the complex amalgam of sublimity and comedy in Haydn's music of the 1790s that appealed to his London audiences.

But how far the English predilection for the picturesque coloured the works Haydn produced for this London audience must remain an open question – clearly it was not in England that Haydn (or for that matter C. P. E. Bach) learnt the art of musical jokes, deceptions and ironic distance, just as he need not have learnt there to appreciate the English garden. To the extent that Haydn was exposed to the aesthetic of the picturesque during his sojourn in England in the 1790s, this surely in some sense affirmed a taste and style which he already knew well; not only was he familiar with the picturesque Sternian mode of narration that characterised C. P. E. Bach's humour (if not with Sterne's novels themselves), but such ideas were less in the air than on the ground and in the daily sights of the fashionable and the aesthetically minded in continental Europe, brought there by people like Zinzendorf. Zinzendorf had taken his experiences of the landscape garden back with him to Vienna and introduced there the pleasurable aesthetic paradox of the English park with its predilection for constructed contrast and surprising disruptions.[84]

---

[81] Uvedale Price, *Essay* (1794), 86–7.   [82] Jean Paul, *School for Aesthetics*, 73.

[83] See Russell, '"Über das Komische in der Musik"'.

[84] Zinzendorf is thought to have had considerable influence on the design of gardens in and around Vienna, where the English style began to appear around 1770. See Hajós, 'The Gardens of the British Isles'; and also his 'Picture and Poetry in Austrian Gardens of the Late Eighteenth Century', in *Garden History: Issues, Approaches, Methods: Dumbarton Oaks Colloquium on the History of Landscape Architecture XIII*, ed. John Dixon Hunt (Washington, DC: Dumbarton Oaks Research Library and Collection, 1992), 203–18.

Indeed, we might better reverse the notion suggested by some recent writers that Haydn learnt of and catered to a particular English taste in the 1790s and that his extrovert London style amounted to an experiment in a new, picturesque, aesthetic. Rather, such a taste, already familiar in Austria as well as Northern Germany in the 1770s and 1780s under the influence of English literature, philosophy and garden art, was returned to England in a musical guise by Haydn. Haydn perhaps saw the opportunity to play up its humorous quirks and disjunctions for an audience particularly receptive to those features, but it was his music, alongside that of C. P. E. Bach, that played the seminal role in the formation among English writers on music of a concept of the musical picturesque; in turn, the concept of the picturesque, in spite of the reservations of critics such as Crotch, crucially enabled the humorous in music, with its contradictory oscillation between melancholy and delight, to achieve the status of high art.

5

Sentiment undone: solitude and the clavichord cult

Zwischen Welt und Einsamkeit liegt die wahre Weisheit in der Mitte
(True wisdom lies at the mid-point between the world and solitude)
Inscription above the door of the garden house next to
Hirschfeld's monument in the Seifersdorfer Tal

'Most living people held for me exactly the interest that the dead have for an anatomist, and it often pained me that one could not once take a truly significant mind with a pair of forceps and put it under a micro-scope.'[1] With this chilling statement Friedrich Rochlitz, editor of the *Allgemeine Musikalische Zeitung*, introduced the magazine's issue of 27 June 1804, confessing to a grim eagerness for laying bare the psyches of remarkable individuals. The story that follows, under the title 'Der Besuch im Irrenhause', is a narrative of music as madness, therapy, and psycho-autobiography, all three presented as functions of pathological solitude.

Embarking on a project to investigate the mentally ill and their care, Rochlitz takes himself off to a lunatic asylum whose name he purpose-fully conceals, partly to protect the inhabitants, but also perhaps to increase the spine-tingling appeal of his tale. He first visits the warden of the institution, and, standing in his office, Rochlitz hears the sound of a piano coming from the adjacent room. It seems as if the instrument has just been tuned, and the tuner, now playing full chords, is checking his work with the greatest care. Glancing through the open door and catch-ing sight of a young man seated at the piano, Rochlitz senses that there is something odd about him. On playing a particularly pure chord, the man sits motionless as the tones fade away, as if in a trance, his eyes gazing blankly towards heaven. The warden explains that this is one of the inmates; though peculiar, he is considered docile and is allowed to move about the place freely; moreover, he is the finest piano tuner the warden has ever encountered. On further questioning from Rochlitz it

---

[1] *AmZ* 6/39 (27 June 1804), col. 645.

Example 5.1   Friedrich Rochlitz, 'Der Besuch im Irrenhause', *AmZ* 6/39 (27 June 1804), col. 650

emerges that the man was not a professional musician before his incarceration, that he is apparently untaught and unable to read music, and is likewise ignorant, or disdainful, of the customary musical forms: yet, he plays the piano, and in a most fantastical way, and the warden urges Rochlitz to listen.

The inmate, 'Karl', is a curious mixture of pride and shyness; pale and fragile, he has the appearance of someone prematurely withered. Rochlitz surmises that his madness is less the symptom of illness than of childhood trauma, on account of his air of cultivation yet profound lack of social grace. When introduced to Rochlitz and asked to play for him, 'Karl' refuses with a disdainful smile. His music, it seems, is not for strangers and he will not be induced to perform. Undeterred in his quest to study the case, and encouraged by the warden, Rochlitz resorts to deception; he makes a show of saying goodbye and leaves the room, only to slip back to the half-open door and hide there, surreptitiously watching as the inmate turns to the piano. Rochlitz eavesdrops with building astonishment as Karl begins to play, tentatively and slowly, wandering through a succession of fragmented sounds. Gradually these ideas take shape and gain coherence as the performer warms up, with triplet figures in the right hand and in the left full chords, which push forward, becoming heavier and more hurried until eventually he is overtaken by an inspired frenzy. The turbulent performance lacks metrical regularity, and is marked by continual crescendi and decrescendi (see example 5.1).

Becoming confused and seeming to tire, 'Karl' then moves into a melancholy Andante which Rochlitz reports as being entirely free and impossible to describe in words or notation; nonetheless he attempts to capture it as best he can, and records a free recitative-like passage in

Example 5.2 Friedrich Rochlitz, 'Der Besuch im Irrenhause', *AmZ* 6/39 (27 June 1804)

Example 5.3 Friedrich Rochlitz, 'Der Besuch im Irrenhause', *AmZ* 6/39 (27 June 1804)

E minor (example 5.2). This develops into a clearer, more recognisably metrical section, in the relative major (example 5.3), which leads back into a crazed Allegro. Rochlitz is both impressed and disturbed by the performance:

As that quick section had strangely stimulated me and this slow one gently moved me, so was I deeply affected by the gradual reawakening of that wild inspiration and power which now gushed out in the most extraordinary Allegro, yet more impassioned; at last I surrendered to a ghastly shudder, especially when I heard how now, in the course of his playing, the sick man began not so much to speak as to hiss, to whisper, with the greatest vehemence, yet softly and utterly indistinctly. This he continued incessantly and with unbelievable fluency.[2]

Rochlitz is so enthralled that he finds that he has unwittingly moved fully into the doorway, and though Karl sits with his back to him, his reflection can be seen in the mirror on the opposite wall. When Karl catches sight of Rochlitz he breaks off instantly, springs up angrily, lunges violently at him, and has to be restrained by the warden, who has been standing quietly by throughout. The dramaturgy of betrayal is so finely executed that one cannot but suspect a degree of staging in Rochlitz's telling of it.

In the denouement of the story, Rochlitz explains that music is the obsession and sole occupation of the incarcerated man. It is Karl's therapy and consolation – when not playing the piano he habitually hums softly to himself. He hardly speaks (though writes maniacally

---

[2] Ibid., col. 651.

when given pencil and paper), and is generally sullen and withdrawn, preferring to keep to himself, suspicious of others. The difference between his usual manner and his behaviour when believing himself to be unobserved at the piano is remarkable, for at the keyboard he is able to express himself freely in music that Rochlitz interprets as the precise record of his mental instability. In a conflation of the identity of performer and musical utterance, Rochlitz understands the fragmented fantasies that Karl improvises as bizarre reflections of his disturbed mind; and thus he claims to have come to know the 'exact exterior and interior history' of the man through this encounter and musical performance. As presented to Rochlitz, the performance is a freak show, and though chastened at being discovered in the act of violating Karl's personal sanctuary, Rochlitz goes further in his betrayal of trust by publishing both the story and a bizarre, inevitably parodic version of the crazed man's music. The strange music with which the inmate fills his private silence is jealously guarded, purely inward reverie, and the tale becomes an extreme example of an unstable mind seeking the protection of solitude for the expression of its innermost feelings.

The lunatic performance described by Rochlitz in 1804 seems marginal, freakish, and musically grotesque, yet it is a logical extension of a bourgeois obsession of the previous decades. The isolated figure at the keyboard would indeed have been familiar to many of Rochlitz's readers, for lonely and obsessive self-indulgence of this sort provided material for not only quasi-scientific case studies, in gothic tales and sentimental novels, but also the most mainstream of musical publications for the least specialised audience. Private music-making at the keyboard was invested in the popular imagination with special, even exalted status, and Karl's performance, the work of a man unhinged from society who can find solace only in himself, through music, is less a fantastic aberration than a disturbing manifestation of a popular cult.

A fascination with inwardness, melancholy and solitude marked Northern German culture in the second half of the eighteenth century, the culture of a repressed, politically impotent and excessively ordered bourgeoisie. Paradoxically, only in the internal world of thought and emotion might the freedom that was lacking in daily political and social life be found. In her seminal work of cross-cultural exegesis, Madame de Staël identified the German character as both solitary and necessarily sensitive: 'the solitary man needs an intimate feeling to take the place of the external movement he lacks'.[3] Nature provided the most reliable form of escape, the contemplation of landscape an exercise in self-

---

[3] Madame de Staël, *De L'Allemagne* (Paris: Didot, 1845), cited in Robert Sayre, *Solitude in Society: A Sociological Study in French Literature* (Cambridge, MA: Harvard University Press, 1978), 57.

reflection and transcendence; likewise, the difficult terrain of the emotions offered rich material for study. Solitude was closely bound up with sensibility, as even the *empfindsam* cult of friendship, with its copious tears and excessive emotionality, served, in Wolf Lepenies' formulation, 'less as a form of contact than as a means of increasing one's rapturous feelings of melancholia'.[4] As Lepenies has noted, 'Bourgeois melancholics longed not for overplanned utopias, but rather for isolation in nature or for passionate activity, even disorder.'[5] While some indulged in group rapture and consolation, others withdrew into the self – the bourgeois music-lover retreating to his (or, more likely, her) clavichord. Indeed, private fantasising at the clavichord offered a counterpart to the solipsistic and paradoxical experience of the picturesque garden; in musical culture the fantasia was not only figured as a landscape garden, offering both poetic indulgence in sentiment and a complex aesthetic problem of planned anarchy, but it too encouraged the pleasures of solitude – pleasures which focussed on, even fetishised, the clavichord itself, that 'thrilling confidant of solitude' ('schauerlicher Vertrauter der Einsamkeit').[6]

Clavichords were relatively cheap, available to the *Liebhaber*, responsive to the enthusiast, and, in their quietness, best heard by the player him- or herself. This 'lonely, melancholy, unspeakably sweet Instrument', as C. F. D. Schubart described it in his *Ideen zu einer Ästhetik der Tonkunst* (*c.* 1785), promised perfect indulgence of the modish inclination for solitary musical reverie.[7] The clavichord not only perfectly matched but was suspected to have inspired the quixotic idiom of C. P. E. Bach, the acknowledged master of the instrument. Moreover, in its inherent intimacy, it encouraged a new kind of listening practice, one predicated on silence and concentration, a profound attention that surely contributed to the changing reception of instrumental music in late eighteenth-century Germany.[8] Even Carl Friedrich Cramer, well informed as he

---

[4] Wolf Lepenies, *Melancholy and Society*, trans. Jeremy Gaines and Doris Jones (Cambridge, MA: Harvard University Press, 1992), 75. See also Leo Maduschka, *Das Problem der Einsamkeit im 18. Jahrhundert* (Weimar: Alexander Duncker Verlag, 1933).

[5] This is Judith N. Shkar's paraphrase, in her foreword to Lepenies, *Melancholy and Society*, xiii and xiv.

[6] Cited by Alfred Kreutz in his afterword to *Carl Philipp Emanuel Bach, Zwei Klavierstücke* (Edition Schott 4013), [p. 18]; also in Arthur Loesser, *Men, Women and Pianos: A Social History* (New York: Simon and Schuster, 1954), 59.

[7] C. F. D. Schubart, *Ideen zu einer Aesthetik der Tonkunst*, ed. Ludwig Schubart (Vienna: Dagen, 1806), 289.

[8] The idea that the quietness of the clavichord may have had a fundamental impact on listening practices in North Germany towards the end of the century was argued by Mary Sue Morrow at the International Clavichord Symposium, Magnano 1999. See *De Clavicordio IV* (forthcoming).

was of musical trends not just in Germany but across Europe, designated the clavichord the 'First among Instruments', praising the fluidity of its effects, the superb quality of its legato, its constantly varying light and shade. Cramer also drew attention to the Germanness of the instrument (Germany was the 'Fatherland of the Clavier'), a common theme among contemporary clavichord enthusiasts, though Cramer's account, written in December 1783, laments what he saw as its declining use in the face of the rising popularity of the fortepiano. Less fashionable, not well suited for 'social music' ('gesellschaftliche Musik'), the clavichord in Cramer's description finds itself confined to a private, even elite realm; citing the relatively poor subscription numbers to the recently published fourth collection of *Kenner und Liebhaber* pieces, Cramer goes so far as to suggest that C. P. E. Bach himself might have been in danger of 'sacrific[ing] himself to the rare private pleasure of a few clavichord players'.[9]

A good clavichord was capable of a wide dynamic range, of singing legato and of striking portato accents; the sensitivity of its action and softness of tone allowed for performances that were both expressive and remarkably intimate. Its particular attraction was *Bebung*, the pulsating vibrato effect obtained by pressing on the key to push the tangent a little harder against the string. As Arthur Loesser so aptly put it, 'What a potent engine of "feeling" this little movement could be! The throbbing heart, the panting breast, the trembling lip, the quivering voice – all this physiognomy of emotion could seem to be in the *Bebung*. Amateurs overdid it ecstatically, to judge from the warnings issued in the instruction books of the period.'[10] Belonging to the private parlour rather than the concert hall, the clavichord promised a transcendent sympathy able to echo and celebrate the emotions of the sensitive player. 'It is true', wrote C. F. D. Schubart,

that you cannot play heavy-fisted concertos, for [the clavichord] cannot hail and thunder like the fortepiano; nor can you, surrounded by your numerous audience, rouse storms with it and use it to drown their cries of applause as if they were mere murmurings of waves. But if your instrument (I mean the clavichord) was created by Stein or Fritz, Silbermann or Späth, tender and responsive to your soul's every inspiration, it is here that you will find your heart's soundboard.[11]

The *Empfindungen* this instrument best expressed were tender and tearful ones, and its finest performances would indulge in the gentlest nuance of light and season, dusk or moonlight:

---

[9] Cramer, review of 'Claviersonaten und freye Phantasien . . . Vierte Sammlung', in Cramer, *Magazin der Musik* 1/2 (7 December 1783), 1247.

[10] Loesser, *Men, Women and Pianos*, 60.

[11] C. F. D. Schubart, *Musikalische Rhapsodien*, 1786. Cited in Hans Neupert, *The Clavichord*, trans. Ann P. P. Feldberg (Kassel: Bärenreiter, 1965), 48.

Sweet melancholy, languishing love, parting grief, the soul's communing with God, uneasy forebodings, glimpses of Paradise through suddenly rent clouds, sweetly purling tears ... Behold player, all this lies in your clavichord. Therefore, pine not, when you improvise by the light of the moon, or refresh your soul on summer nights, or celebrate the evenings of spring; ah, then pine not for the strident harpsichord. See, your clavichord breathes as gently as your heart.[12]

The intimate relationship with the instrument described here by Schubart was not the exclusive domain of poets and enthusiastic amateurs. According to Pohl, the young Haydn too found solace at the clavichord: 'his poverty isolated him from his fellow men, and he therefore sought all the more his only joy with his clavichord, which best understood him'.[13] In a gloss on a similar story regarding Handel, Friedrich Chrysander emphasised the 'secrecy' of clavichord playing; the clavichord, he explained, for his mid nineteenth-century readers, is 'a sort of keyboard instrument, small enough for an active man to take under his arm, and its tone just barely exceeds mouse music, and must be accounted especially welcome to the musician who wishes to play secretly'.[14]

The ultimate envoicing of this instrument was achieved, of course, by C. P. E. Bach, who was not only admired as the greatest clavichordist of his era, but was famed for his intimate affiliation with one particular musical companion, his renowned Silbermann clavichord. Bach's performances on the instrument were legendary, inspiring proto-mythical accounts. Burney described how from this, 'his favourite instrument', Bach was able to produce 'a cry of sorrow and complaint, such as can only be effected upon the clavichord, and perhaps only by himself';[15] Reichardt reported from Hamburg in 1774 that Bach's playing of adagios on this clavichord would put all other players to shame, for he had such command of the instrument that he could sustain the sound for the duration of six quavers in a slow tempo, with all manner of shadings, of swelling and ebbing, both in the bass and in the treble; but this is only possible, Reichardt insists, on his 'very beautiful Silbermann clavichord' ('Dieses ist aber auch wohl nur allein auf seinem sehr schönen Silbermannschen Claviere möglich . . .') which could take fortissimos that would destroy another instrument, and pianissimos which, on any other, would never sound.[16]

It is as if, in these reports, the Silbermann clavichord has its own particular powers of agency, even of inspiration – and indeed, Bach was said to have composed many of his finest works at this instrument. In

---

[12] Ibid.   [13] Quoted in Neupert, *The Clavichord*, 46.

[14] Friedrich Chrysander, *G. F. Händel*, 3 vols. (Leipzig: Breitkopf & Härtel, 1858), I, 15.

[15] Charles Burney, *The Present State of Music in Germany, the Netherlands and the United Provinces* (London, 1773), 269–70.

[16] Johann Friedrich Reichardt, *Briefe eines aufmerksamen Reisenden die Musik betreffend* (Frankfurt and Leipzig, 1774–6), 17.

its wonderful capacity to 'speak', the clavichord itself becomes not only the vehicle for, but the originator of, an intensely expressive musical style endowed with its own identity. As the writings of Burney and Reichardt suggest, the idea of a mythic fusion between composer/player and oracular clavichord was not just for dilettantes and poets. No less reliable a theorist than Johann Nikolaus Forkel concurred, claiming in his unpublished treatise 'Von der wahren Güte der Clavichorde', that 'the power active within the instrument' has stimulated the imagination of many a composer, for 'a beautiful instrument can be counted among the sources of inspiration, and indeed not the least fruitful of them'. The clavichord, approximating the quasi-divine status of Music itself, seems to take on the powers of invention, as the composer/improviser finds his creative powers 'stimulated by a beautiful instrument, pouring out well-developed and coherent ideas, inspiring wholehearted admiration in the listener'.[17]

In 1781 Bach passed this clavichord on to his ex-student, the young nobleman Dietrich Ewald von Grotthuß, then living in Courland, and sent along with the instrument a testament to his affection for it, the wonderful sorrowing rondo, *Abschied von meinem Silbermannischen Claviere*.[18] Bach's accompanying note to Grotthuß referred to the clavichord as if it were a beloved child: 'Here you receive my favourite, and so that this sonata could be soon in your hands I have copied it myself from my first manuscript. It is a proof that one can also write plaintive rondos, and it can be played well on no other clavichord than yours.'[19] According to Grotthuß, it was as if Bach had given up a beloved daughter, grateful that she was going into good hands, yet, grieving at her loss, investing his *Farewell* with profound personal significance. Bach himself reinforces the myth of this particular instrument with his claim that the *Abschied* will only truly sound on the very clavichord for and on which it was conceived.

With its careful exploration of the different registers and dynamic shadings of the instrument, and its continual throbbing *Bebung* at each return

---

17 Forkel, 'Von der wahren Güte der Clavichorde', quoted in Neupert, *The Clavichord*, 77–8.

18 Although the instrument was presumably sold by Bach to Grotthuß, the circumstances of this transaction remain murky, partly because the documents pertaining to it have remained inaccessible in a museum in Mitau (now Jelgava, Latvia). They were described in Otto Vrieslander's book *Carl Philipp Emanuel Bach* (Munich: R. Piper, 1923), 95–6 and by Alfred Kreutz (drawing on Vrieslander) in the afterword to his 1950 edition of Bach's *Abschied* Rondo and F♯ minor fantasia, *Carl Philipp Emanuel Bach, Zwei Klavierstücke* (Edition Schott 4013). See also Bernard Brauchli, *The Clavichord* (Cambridge: Cambridge University Press, 1998), 217–21.

19 Quoted in afterword to Alfred Kreutz, ed., *Zwei Klavierstücke*. See also Ernst Suchalla, ed., *C. P. E. Bach: Briefe und Dokumente, Kritische Ausgabe*, 2 vols. (Göttingen: Vandenhoeck & Ruprecht, 1994), II, 891. Translation from Brauchli, *Clavichord*, 220.

Example 5.4   C. P. E. Bach, *Abschied von meinem Silbermannischen Claviere in einem Rondo*, H. 272, bars 1–14

of the rondo theme, this heartfelt *Farewell* both fully displays to its new owner the Silbermann clavichord's expressive scope, perhaps reassuring Grotthuß that he had made a good buy, and testifies to the poignant departure of a lifelong friend. Melancholy is built into the E minor rondo theme itself, which, at its first appearance, descends for four bars through the dark tenor register to a half cadence on V (example 5.4); the soprano – a ground bass elevated to the status of melody, the sparsest of elemental figures encircled by decorative chromaticisms – traces the descending tetrachord E–B, the conventional signal of musical lament. The absence of a strong opening statement of the tonic chord (nothing new for Bach) hints at instability; the tonic is merely touched upon, in first inversion, in the briefest of semiquaver upbeats to the first bar, and the theme, which is constructed on a series of descending 6–3 chords, emerges *in medias res*, as if we have stumbled into the midst of a scene of sorrow.

Given Bach's famous gifts for harmonic adventuring, this piece shows remarkable restraint. The rondo theme returns only in closely related keys – in E minor, in B minor, after an idyllic episode in E major in G♯ minor, and again in E minor;[20] but the three enharmonic detours that expand first the G♯ minor statement of the theme, then the penultimate E minor statement, and finally the last phrase itself, ensure that Bach's dark idiosyncrasies find expression. Each of these excursions pulls away from the predominant sharp keys to the flat side; the first (example 5.5a) shockingly juxtaposes a D major chord (in first inversion) with a chord of B♭ major in second inversion, only to find its way to A minor a bar and a half later, and then eventually to a cadence in B; in the second (example 5.5b), E minor metamorphoses suddenly into B♭ minor, a move which prefigures the potentially catastrophic turn to come at bars 79–80. There (example 5.5c) a glimpse of C major veers via A minor and a dominant seventh on F to another B♭ minor chord which is transformed, as the bass moves up a semitone, into the dark and

---

[20] I borrow Elaine Sisman's apt designation of this section as an 'idyll', made in her paper 'Melancholy, the Enlightenment and C. P. E. Bach' presented at the conference 'German Orpheus: C. P. E. Bach and Musical Culture in the late 18th Century' at Cornell University, February 1999.

Example 5.5a   C. P. E. Bach, *Abschied von meinem Silbermannischen Claviere in einem Rondo*, H. 272, bars 57–60

Example 5.5b   C. P. E. Bach, *Abschied von meinem Silbermannischen Claviere in einem Rondo*, H. 272, bars 72–4

Example 5.5c   C. P. E. Bach, *Abschied von meinem Silbermannischen Claviere in einem Rondo*, H. 272, bars 78–84

remote G♭ major; this chord is pointedly restruck under the insistent portato accents of the repeated soprano B♭s, as if to underscore the difficulty of finally relinquishing the beloved object of the farewell itself, before a return, via a diminished seventh on E (D♭=C♯, B♭ = A♯), to a B major chord and a resigned, faltering cadence in the tonic E minor.

To the end, the qualities of the renowned Silbermann clavichord are brought fully to the attention of the new owner: the carefully notated *Bebung* is an integral feature of the theme, and the piece evokes the melancholy of parting not as a single affect, but as a dappled and subtly shaded palette of colours. Variety is achieved most particularly in the contrast between the various registers of the instrument itself (another Bachian device), especially the repeated explorations of the tenor and the delicate sighing cadences in the treble (bars 62 and 68); at bar 42 high treble and low bass are juxtaposed to beautiful effect, as the sustained low B minor cadence is succeeded by the ethereal E major theme radiant high above (example 5.6).

Example 5.6   C. P. E. Bach, *Abschied von meinem Silbermannischen Claviere in einem Rondo*, H. 272, bars 38–46

The final note of the whole piece, though, is perhaps the most ventriloquistic of all, for here the famous ability of Bach's Silbermann clavichord to sustain long notes is displayed and exploited as the instrument is made to express the final leave-taking, and its departing sound enacts the dying away of farewell. Bach asks that the act of *Bebung*, the deeply physical engagement of the player with the instrument, continue beyond the lapsing of the tone; this rupture between touch and sound is highlighted by the crotchet chord in the soprano which is cut off (pp) above the dying of the bass note (example 5.5c). The actual letting-go is made difficult, the moment of parting is rendered decisive and laden with sorrow. Here the beloved clavichord itself is admitted into the most intimate friendship circle; it is the object of the leave-taking, but also the superbly vivid means of its expression. It is as if the instrument, with its uncanny powers of expression, has incorporated into itself the echo of its former owner's voice.

The centrality of the clavichord to the German bourgeois world of intensely private emotion, of *Empfindsamkeit* and *Einsamkeit*, sentiment and solitude, is vividly reflected in the multitude of poems and songs addressed 'An das Clavier' ('To the Clavichord') which flooded into the new market for such publications in the second half of the eighteenth century. As Max Friedländer and J. W. Smeed have shown, the period witnessed the publication of at least thirty-two different poems on this single theme, providing the texts for over seventy different song settings.[21] Their approach is remarkably uniform, as a selection of their first

[21] See Max Friedländer, *Das deutsche Lied im 18. Jahrhundert*, 3 vols. (Stuttgart and Berlin, 1902; reprint edn Hildesheim: Olms, 1962), I/1, 379ff., and J. W. Smeed, '"Süssertönendes Klavier": Tributes to the Early Piano in Poetry and Song', *Music and Letters* 66/3 (July 1985), 228–40. Attention was also drawn to these songs by Loesser in *Men, Women and Pianos*.

lines indicates: 'At the sweet-toned clavichord' ('Am süss tönenden Klavier') (anonymous, 1782); 'With you, clavichord, the hours dissolve away' ('Bei dir, Klavier, entschweben die Stunden') (anonymous; date uncertain); 'You gentle child of sorrow' ('Du holdes Kind der Trauer') (anonymous, date uncertain); 'Give relief to my sorrows' ('Erleichtre meine Sorgen') (Henriette von Hagen, by 1773); 'Companion of my solitude' ('Gefährtin meiner Einsamkeit') (Loder, by 1780); 'O my tender clavichord' ('O mein zärtliches Klavier') (anonymous, before 1787) and 'When I weep solitary tears' ('Wenn ich einsam Tränen weine') (anonymous, by 1782). With their ubiquitous references to quivering strings and *Bebungen*, these poems clearly refer to the clavichord, although they have been mistakenly interpreted in some modern criticism as homages to the early piano; as many contemporary sources attested, however, the fortepiano of the 1760s–80s was no match, in expressive terms, for the clavichord.[22]

The model for these, published in 1754, was Justus Friedrich Wilhelm Zachariae's poem 'An mein Klavier', in which the clavichord is addressed both as sympathetic friend and consolation for self-indulgent love-sickness. Zachariae's 'An mein Klavier' begins as follows:

Du Echo meiner Klagen,	Oh echo of my laments,
Mein treues Saitenspiel,	My faithful stringed instrument,
Nun kommt nach trüben Tagen	Now after dismal days comes
Die Nacht, der Sorgen Ziel.	The night, the goal of sorrows.
Gehorcht mir, sanfte Saiten,	Obey me, gentle strings,
Und helft mein Leid bestreiten,	And help combat my suffering;
Doch nein, laßt mir mein Leid,	But no, leave me my pain,
Und meine Zärtlichkeit.	And my tenderness.
Wenn ich untröstbar scheine,	If I appear to be inconsolable,
lieb ich doch meinen Schmerz;	Nonetheless I love my pain;
Und wenn ich einsam weine,	And if I cry alone,
Weint doch ein liebend Herz . . .	Nonetheless it is a loving heart that cries . . .[23]

Zachariae establishes the dominant theme of these poems – the clavichord as a sonic mirror of the sufferer's psyche, both sensitive and compassionate, even potentially curative. In addition, the instrument mediates the tension between pain and pleasure; it is a useful tool for the seemingly perverse enjoyment of the turmoil of unrequited love.

---

[22] Smeed is one of those who understands 'Clavier' to mean piano, as demonstrated by the title of his article '"Süssertönendes Klavier"'. For revealing comments on the difference in expressive capabilities between piano and clavichord in the 1780s, see especially Cramer, review of 'Claviersonaten und freye Phantasien . . . Vierte Sammlung', 1245–7.

[23] J. F. W. Zachariae, 'An mein Klavier' (*Scherzhaften Epischen Poesien nebst einigen Oden und Liedern*, Braunschweig, 1754). Translations mine, unless otherwise noted. A number of these poems are cited in Loesser, and in Friedländer, *Das deutsche Lied*.

C. F. Weisse's poem 'Sweet-toned clavichord' ('Süssertönendes Clavier', 1766) likewise appealed to the clavichord as a pliable companion and emotional double: 'If I am merry, a playful song resounds from you to me; / If however I feel sad, sorrowing you attune yourself to me; / If I raise up pious songs, how sublime you then sound!'[24] The clavichord is all things to all people, the perfect emotional crutch for an *empfindsam* generation.

In general, Zachariae's imitators pursued self-indulgence and pathology in like measure, and in all of them the clavichord provides the crucial medium for secret confession, the object of tender confidences, even a substitute for the absent lover. In the first verse of Philippine von Gatterer's 'An das Klavier' (1776) a lovesick girl retreats from society to the embrace of her clavichord which offers a surrogate solace: 'With silent grief in my breast / I steal away to you, / Bring harmony and joy to me / You lovely clavichord!'[25] In the anonymous poem 'To the clavichord, from a bride on her wedding day' ('An das Klavier, im Namen einer Braut an ihrem Hochzeittage', by 1780) the clavichord performs a similar function: the young bride addresses the instrument as 'Sympathetic friend' ('O sympathet'scher Freund') and openly admits the strange equivalence between husband and clavichord; gently and somewhat regretfully she banishes the now superfluous instrument to the corner;[26] the clavichord is personified as a loyal childhood friend, neglected after the owner's marriage, yet forced mutely to observe the new relationship; only at moments of marital strife will the instrument come into its own again, asked to perform its old role of confidant and consolation, this time for the spouse too: 'Only when his black look / Unintentionally betrays his ill humour to me, / Will I turn back to you to soothe his temper!'[27] Johann Timotheus Hermes' poem, 'Sei mir gegrüßt, mein schmeichelndes Clavier!', from his novel *Sophiens Reise von Memel nach Sachsen* (Leipzig, 1769) explores similar themes; the poem is suffused with a secret 'sickness', but here the emotional turmoil of the sufferer, confided to the clavichord, is figured as intrinsic to the instrument itself:

Sei mir gegrüßt, mein schmeichelndes Clavier!	Greetings to you, my flattering clavichord!
Was keine Sprache richtig nennt,	What no language can properly name,

---

[24] Quoted in Smeed, '"Süssertönendes Klavier"', 232.

[25] 'Mit stillem Kummer in der Brust / Schleich ich mich hin zu dir, / Bring Harmonie in mich und Lust / Du liebliches Clavier!'

[26] 'Bald wirst du, Monden lang, / Im Winkel, einsam, stehen; / Mich doch voll Wonne sehen'. Quoted in Smeed, '"Süssertönendes Klavier"', 233.

[27] 'Nur, wann sein finstrer Blick / Mir Unmuth, wider Willen, / Verräth, um ihn zu stillen, / Kehr' ich zu dir zurück!' Ibid.

Die Krankheit, tief in mir,	The sickness deep in me,
Die nie mein Mund bekennt,	Which my mouth never confesses,
Die klag ich dir!	I cry to you.

Dich, o Klavier, erfand ein	You, O clavichord, were invented by
Menschenfreund,	a friend to humankind,
Ein Mann, der traurig war, wie ich;	A man who was wretched, like me;
Er hat, wie ich geweint,	Like me, he wept;
Voll Kummer schuf er dich	Full of sorrow he created you
Für sich, und auch für mich.	For himself, and also for me.

Und Heil sey ihm, Vertrauter meiner	And hail to him, confidant of my
Brust,	breast;
Heil sey dem Mann der dich erfand!	Hail to the man who invented you!
Hat ihn, der Schmerz und Luft	Has no memorial stone named him
An deine Saiten band,	Who combined pain and sighs
Kein Stein genannt?²⁸	Into your strings?[28]

Resonating in sympathy with both the current player and the original inventor, the instrument acts uncannily as a medium, transmitting the sorrows of one soul to another. The clavichord transcends unspeakability and brings a communication from the grave, like the tombstone from which the voice of a dead man speaks. The maker is surreptitiously named by the very stone mentioned here, a play on the name of Stein, the famous Augsburg keyboard maker ('Hat ihn, der Schmerz und Luft / An deine Saiten band, / Kein Stein genannt?'). This is the typical *empfindsam* exchange, a communing of souls over an unbridgeable gap which, paradoxically, serves merely to reinforce emotional isolation.

The appropriateness of these texts as songs is obvious, especially as domestic music for performance by a single musician taking private delight in accompanying him- or herself at the clavichord. The music, as commentary, has the potential to enact the text in an unrelenting series of solipsistic reflections; and to a certain extent it succeeds, for the prevailing gentle sweetness of most of the songs nicely conjures soothing consolation. And yet, it is striking that the musical settings tend to make little of the texts' dark anguish. Indeed, were it not for their clear earnestness one might even be tempted to interpret the simple naivety of the songs as ironic. Take, for example, Ernestine von Hagen's poem 'An das Clavier' in its setting by Johann André (*Lieder, Arien und Duette beym Klavier*, I, Berlin, 1780):

Erleichtre meine Sorgen,	Assuager of my cares,
Sanfttröstendes Clavier!	Softly consoling clavichord!

---

²⁸ Johann Timotheus Hermes, 'Sei mir gegrüßt, mein schmeichelndes Clavier!' (Leipzig, 1769).

Example 5.7   Johann André, 'An das Clavier', *Lieder, Arien und Duette beym Klavier*, I (Berlin, 1780), 34

Der Hoffnung lichter Morgen	The bright morning of hope
Verhüllet sich vor mir.	Veils itself before me.
Laß deine treue Saiten	Let your faithful strings
Mein Herz zur Ruhe leiten,	Calm my heart,
Dem ein geheimer Gram	Which a secret sorrow
Längst alle Ruh benahm.	Has for a long time deprived of all tranquillity.
In kummervollen Tagen	In troubled days
Hast du mich oft erquickt.	You have often refreshed me.
Noch muß ich Fesseln tragen;	Yet I must still endure my fetters;
Noch bin ich unbeglückt.	I have not yet been made happy.
Hilf mir mein Leid versüßen.	Help me sweeten my suffering.
Die Welt soll es nicht wissen;	The world shall not know it;
Dir klag' ich es, nur dir:	I lament it to you, only you:
Du seufzest ja mit mir.	Indeed, you sigh with me.
Auf weichgedämpften Chorden	On softly muted strings
Ertönet dein Gesang	Your song resounds,

Voll rührender Accorden,	Full of touching chords,
Im holden Lautenklang.	In lovely lute-like sounds.
Gieb meine Trauerlieder	Return my laments
Den stillen Nächten wieder	To the silent nights;
Sing', bis Aurora scheint,	Sing, until dawn appears,
Und bis ich ausgeweint.	And until I can cry no more.

On the Zachariae model, the musical lover laments a 'secret sorrow' with a sympathetically sighing clavichord. The poem touches on the idea of inexpressibility, but André's setting of this text makes little of its claim to emotional intensity; instead, the music works to cast the poetic angst as sentimental effusion. The song is to be performed in a 'sweetly plaintive' ('zärtlich klagend') manner, and its affect is one of charming, if somewhat banal, consolation: a simple melody flows smoothly over a reassuringly regular Alberti bass; the phrases answer one another in a symmetrical antecedent–consequent structure; and the stable G major tonality is tinged only slightly by minor inflection in the third phrase, at the 'Ruhe' which proves so elusive (example 5.7). The effect is one verging on complacency – and the performer, too, can relax here, for there is little to challenge even a tentative amateur. In the manner of most of these songs (and the 'volkstümlich' lied of the period in general), keyboard and voice parts are one, and it was a feature of such songs that they could be played simply as small keyboard pieces, or alternatively the melodies sung alone, without accompaniment.[29]

A more poignant, though hardly more profound, rendering of this theme is to be found in a setting by Johann Adam Hiller of another popular 'An das Clavier' poem by Hermes (the poem appeared in Hermes' novel *Die Geschichte der Miß Fanny Wilkes* (1766)). Hiller's song, published in his *Wöchentliche Nachrichten und Anmerkungen die Musik betreffend*, 1769, makes rather more of the plangent music-making described in the text:[30]

Bereite mich zum Schlummer,	Prepare me for sleep,
Sanft klagendes Clavier!	Softly lamenting clavichord!
Ermüdet durch den Kummer,	Wearied by cares
Komm ich betrübt zu dir.	I come dejected to you.
Dir sing ich meine Klagen;	To you I sing my laments;
Vermindre du die Plagen!	Diminish my cares!
Und du, gebeugtes Herz,	And you, oppressed heart,
Vergiß nun deinen Schmerz!	Forget now your pain.

---

[29] This is stated explicitly in the preface to Johann André's *Neuer Sammlung von Liedern* (Berlin, 1783); quoted in Friedländer, *Das deutsche Lied*, i/I, 219.

[30] This is Hiller's second published setting of the poem, the first having appeared in his *Wöchentliche Nachrichten* in 1767.

Example 5.8   Johann Adam Hiller, 'An das Clavier', *Wöchentliche Nachrichten und Anmerkungen die Musik betreffend*, III (27 February 1769), 276

Be - rei - te mich zum Schlum - mer, sanft kla - gen - des Cla - vier! Er - mü - det durch den Kum - mer, komm ich be - trübt zu dir. Dir sing ich mei - ne Kla - gen; Ver - min - dre du die Pla - gen! Und Du ge - beugtes Herz, Ver - giß nun dei - nen Schmerz! Ver - giß nun dei - nen Schmerz!

Genieße dieser Stunde	Enjoy these hours,
Wo keine Thräne fließt!	In which no tear flows!
Und fühle nicht die Wunde	And do not feel the wound
Die sonst so schmerzhaft ist.	Which is otherwise so painful.
Dann sinkt durch sanfte Lieder,	Then, through gentle songs,
Mein Busen ruhig nieder,	My breast, into which pain has
	poured itself,
In den der Schmerz sich goß,	And which has locked up the pain,
Und der den Schmerz verschloß.	Sinks calmly down.
Ja Seele! werde stille!	Yes my soul, be still!
Sey demuthsvoll gerührt,	Be humbly touched
Wenn dich des Schöpfers Wille	When the Creator's will
Auf dunklen Wegen führt;	Leads you on dark paths;
Und trotze nicht in Leiden!	And do not be defiant in pain!
Sey sanft wie diese Saiten!	Be gentle, like these strings!
Und geh in Wehmuth hin,	And continue in melancholy
Bis ich getröstet bin.	Until I am consoled.

Here pulsating pairs of sighing appoggiaturas dominate the texture; a tremulous shake evokes the sought-after 'Schlummer' in the first phrase, while a plaintive reiteration of the rising appoggiatura figure

161

enacts the musical lament at 'klagendes' in the second half of that phrase (example 5.8). The more highly-profiled melodic line rises to its highest point in the fifth measure to accompany 'sing ich', and in quasi-dramatic fashion leaps downward a major sixth to the G♭, a not atypical mixture of the minor mode, for 'Plagen'. For the final line of text, which Hiller repeats, the edgy chromaticisms dissolve into diatonic simplicity as the oppressed heart is encouraged to forget its pain. It is a charming enough song, to be performed, as usual, 'slowly and tenderly' ('langsam und zärtlich'), yet in its conventional sentimentality it comes close to portraying solitary weeping at the keyboard as polite behaviour.

Perhaps the most striking example of such a disjunction between text and musical setting is to be found in the Weimar Kapellmeister Ernst Wilhelm Wolf's setting of the poem 'Phyllis an das Clavier' by H. W. von Gerstenberg, published by Wolf in his *Ein und fünfzig Lieder der besten deutschen Dichter* (Weimar, 1784). The poem was composed sometime before 1762 and was later published as 'Die Clavierspielerin' ('The (Female) Clavichord Player'), and indeed, it describes intense communion with the clavichord and that instrument's unique performative characteristics. The poem plays off muteness against vocality, public reticence against private soliloquy, the silence of a woman before her would-be lover contrasted with her exultant lack of inhibition in solitary fantasising, not so much at her instrument as with it. A young woman, distraught and sick with love, sits alone in her room; in solitary anguish, riven with a passion she cannot express, she turns to her trusted clavichord:

Bestes, kleines Klavier,
Schalle, schalle
Lauter Liebe!
Lauter süße Liebe
Sei dein schmelzendes Saitenspiel!

Dear, little clavichord,
Resound, resound
With nothing but love!
Pure sweet love
Be your melodious string-music!

Denn ich fühl' s, ich fühl's,
Dieser Busen
Schmilzt vor Liebe:
Ach! wie wallt, wie wallt er,
Unaussprechlich empfindungsvoll!

For I feel it, I feel it,
This bosom
Melts with love:
Ah! how it seethes, it boils,
Inexpressibly full of emotion!

Aber, Theon, du weinst,
Nennst mir kälter
Als das Eismeer:
Und, Grausamer! siehst nicht,
Wie ich zittre dich anzusehn!

But Theon, you weep,
Call me colder
Than the arctic ocean:
And more cruel! You do not see
How I tremble to look at you!

Wie die Wange mir glüht!
Und die Stimme

How my cheek burns!
And my voice

Itzt dahin stirbt!	Now dies away!
Und der Finger bebend	And the quivering of my finger
In die Töne hinüberfliegt.	Is translated into the realm of
	sounds.
Weh mir! wenn er nun kommt!	Woe is me! If he should come now!
Und nun sprachlos	And if he speechless
Horcht und seufzet,	Listens and sighs,
Und nun meine Seele	Whilst my soul is
Ganz im Feuer der Liebe strömt!	Gushing entirely in the fire of love!
Welchen leisesten Ton	Which softest tone
Soll ich, Himmel!	Shall I, O God!
Soll ich wählen,	Shall I choose,
Der doch ganz ihm sage:	With which to tell him truly
Bester Jüngling! ich liebe dich!	Dear youth! I love you!
Ach! die Wange wird glühn,	Ah! My cheeks will flush,
Und die Stimme	And my voice
Wird verstummen,	Will fall silent,
Und der Finger bebend	And the trembling of my finger
In die Töne hinüberfliehn.	Will be translated into tones.
Und der silberne Laut,	And the silvery sound
Zittern wird er	Will become a shivering
Auf der Saite,	On the string,
Noch ersterbend sagen:	Still saying as it dies away:
Bester Jüngling, ich liebe dich!	Dear youth, I love you![31]

Pleading to the clavichord itself to act as intermediary and to proclaim her love, the *Clavierspielerin*, like a shy improviser who abjures a public hearing while simultaneously yearning for it, fears being exposed in the 'gushing fire' of her passion to a man who might himself be dumbfounded by her display. Only too aware of the impropriety of demonstrating emotion, rendered all the more transgressive when animated by music, she rejects the free fantasy and sublimates these desires, accepting instead a 'soft tone' in which to express her feeling. But this is bound to fail, and, floundering in confusion as the voice chokes, losing her shaking self in the clavichord, the *Clavierspielerin* sounds out only an overwrought *Bebung*; what remains finally is the dying, toneless vibration of the string itself. In this atmosphere of heightened emotion, with its identification of musician with instrument, it is as if the fading sound, with its ghostly after-echo whispering in the strings, hints at the death of the love-sick girl herself. The clavichord is endowed here with strange powers: no longer a mere machine, a box of strings, it metamorphoses

---

[31] H. W. von Gerstenberg, 'Phyllis an das Clavier' (before 1762); published as 'Die Klavierspielerin', in 'Poetisches Wäldchen', *Vermischte Schriften*, 3 vols. (Altona: Hammerich, 1815), II, 122ff.

Example 5.9   Ernst Wilhelm Wolf, 'Phyllis an das Clavier', *Ein und fünfzig Lieder der besten deutschen Dichter* (Weimar, 1784)

into a quasi-human presence, a trusted confidant, consoling friend and potential intermediary. Rarely has an instrument been asked to endure so much.

Nevertheless, in what amounts to a fine misrepresentation of Gerstenberg's poem, Wolf's song setting is a charming and lighthearted tale of musical love; far from foundering in private emotion and the agony of the unspeakable, Phyllis and her clavichord engage in an extroverted and confident performance. The song is in D major, in a vigorous 2/4, marked 'Herzig', its jaunty melody one of confident leaps and lively dotted rhythms, and only a momentary gesture towards a softer affect with a chromatic inflection and hint of B minor at 'süße Liebe' in bars 5–6 (example 5.9). But most drastically, in addition to a number of small changes in the text, the song substitutes a new ending for the tragic dying away of Gerstenberg's final two stanzas; instead of the muted voice, trembling finger, and shivering of the strings, Wolf's song transforms the tense and faint echo of an 'I love you' into a confident declaration, sweet and charming as befits the clavichord and its player, but unambiguously successful: 'And in the most moving tone, softly enchanting, soft and languishing, my playing will say to him: dear youth, I love you!' ('Und in rührendsten Ton, / Sanft entzückend, / Sanft und schmachtend, / Wird mein Spiel ihm sagen: / Bester Jüngling, ich liebe dich!') Wolf's energetic song recasts the poetic angst of Gerstenberg's poem as sentimental effusion. The genteel music of the 'An das Clavier' songs renders 'Leid' and 'Schmerz' as forms of bourgeois delectation ('if I appear to be inconsolable, nonetheless I love my pain'); although such emotional distress might threaten a free collapse, it is staged here as a refined pursuit.[32]

---

[32] Preface to Johann André, *Neuer Sammlung von Liedern* (Berlin, 1783); reprinted in Friedländer, *Das deutsche Lied*, I/1, 219.

In the preface to his *Sammlung von Liedern beym Clavier zu singen* (Pförten, 1784) Johann Gottlieb Naumann drew attention to the private musical experience such songs encapsulate: 'They have not been written down for the public . . . – No, they are outpourings of [the composer's] heart, only transcribed for his circle of friends, and until now only by them tenderly felt again and yet again.'[33] Given the burgeoning market for such publications this statement may be considered somewhat disingenuous, yet Naumann stresses that his own emotional integrity is intact, that rather than addressing a critical public, the collection is simply a window onto a private exchange between friends. Still, Naumann makes considerable claims for his work, suggesting that it covers the gamut of fashionable aesthetic categories: 'One will not miss, even in these small products, the sublime and the moving, the sweet and the soft, the simple and pleasant, which characterises the rest of his works.'[34] Whether or not they achieve their aim of representing even the 'sublime and moving', songs such as these present the heart's outpourings in respectable commodified versions; tidily confined within the strophic form, they offer a popularised, safely appealing representation of solitary musical ravings. There is a whiff of authenticity now and then, perhaps, but this only reinforces an entirely unthreatening musical discourse, serving to titillate and protect the player from any disturbing complications. The emotional turmoil of the 'An das Clavier' song is about as threatening as the grotto in a landscape garden, or the painting of a sublime landscape hanging from the picture rail, whose chasms only confirm the safety of the viewer, the calm of the household.

For all their intense adulation of the clavichord, the private, impassioned music that is evoked in the poetic texts is only palely represented in the song settings 'An das Clavier'. The clavichord, whose ability to express otherwise unspeakable emotional experience is the subject of these poems, sounds in the songs in only the most conventional language; indeed, its music of lament and emotional excess, sickness, even madness, is conspicuously absent. The problem is partly generic, for there is little room within the parameters of the newly popular German lied for display at the keyboard. Johann Gottlieb Naumann's setting (Pförten, 1784) of Zachariae's 'Du Echo meiner Klagen' offers a case in point. Here, keyboard and voice have separate lines, though hardly independent parts, for they enact the animating idea of the poem in which the clavichord echoes the griever's laments. But this attempt at bringing the clavichord itself into the foreground is hindered by an overwrought complexity in the setting, with its extensive vocal melismas (example 5.10). Indeed, Naumann's keyboard flourishes mimic a

---

[33] Johann Gottlieb Naumann, Preface to *Sammlung von Liedern beym Clavier zu singen* (Pförten, 1784).   [34] Ibid.

Example 5.10   J. G. Naumann, 'An mein Clavier', *Sammlung von Liedern beym Clavier zu singen* (Pförten, 1784), 50

vocal virtuosity that seems to invoke the showy world of opera – ironically, exactly the performing space which the third stanza of Zachariae's poem rejects:

Ihr holden Saiten, klinget, / In Sanfter Harmonie! / Flieht, was die Oper singet, / Und folgt der Phantasie. / Seyd sanft, wie meine Liebe, / Besinget ihre Triebe, / Und zeigt durch eure Macht, / Daß sie euch siegend macht.

Ye gentle strings, resound / In soft harmony; / Flee what the opera sings, / And follow fantasy. / Be gentle, as my love, / Celebrate its desire, / And show through your power / That love makes you victorious.

There is surely a musical pun here, in the opposition between opera and *Phantasie*, between the most glamorous and public of musical genres and that most private one, in which the clavichord's expressive capabilities are fully exploited – the free fantasia. This tension recapitulates the polarity more obliquely depicted in Gerstenberg's poem, between the decorous music of the human voice and the geyser of private passion at the keyboard. But while the songs 'An das Clavier' lay claim to a uniquely sympathetic identity between poet, performer and instrument, and assert the compelling power of the clavichord itself, their mild-mannered accompaniments generally fail to evoke this instrument's uniquely expressive and communicative music. In its complexity and ambiguity, its improper flirtation with chaos, the fantasia must necessarily be excluded from the simple lied accompaniment.

There is, though, an astonishing exception to the usual 'An das Clavier' song (the exception that proves the rule, perhaps), in which strophic song and free fantasia are brought together in an attempt at representing precisely that emotional and unstable world associated with the clavichord cult. In Christian Michael Wolff's setting of Ernestine von Hagen's 'An das Clavier' poem 'Erleichtre meine Sorgen', published in his *Sammlung von Oden und Liedern zum Singen beym Clavier und Harfe* (Stettin, 1777), an extensive keyboard introduction, interludes and postlude, replete with chromatic harmonies and wild passagework, bizarrely disrupt the generic boundaries of the lied while supporting with great intensity the poetic text (example 5.11).[35] The song, in A minor, opens with a fourteen-bar prelude for the clavichord which is unstable and chromatic and immediately establishes a dark and searching mood. It begins with a question, its opening chord a diminished triad (A–C–D♯) on an upbeat leading to a heavy appoggiatura, the chromatically inflected soprano rising to scale degree 5, onto an E major chord in first inversion – the dominant; thus at the start the home key is far from clear; indeed, the long-awaited cadence to an A minor chord is arrived at for the first time only weakly in bar 9, by a series of unsettling chromaticisms. Even the Alberti bass, so familiar to the lied accompaniment (compare this with André's setting of the same text) which begins at bar 4, is as turbulent as the rest, undermining its evocation of a lullaby by turning soon to continued chromatic exploration. One thing this prelude does not do is introduce the melody of the song to come – instead the overtly fantastic introduction immediately establishes the unusual primacy of the keyboard over the voice, for this is indeed a piece about keyboard playing.

Once the voice enters the keyboard part is supportive for the first two couplets, though breaking out into its own more flamboyant voice in the intervening gaps, most notably after the second couplet. Here, the shining transformation to the relative major that accompanies the text's glimmer of hope, an idyll comparable to the central section of Bach's *Abschied*, is dramatically counteracted by an avoided cadence at bar 28

---

[35] Other virtuosi, such as the blind pianist Maria Theresia von Paradis, tried for a more active role for the keyboard; in general, however, such writing is rare and not altogether successful (in the Paradis setting of Zachariae's 'Du Echo meiner Klagen' the keyboard part, while more virtuosic than usual, consists of essentially rather tame arpeggios and broken chords). For some discussion of this point, see Smeed's article.

Example 5.11   Christian Michael Wolff, 'An das Clavier', *Sammlung von Oden und Liedern zum Singen beym Clavier und Harfe* (Stettin, 1777)

Example 5.11 (*cont.*)

Example 5.11 (*cont.*)

and the descent to ♭VI, an A♭ chord, instead of the anticipated C major; this thoroughly Bachian gesture introduces a momentary escape into pure fantasy, with its diminished harmony and potentially free metre (not notated as such, but surely implied to anyone familiar with Bach's C minor *Versuch* fantasy), before the affirmative cadence in C major. As the voice enters again, however, things break down further and the clavichord launches into manic *Sturm und Drang* figuration, frenzied passagework meant perhaps to enact the music of the 'calming' strings, but working instead to overpower the text and render it ancillary in the manner of the interpretative texts added by Gerstenberg to Bach's C minor fantasy. In making the song the vehicle for the clavichord's music itself Wolff has created here a strange creature: not only does he identify the private emotional discourse of the instrument with the free fantasia, but, in a bizarre integration of song and fantasy, he makes repeatable the manic passagework and 'original' modulations, thus inventing the conceptually impossible strophic fantasy.

The more usual reticence of the clavichord in these songs parallels the silencing of the women who populate the 'An das Clavier' poems. This aspect of the clavichord cult was indeed pointedly gendered, for the instrument and its songs suited both the confines of female domesticity, as well as the curiously repressive emotionalism of the contemporary culture of sensibility, with its version of the male hero the effeminate and tearful Man of Sentiment. The simplicity of the 'An das Clavier' songs, as of the lied in general, made perfect music for the female amateur; and yet the clavichord promised a private emotional release in a repressive world, a lion's roar conveniently disguised as mouse music. There was perhaps even a hint here of the danger of giving a clavichord to a woman – would she stick to the notes while her husband was away? Grounded as it was in the polarisation that characterised late eighteenth-century culture, the clavichord cult embodied an implicit opposition between the depressed post-adolescent female (or *empfindsam* male amateur) and the professional musician or connoisseur, represented most clearly by C. P. E. Bach and the circle which included Johann Nikolaus Forkel, Carl Friedrich Cramer and Johann Friedrich Reichardt; written into the poems, songs and the contemporary culture of clavichord music was the assumption that the clavichord (even music itself), though multifaceted, moving, expressive, could find its true voice only at the hands of the male *Originalgenie*, most particularly in his improvisations.

In his magisterial and widely circulated treatise *Über die Einsamkeit* (1784), Johann Georg Zimmermann explained that only in solitude is the artist able truly to express himself, without regard for the constraints of convention. In an indirect attack on the repressive nature of contemporary German society, Zimmermann suggested that solitude is essential to an artist's integrity:

> To entertain readers it is, in my opinion, only necessary to deliver freely in writing that which in the general intercourses of society it is impossible to say either with safety or politeness. This is what I call LIBERTY; an inestimable treasure! which, under a wise and moderate administration, every one enjoys who lives in solitude. . . It is precisely this love of liberty which leads men into Solitude, that they may throw off the chains by which they are confined in the world: it is from this disposition to be free, that he who thinks in Solitude boldly speaks a language which perhaps in society he would not have dared openly to hazard.[36]

At the heart of Zimmermann's manifesto is the notion that solitude is a necessary condition not just for self-expression but for a therapeutic examination of the self; retreating into himself, or into nature, the solitary figure is able to reflect on, and come to a higher awareness of, the course of his own sensibilities. 'Man discovers with deeper penetration the extent and nature of the passions by which he is swayed, when he reflects on their power in the calmness and silence of solitude, where the soul, being less frequently suspended between hope and fear, acts with greater freedom' (47). Once alone, the artist can release his creative genius and express ideas that would be unspeakable in public. Indeed, Zimmermann identifies liberating solitude as the basis for the new 'free and easy' style of writing, whose 'ramblings, extravagances and digressions' he defends as the work of unconstrained originality.

The English garden stood as a central metaphor in North German culture for the mediation between the private and public spheres. Though ostensibly a public space, the garden represented a private utopia of liberty, offering a site of imaginative freedom in which to indulge in the pleasures of solitude and private feeling.[37] To walk alone

---

[36] Johann Georg Zimmermann, *Solitude Considered, with Respect to its Influence upon the Mind and the Heart . . .*, trans. from the French by J. B. Mercier (London: C. Dilly, 1791), 190–1 and 171.

[37] See Linda Parshall, 'C. C. L. Hirschfeld's Concept of the Garden in the German Enlightenment', *Journal of Garden History* 13/3 (1993), 125–71; Siegmar Gerndt, *Idealisierte Natur: Die literarische Kontroverse um den Landschaftsgarten des 18. und frühen 19. Jahrhunderts in Deutschland* (Stuttgart: J. B. Metzler, 1981); and Lepenies, *Melancholy and Society*.

Figure 5.1   Lonely garden hermitage, C. C. L. Hirschfeld, *Theorie der Gartenkunst*, vol. III (1780)

through the changing scenes of a landscape garden was to traverse the complex terrain of the ever-changing emotions,[38] and immersion in nature offered the opportunity for reflection on the self. This was one of the guiding themes of C. C. L. Hirschfeld's *Theorie der Gartenkunst*, whose descriptions conjured a picture of the English garden as a site of sociable pastime but also of liberating release from social life. At the park at Gut Schierensee (Schleswig-Holstein), seat of the erstwhile Russian minister Caspar von Saldern, for example,

everything breathes tranquillity and freedom. Each guest is the master of his time and his movements. He troubles no one, nor is he troubled . . . Occupations, pastimes, conversations, solitary amusements succeed each other in turn, until the chime of the bell at the appointed hour calls back the scattered guests out of their hermitages [Einsiedeleyen] or from their companionable walks to the great pavilion on the summit for dinner.[39]

Hirschfeld's accounts of the English-style gardens created according to the precepts of modern *Gartenkunst* are imbued with a heady mix of solitude, sentiment and tearful fantasy (figure 5.1). *Gartenkunst* manipulated the emotions of the visitor in a therapeutic landscape for the soul.

The first volume of the *Theorie* was dedicated to Johann Georg Sulzer; Sulzer had died as Hirschfeld was writing the second volume, and as a tribute to the man who had first promoted *Gartenkunst* as a fine art in Germany, Hirschfeld created an imaginary monument such as might have been found in any landscape garden, a focal point for solitary and sentimental experience (figure 5.2):

What judicious friend of lonely walks must not be keenly moved when, in a wooded area he stumbles upon a monument consecrated to the memory of a man he can treasure. The moon rises over the shrubs with its solemn light . . . No sound is heard, all around deep stillness and solemnity. Overcome by the impression of this scene, sunk in his reflections and his melancholy, the sentimental onlooker leans against an oak standing opposite, looks towards the place where the moonlight illuminates the name of his Sulzer, looks away again, and a tear falls.[40]

The picturesque garden becomes the site for lonely, nocturnal wanderings, a refuge from society as well as the ideal stage for emotional indulgence and morbid reflection.

C. P. E. Bach was famously aware of the distinction between public

---

[38] See Max Becker, *Narkotikum und Utopie: Musik-Konzepte in Empfindsamkeit und Romantik* (Kassel: Bärenreiter, 1996).

[39] C. C. L. Hirschfeld, *Theorie der Gartenkunst*, 5 vols. (Leipzig: Weidemann & Reich, 1779–85; reprint edn, Hildesheim: Olms, 1973). Cited in Adrian von Buttlar, *Der Landschaftsgarten: Gartenkunst des Klassizismus und der Romantik* (Cologne: DuMont, 1989), 169.

[40] Hirschfeld, *Theorie der Gartenkunst*, II (1780), 60f. In Buttlar, *Landschaftsgarten*, 153.

Figure 5.2 Imaginary monument to Sulzer, C. C. L. Hirschfeld, *Theorie der Gartenkunst*, vol. II (1780)

and private spheres, stressing in his short 'Autobiography' published in the German translation of Burney's *Travels* that he had had to make many compromises in providing music for general consumption, and that in only a small number of pieces written for himself had he been able to be truly free. Bach candidly admitted the difficult nature of the fantasia, frankly claiming his fantasies as music written essentially for himself, without an eye to the general market. He went so far as to suggest that the preparation of fantasias for publication amounted to as much of a waste of time as composing popular 'accompanied sonatas':

At the moment I have little inclination for [the publication of a collection of fantasies], as little as for writing keyboard sonatas with an accompanying instrument in the current tedious fashion. Though certainly the latter non- or half-entity could be more lucrative than any dark fantasia.[41]

Fantasias were difficult, uncompromising and private, and Bach's statements emphasise solitary performance and understanding of this music over its public reception, while hinting at the contradictions inherent in its commodification.

Not only did Bach's fantasies represent the apotheosis of the clavichord cult, their picturesque landscapes likewise offered a musical corollary to Zimmermann's uninhibited productions of artistic solitude. For devotees of the fantasia, improvising at the keyboard offered escape from the tedium of daily life, an outlet for overheated sensibilities, and inspiring exercise for the creative imagination. In his autobiographical novel *Hesperus*, Jean Paul, who devoted 'many hours to an old out-of-tune clavichord, whose only tuning lever and tuning master was the weather', described improvisation at the clavichord as a rapturous aid to poetic invention, as well as quasi-erotic arousal and release:

When I want to express a particular feeling that seizes me, it strives to find not words but sounds, and I crave to express it on my clavichord. As soon as I shed tears at the clavichord over my invention, the creative process is over and feeling takes command. Nothing exhausts me as much, nothing soothes me more than improvising at the clavichord. I could improvise myself to death.[42]

As contemporary writers noted, most often in connection with C. P. E. Bach, such improvisation verged on both the indecorous and the pathological: fantasia veered easily into fever and madness.

The free fantasia was celebrated as private, even secret music; to listen to a fantasia was to be either an initiate into an elite circle, or else a lucky eavesdropper, one 'who by accident has the luck to serve, unnoticed, as an observer' ('wer von ohngefähr das Glück hat, unvermerkt einen

---

[41] Letter to Forkel, 10 February 1775, in Suchalla, ed., *Bach: Briefe*, 486.
[42] Cited in Neupert, *The Clavichord*, 51.

Zuschauer abzugeben'),[43] as J. F. Unger, inventor of the Fantasy Machine, explained – a view reinforced by Rochlitz's account of the madman Karl. If the fantasia could represent the revelation of the private sensibilities of the artist, then to fantasise at the keyboard in public was to expose naked consciousness. The musical fantasia could constitute a uniquely personal utterance, offering an intimate view into the emotional life of the improviser, one perhaps epitomised by the final, unpublished, fantasia composed by C. P. E. Bach in the year before his death, the free fantasia in F♯ minor (H. 300), entitled *C. P. E. Bachs Empfindungen*.

This is an extraordinary work, the longest of Bach's fantasias and perhaps the most difficult for both performer and listener, a rhapsodic piece which carries to an extreme the characteristic features of the genre, and one in which the clavichord holds forth in a fluent and virtuosic, if opaque, language. Marked 'Sehr traurig und ganz langsam', the piece evokes a dark, private and extremely melancholic world and, unlike Bach's other late fantasias it is less a witty play with form than an expression of unmediated pathos. The fantasia is largely unmeasured, although the pulsing theme with which it opens, and the pathetic Largo 'second' theme tend to be barred in their appearances during the course of the piece, marked as 'thematic' in contrast to the web of ambiguous diminished chords, continual modulation, avoided cadences, and brilliant passagework in which they are set (figure 5.3). Constant interruptions in the texture and restlessly shifting dynamic levels contribute to the bewildering effect of the fantasia, whose points of climax are articulated, in Diether de la Motte's apt formulation, by 'enharmonic catastrophe'.[44] The formal patterning of this fantasia, with its central 'development' of the opening motive, its subsequent wholesale reprise of the opening, and its structural opposition of two relatively stable thematic groups, alludes to a sonata form built around fourth relationships, and takes the fantasia well beyond the realm of the purely improvisatory.[45] Yet it is simultaneously a brilliant exercise in disruption, undermining any sense of teleological patterning. Here reiteration is random, recollection uncertain; in its constant flux, its fragmentary echoes and

---

[43] Johann Friedrich Unger, *Entwurf einer Maschine wodurch alles was auf dem Clavier gespielt wird, sich von selber in Noten setzt* . . . (Braunschweig, 1774); cited in Schleuning, 'Die Fantasiermaschine: Ein Beitrag zur Geschichte der Stilwende um 1750', *Archiv für Musikwissenschaft* 27 (1970), 200.

[44] See Diether de la Motte, 'Spezialanalyse: C. P. E. Bach, Freie Fantasie für Klavier', in his *Musikalische Analyse, mit kritischen Anmerkungen von Carl Dahlhaus* (Kassel: Bärenreiter, 1968), 95–105.

[45] De la Motte's detailed 'dialectical' analysis beautifully highlights the tension between compositional planning and improvisatory freedom in this fantasy. See also the analysis of this piece in Peter Schleuning, *Die Freie Fantasie: Ein Beitrag zur Erforschung der klassischen Klaviermusik* (Göppingen: Kümmerle, 1973), 263–83.

Figure 5.3   C. P. E. Bach, Free fantasia in F♯ minor, H. 300.
Autograph

allusions, the F♯ minor fantasia seems to work by a process of association, like the imagination itself.

The unprecedented title *C. P. E. Bachs Empfindungen* which Bach himself gave to the work seems to advertise it as the self-conscious expression of the emotions of the aged composer. Whether a melancholic meditation on impending death, or simply the introspective moodiness of a famously *launig* composer in his old age,[46] such focus on feeling would appear finally to belie the ironic-fantastic and to posit the apotheosis of sentiment; as Diether de la Motte notes: '[The title] *C. P. E. Bachs Empfindungen* . . . suggests the absorption of the player in the personal, private emotion of the composer. Not what he might be able to feel but what he has felt and has exorcised in tones is expressed there. In this respect the title reads like a justification, an apology even, for a composition whose events shun the clear light of general intelligibility and civility'.[47] Picturesque in its confrontation of form with freedom, this fantasia seems far from humorous or ironic; rather, it is steeped in the sincerity admired and promoted by mid-century clavichord enthusiasts. The fantasia stands as a monument to its composer, like Hirschfeld's to Sulzer, an imaginary locus for nocturnal reflection and indulgence in tearful emotion. In this late, great unpublished work, music 'for himself alone', Bach conjures up an intimate emotional self-portrait, whose title presents it as a reverie of self-consciousness. It is the apotheosis of the private address to the clavichord, and of the intense and uninhibited music of solitude, as if here, in Bach's last fantasia, Zimmermann's lonely artist is to be found examining, and expressing, the course of his own emotions in complete freedom.

But surely this is too easy an interpretation. Zimmermann posited solitude and its attendant opportunities for introspection as the context for boldly unconventional utterance. To take Bach's last fantasia at face value would be to underestimate both the conflicted mediation between private and public that constitutes the fantasia as genre, and the contemporary aesthetic context within which this ambitious and highly self-conscious composer worked. In its radical and uncompromising exploration of the limits of fantasy, *C. P. E. Bachs Empfindungen* may be read less as the withdrawn musings of an old man, than as the critical utterance of a revolutionary, expressing the unspeakable in opaque music that not only is resistant to, but, in the manner of Sterne or Jean Paul, constitutes an ironical commentary on, the demands of fashion-

---

[46] Schleuning notes that in a number of Bach's songs the performance indications 'sehr traurig' and 'sehr langsam' are attached to settings of texts on the subject of mourning, pain or parting; furthermore, the key of F♯ minor, designated 'dark' by C. F. D. Schubart, is exceptional, appearing as the principal key in only one other instance in all of Bach's keyboard works or songs (the Sonata, H. 37, 1763). See Schleuning, *Freie Fantasie*, 278–9.

[47] De la Motte, 'Spezialanalyse', 96.

able taste. The history of *C. P. E. Bachs Empfindungen* is more complicated than my account has allowed, for the piece entitled *C. P. E. Bachs Empfindungen* is, strictly speaking, neither the intimate clavichord fantasia described above, nor did it remain unknown in Bach's lifetime. Bach made two versions of the fantasia in the same year. The first was a fantasia for clavichord alone, whose autograph bears the simple inscription 'Freye Fantasie von C. P. E. Bach, fürs Clavier, H[amburg] 1787' (H. 300); its tempo indication (which appears to have been added by another hand) is 'Adagio' (see figure 5.3). The second version, that which the composer entitled *C. P. E. Bachs Empfindungen*, and designated 'Sehr traurig und ganz langsam', is an arrangement of the fantasia for clavichord with accompanying violin (H. 536) (see figure 5.4). Though both pieces remained unpublished (until the twentieth century), they were not unknown to Bach's contemporaries and a number of copies were in circulation.[48]

The keyboard part remains substantially the same in both versions, but the addition of the violin amounts to a metamorphosis into that most fashionable and popular genre so disparaged by Bach, the accompanied sonata. The fantastic itself seems to be severely compromised in the version with added violin which, far from being unmeasured, is barred throughout – a concession to the demands of ensemble playing, and to the fact that this is no longer music for solitary indulgence in the whims of the imagination. Worse still, at the end of this version of the fantasia there is a short segue into a jolly A major Allegro in 6/8 (example 5.12). One might perhaps interpret the duo version of the fantasia as maximum indulgence in sentiment – the social, shared emotionalism that was suggested by the epistolary novel and Naumann's song-collection prefaces – but a sincere commitment to dark emotion is rendered highly problematic by the jovial movement that follows. Brushing aside the profound melancholy of the fantasia, even recasting it as ludicrous posturing, the Allegro effects a plunge into bathos; it is not even as if, in a further exploration of his feelings, Bach developed the idea of the sunny conclusion out of what had come before, for the tacked-on ending is indeed just that, having been taken wholesale from an unpublished sonata in B♭ (H. 212) for which it constituted an alternative third movement, written twenty years earlier in 1766.[49]

Not surprisingly, the critical literature has tended to dismiss this awkward arrangement, viewing the 'accompanied sonata' version of the F♯ minor fantasia as an embarrassment, a capitulation to popular taste

---

[48] Of extant copies one of each is to be found in the Esterházy archive in Budapest. Did Haydn know this fantasy?

[49] Bach had written on the score of this movement 'hat noch niemand', as if the piece were part of a store of works for potential use. My thanks to Richard Kramer for drawing my attention to this piece.

Figure 5.4   *C. P. E. Bachs Empfindungen*, H. 536. Autograph

Example 5.12   C. P. E. Bach, *C. P. E. Bachs Empfindungen*, bars 99–106

or the ill-advised request of a friend, perhaps the worst of Bach's long career of making money off the *Liebhaber*.[50] But this is surely to underestimate the irony inherent in *C. P. E. Bachs Empfindungen*. As the freest of musical genres finds itself confined in the decorous duet, rearranged for bourgeois consumption, the unyielding individuality of the piece – and its composer – are recast in a mediation between private and public. *C. P. E. Bachs Empfindungen*, Karl's fantasies in Rochlitz's fragments and

---

[50] There is little discussion of this movement in the literature, besides offhand acknowledgement of the mere existence of the violin version.

parlour songs 'An das Clavier' are all representations of solitude which can be enjoyed and shared in company. They invoke solitude even while they deny it, explore sentiment while enforcing an anti-sentimental critical distance.

In 1785, when Elisa von der Recke and Sophie Becker paid a visit to Bach in Hamburg, the old man sat down at the keyboard and played for them before a hearty dinner; what they were treated to was an 'Abschiedsrondeau'.[51] On the assumption that this was the work Bach wrote for Grotthuß, it is surely significant that now its representation of parting regret, performed on some other instrument than the Silbermann clavichord, could have provided an early-evening entertainment, whetting the appetite for a good meal. The sorrows of this farewell, like the private musical enjoyment of lovesickness, reflect emotional experience at a distance; in their intricate evocations of pain, both are perfect manifestations of the polite art of sentiment. Bach's *Farewell* and *Empfindungen* conjure up the intimate sound world described in the 'An das Clavier' poems, and realise the emotive musical potential that the songs themselves seem to shy away from; yet rather than expressing emotional effusion in the Romantic autobiographical sense, Bach's musical explorations of sorrow are deeply moving but finely balanced representations of such feeling, no less contrived than the fervent staging of emotion, the intimate gestures of sentiment, evoked in the 'An das Clavier' songs. Indeed, in the *Abschied* the choice of a rondo as the genre in which to say goodbye carries with it its own irony, for the rondo is built around the narrative structure of return. More overtly, the almost unbearably light-hearted Allegro of the *Empfindungen* punctures the atmosphere of melancholy with so decisively 'annihilating' a humour that it renders ironic the earlier emotional intensity, framing private sorrow as an aesthetic experience, distanced and commodified. The violin accompaniment to the fantasy itself works to support this: difficult to count and difficult to follow, the added voice serves less to render the fantasy banal than to heighten it, serving as a ghostly commentary on the author's soliloquy, and intensifying the dramatic, uncompromising utterances in what amounts to meta-fantasia at its most unsettling. It is the paradox of *C. P. E. Bachs Empfindungen* that although it presents an approachable, public solitude, performing an ironic commentary on the very notion of *Empfindsamkeit*, as an object of contemplation contained within the picturesque frame it remains as strange – even disturbing – as Karl's feelings, ultimately distant, baffling, lonely.

---

[51] Elisa von der Recke, writing in the third person, recounts that: 'Einmal speisten sie bei ihm; vor dem Essen spielte er ihnen ein Abschiedsrondeau; Frau Bach aber, eine geschäftige Martha, "gab sich alle Mühe, ihren Gästen so viel Essen einzupfropfen, als nur immer Raum hat".' In Suchalla, ed., *Bach: Briefe*, 1118–19.

6

Picturesque Beethoven and the veiled Isis

The customary form of observation of nature is thoughtless and seems to expect that she will reveal her secrets all by herself. That is impossible, for the veil, the robe, is essential to her. Only the naive and chaste mind is granted the privilege of being allowed to lift the veil of Isis and to throw a glance into the mysteries.

(C. A. Eschenmayer, *Psychologie*, 1817)

A monument is a ruin twisted forward, just as a ruin is a monument twisted backward. (Schumann, 'Monument für Beethoven',
Neue Zeitschrift für Musik, 1836)

I

Karl, the manic improviser and compulsive writer, pathologically inclined to solitude, is deranged and traumatised; yet he functions both as a weirdly logical outcome of the late eighteenth-century North German keyboard cult, and as a totem of a literary obsession around 1800 with musical fantasy and its trappings. Rochlitz's account from the lunatic asylum of 1804, which, perhaps predictably, caught the attention of that master of the strange, E. T. A. Hoffmann, puts on public display an intensely disturbing figure; but Karl is in no sense safely confined to the past. Rather, the lunatic Karl shadowed the centre of contemporary musical culture; with only a slight deflection of the line dividing mental balance from insanity, he both mirrors and prefigures Beethoven, performing the role of a twisted Doppelgänger to the great improviser, musical solitary, and constant scribbler whose own indulgence in musical fantasy, already the topic of some debate, was to provoke heated reaction with the appearance of the *Eroica* Symphony in this same year.

Already by 1802, plagued by impending deafness, Beethoven had become increasingly misanthropic, anxious for his health and sanity, fearing, yet resigned to, social isolation. Needless to say, his deafness exacerbated his distaste for being on public display, and his almost mythical reluctance to improvise in public had begun to colour, paradoxically, the image of a virtuoso whose reputation was based in no small part on the brilliance of his fantasising.[1] Commentators agreed that Beethoven's improvisations constituted revelatory, if occasionally unfathomable, musical utterances, and that his genius was only fully to be understood in his extemporaneous performances at the keyboard; his improvisations had experts such as Johann Schenk marvelling at their 'profound psychological pictures' and the brilliance and variety of ideas combined so skilfully in them, while their emotional power moved amateurs and experts alike.[2] Yet in extended dramas of trickery and deceit, similar to that between Rochlitz and Karl, such performances, increasingly and excitingly, had to be wrung out of the great genius. Sir John Russell visited Beethoven in 1821 and described a by now familiar charade: how, at a soirée at the house of one of Beethoven's acquaintances the whole party pretended to leave, withdrawing into the next room; there they waited in excited anticipation while their host, left with Beethoven at the piano, disingenuously enticed the musician to the piano. Beethoven having begun to play, the friend too hid himself in the next room, while Beethoven, beginning tentatively with only 'a few hurried and interrupted notes, as if afraid of being detected in a crime', proceeded to improvise an extended fantasy, 'in a style extremely varied, and marked, above all, by the most abrupt transitions'. The amateurs 'were enraptured'.[3]

A crucial conclusion to such tales, and fully in line with the story of Karl, is the rage of the composer on discovering that he has been tricked and overheard. Beethoven scorned the banality of weeping and fainting – keynotes of *empfindsam* behaviour now reduced to mere *Empfindelei* – that accompanied his listeners' effusive enthusiasm for his improvisation; as Czerny reported: 'When he had concluded an improvisation of this kind, he was capable of breaking out into boisterous laughter and of mocking his listeners for yielding to the emotion he had called forth in them. He would even say to them: "You are fools". At times he felt insulted by such manifestations of sympathy.'[4] Aggressively antisocial, jealously guarding his private musical fantasy, Beethoven is portrayed in such accounts as a freak of nature, fantastically compelling, even inspirational, yet simultaneously marginal, odd and disturbing.

In the reception of Beethoven's instrumental works, both in his lifetime and posthumously, the musical fantastic likewise occupies an ambiguous

---

[1] As early as 1801 Beethoven wrote to his friend Karl Amenda that 'when I am playing and composing, my affliction still hampers me least; it affects me most when I am in company'. Emily Anderson, ed., *The Letters of Beethoven*, 3 vols. (New York: St Martin's Press, 1961), I, 65 (1 July 1801); quoted by William Meredith, 'Beethoven's Creativity: Improvisations', *The Beethoven Newsletter* 1/2 (Fall 1986), 25–8.

[2] Cited in O. G. Sonneck, ed., *Beethoven: Impressions by his Contemporaries* (New York: Schirmer, 1926), 15. See also Meredith, 'Beethoven's Creativity'.

[3] Cited in Sonneck, *Beethoven*, 115–16; see also Cipriani Potter's report dating from 1818, in ibid., 110–11.   [4] Cited in ibid., *Beethoven*, 31.

position. In paradoxically parallel critical positions, Beethoven's contemporaries grappled, often reluctantly, with what they understood to be a wild incursion of the fantasy into other genres, while modern commentators, more at home with Beethoven's sometimes grotesque games with formal paradigms, have tended to regard with suspicion, and even to dismiss, pieces actually designated by Beethoven as fantasias. The *Eroica* Symphony, unmasked by the *AmZ* in 1805 as 'really a very extended, daring and wild fantasia',[5] and the late piano sonatas, imbued with the formal dislocations and ambiguities of the fantasy as they are (and were understood to have been), have, of course, generated a massive modern critical literature; the *Fantasie*, Op. 77 and the Choral Fantasy, Op. 80, by contrast, tend to be shrugged off with a hint of boredom. But despite the fact that these are relatively slight works, their position in the culture of fantasy in which Beethoven's oeuvre is embedded deserves closer attention; indeed, the significance of fantasy itself within the discourse especially of a number of the piano sonatas and their accompanying nineteenth-century critique richly repays investigation.

In the late eighteenth century the complex and opaque utterances of the free fantasia found their popular counterpart in the pyrotechnical display of such charlatan artists as Abt Vogler, whose speciality, virtuoso storm scenes, presented magnificent parodies of the sublime. Around 1800, with public (published) improvisation increasingly intent on being impressive in large halls rather than expressive in small chambers, the genre of free fantasia proper faded from the published repertory, to be replaced by the virtuoso pot-pourri (variations on a mixture of familiar tunes).[6] Czerny's *Systematic Introduction to Improvisation on the Pianoforte* (1836, written in the late 1820s) focusses largely on keeping the audience awake, and does not shy away from advising the performer on the differences between the old 'very interesting' and 'distinctive' style of free improvisation and the new pot-pourri variation style: the former, thanks to the 'very destructive fear of boring the audience' and to the general ignorance of a 'largely heterogeneous public' is inappropriate for improvisation before a large crowd; rather, 'the majority will be entertained only by pleasant, familiar tunes and will be sustained in spirit by piquant and glittering performances'.[7] In 1799 critics in the *AmZ* attacked the most recent fantasia

---

[5] *AmZ* 7/20 (13 February 1805), col. 321; translation from Peter Schleuning, *The Fantasia*, vol. II: *18th–20th Centuries*, trans. A. C. Howie (Cologne: Arno Volk, 1971), II, 15.

[6] On the fantasia at the turn of the nineteenth century see Schleuning, *The Fantasia*, 15–17.

[7] Carl Czerny, *A Systematic Introduction to Improvisation on the Pianoforte*, Op. 200, trans. and ed. Alice L. Mitchell (New York and London: Longman, 1983), 23, 86. Czerny's own example of the pot-pourri in his *Systematic Introduction* has a peculiar academic integrity, offering a chronological survey of musical style, from Bach to Beethoven, via Handel, Gluck, Haydn, Mozart and Cherubini.

publications for their nonsensical wanderings, their random 'jangling through' various emotional states without connection or direction. In a proto-formalist twist, they blamed composers of modern fantasies for misjudging the limits between the private and the public spheres: pandering to ignorant audiences demanding pyrotechnic display and cheap effects, their fantasies were without 'the slightest connection, order, without once an actual idea as the foundation'; in the privacy of one's own room such abandon to accident and strange wandering might be natural, but fantasies designed for 'general entertainment' must have harmonic coherence and a sense of direction, 'a natural underlying connection, despite apparent diversity on the surface'.[8]

This shift parallels the popularisation of the picturesque, in which the academic discourse of a connoisseur's category of irregularity found its counterpart in the chatter of a regularised popular cult. By the turn of the nineteenth century, *Gartenkunst* had become enormously fashionable in German-speaking lands, widely available in both theory and practice. 'Englished' gardens were open to the public or accessible through often heavily poeticised descriptions in pamphlets, books and magazines, such that the theorist August Hennings could claim that an education in *Gartenkunst* was the modern equivalent of the *Bildungsreise*: just as people used to travel to see the monuments, palaces, churches and the ruins of ancient Rome, they now visited the most famous gardens, or toured them vicariously, in a kind of education of the imagination, with the help of publications in which the grand garden circuits had been so accurately described that, simply by reading, one could achieve the sense of losing oneself in 'a labyrinth of beauties'.[9] So popular, indeed, had *Gartenkunst* become that Hennings, fearing its debasement, claimed for it a place beside the equally fashionable philosophy of Kant, both

[8] See the reviews of a 'Fantasia' by Gottfried Rieger, *AmZ* 2/8 (20 November 1799), cols. 154–5, and a Capriccio by Luigi Lodi, *AmZ* 2/2 (9 October 1799), cols. 27–9. Wenzel Tomaschek reported having heard Beethoven comment similarly about contemporary pianists, those who 'only run up and down the keyboard in passages learned by heart, thump-thump-thump. What's the use of that? When the true virtuosi played, it was something coherent, something whole; written down on the spot, one would have regarded it as a well-executed work. That can be called playing the piano, the rest should be called nothing.' In Michael Hamburger, ed., *Beethoven: Letters, Journals and Conversations* (London: Thames and Hudson, 1984), 132.

[9] August Hennings, ed., 'Über Baummahlerei, Garten Inschriften, Clumps und Amerikanischen Anplanzungen', *Der Genius der Zeit* 10/1 (1797). Such publications included both specialised (and widely-circulating) garden magazines such as W. G. Becker's *Taschenbuch für Garten-Freunde* (Leipzig, 1795–99), and Johann Gottfried Grohmann's *Ideenmagazin für Liebhaber von Gärten, Englischen Anlagen und für Besitzer von Landgütern und Gärten* (Leipzig, 1779–1805), and more general publications such as the *Journal des Luxus und der Moden*. See Siegmar Gerndt, *Idealisierte Natur: die literarische Kontroverse um den Landschaftsgarten des 18. und frühen 19. Jahrhunderts in Deutschland* (Stuttgart: J. B. Metzler, 1981), 116–19.

being much more than 'simply fashion and trivial pastime'.[10] In addition, *Gartenkunst* could act as a potential agent for subversive ideological influence, inculcating radical new ways of thinking about both politics and aesthetics: 'It is very possible that, whilst the political reformer works in vain to bring about a revolution in people's way of thinking, beautiful *Gartenkunst*, unnoticed could effect a complete reformation in the attitudes and in the ideas of people.'[11] Perhaps by a subtle influence, the natural freedoms of the English garden could encourage their own revolution: a surreptitious, but no less radical one, as such landscapes educated tastes and moral sensibility, in turn moulding social and political ideals (figure 6.1).

In Austria, the despotic rule of the Emperor was mirrored, and advertised, by the magnificence of the Baroque garden even in late eighteenth-century Vienna, where the authorities were all too aware of the political implications of the English park. When Joseph II opened the Prater to the public in 1766 the 'too remote parts and dense woodlands' were closed off, 'for fear of mischief and misuse'. The Augarten was completely opened to the public in 1775, but, exceptionally, this imperial garden was not modernised according to the English taste. The subversive dangers of the English style did not diminish with time. After Napolean's retreat from Vienna in 1809 a heated debate arose over whether to lay out the Volksgarten in the formal French or the more natural English style; the decision was taken in favour of the French, for pragmatic rather than aesthetic reasons – the public could be controlled more easily in the ordered and open walks of a French garden, than in the irregular, secluded paths of an English one.[12] In Henning's Altona paper *Genius der Zeit* (1800), Joseph Rückert celebrated the levelling effect of the English garden as he described the famous park at Weimar: 'The prince may not display himself in the open countryside; that would disturb nature's pure impression; he may only be present as a human being, and everything that surrounds him must display the reflection of a freely feeling soul, the purely human, if it is to please. Nature is republican and proudly and disdainfully casts aside crowns, feudal hats, courtly pomp and vain glitter, and our heart is formed after its sense. The simpler, the more beautiful, the more

---

[10] Hennings, 'Über Baummahlerei', 20.

[11] Ibid., 20. Hennings' essay is quoted in Gerndt, *Idealisierte Natur*, 116 and also Adrian von Buttlar, *Der Landschaftsgarten: Gartenkunst des Klassizismus und der Romantik* (Cologne: DuMont, 1989), 171.

[12] See Géza Hajós, 'Picture and Poetry in Austrian Gardens of the Late Eighteenth Century', in *Garden History: Issues, Approaches, Methods: Dumbarton Oaks Colloquium on the History of Landscape Architecture XIII*, ed. John Dixon Hunt (Washington, DC: Dumbarton Oaks Research Library and Collection, 1992), and his *Romantische Gärten der Aufklärung: Englische Landschaftskultur des 18. Jahrhunderts in und um Wien* (Vienna: Böhlau, 1989).

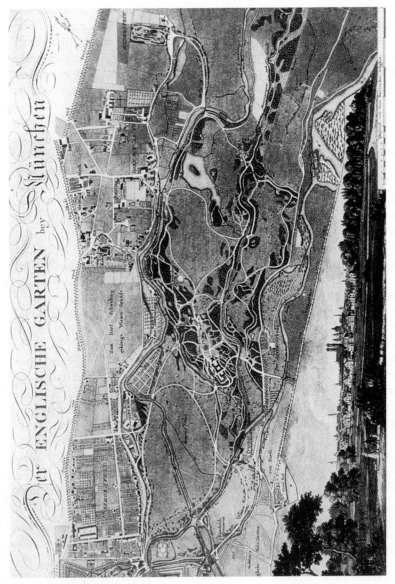

Figure 6.1   Plan of the English garden at Munich, the first public garden in Germany (1790s)

welcome.' On Sundays this park was open to the public, to create 'a republican holiday for the whole of Weimar'.[13] In most cases, of course, the English garden was the plaything of the aristocracy; although open to the public on a limited basis, it had been laid out at tremendous expense and functioned as a symbol of the wealth and status of its fashionable owners.[14]

The English garden stood for a liberation of taste from the despotic rule of the Francophile neo-classicists, yet in aesthetic terms the freedoms of the English garden were themselves increasingly the object of critique towards the turn of the nineteenth century. By the 1790s reformers such as Hennings were calling for a curb on too much wildness in gardens, warning that 'the propensity for Nature must not transform us into aimless dreamers of fantastic visions';[15] likewise, in their 'Fragment über den Dilettantismus' (1799), Goethe, Schiller and Heinrich Meyer scathingly rebuked the current faddish enthusiasm of garden *Liebhaberei* which 'promoted sentimental and fantastic nothingness'. Debasing the sublime in weak imitations of grand landscapes, it merely perpetuated what they called 'the ruling bad habit' of the age, to be committed in aesthetic matters to 'spontaneity and rulelessness' and to 'arbitrary fantasising'.[16] Already in 1795 Schiller, previously a strong advocate for the English 'garden of freedom', had demanded a German national style that would mediate between the overly natural English and the overly artifical French. A well-composed landscape, he proposed, was one in which the individual elements worked together in a free play to constitute a unified whole, the stress lying on the unity rather than the diversity of individual elements.[17] Complaining that *Gartenkunst* and dramatic arts had suffered similarly from overwhelming German deference to foreign cultural influence, he rejected the models both of the 'tyranny of rule' in French gardens and French tragedies, and of the 'wild rulelessness' of English parks and 'their' Shakespeare.

---

[13] Joseph Rückert, 'Bemerkungen über Weimar' (1799), in August Hennings, ed., *Genius der Zeit*, 21 vols. (1794–1800; reprint edn Nedeln/Liechtenstein: Kraus Reprint, 1972), 20 (May 1800), 1–28; cited by Gerndt, *Idealisierte Natur*, 123.

[14] Such projects of improvement were often taken to absurd lengths, and in their manipulation and distortion of the landscape were anything but a celebration of the natural. Prince Hermann von Pückler-Muskau famously ruined himself as the result of the overambitious 'Englishing' of his park. But as Ann Bermingham has shown, the picturesque discourse of the 1790s and on was in many ways one of reaction rather than revolution; see her *Landscape and Ideology* (Berkeley and Los Angeles: University of California Press, 1986).   [15] Hennings, 'Über Baummahlerei', 17.

[16] Johann Wolfgang Goethe, Friedrich Schiller and Heinrich Meyer, 'Fragment über den Dilettantismus' (1799), cited in Buttlar, *Der Landschaftsgarten*, 163.

[17] See Friedrich Schiller, 'Über den Gartenkalender auf das Jahr 1795', in *Werke*, vol. XXII (Weimar: Böhlaus, 1943), and Gerndt, *Idealisierte Natur*, 112–13.

The language of cultural politics proved astonishingly intact, when, as late as 1828, G. W. Fink explained to his German readers how Beethoven had been received in France, signifying the opposing sensibilities of French and Germans, their very different responses to the unconventional and fantastic elements in Beethoven's music, by referring to landscape aesthetics. Explaining that the landscape of Beethoven's imagination constituted a wilderness that is intrinsic to his nature, so that what in others would be aberrations are natural to him (indeed, the lack, or 'correction', of his excrescences would itself constitute unnaturalness), Fink compared sudden contrasts in Beethoven's monumental music to being 'led out from the wild rocky shores to the most pleasant valleys'. Not without humour, Fink proposed an extended landscape analogy for Beethoven's instrumental music, one whose appeal to nature incorporated the interruptions, distortions and even irritations of a determinedly realistic natural world:

Certainly many frogs hop in the grass, many midges buzz around the ear and all sorts of game runs through the green forest, while, in most beautiful May the lovely army of feathered singers sounds out its song of praise from the spray of blossoms and enchants us to joy and to thanks. If [Beethoven] sometimes leads us through small swamps, this is only in order to show us even more charming groves.

The analogy emphasises the pleasures of surprising contrast, as the sweet is made sweeter after a difficult patch, and the composer quite deliberately 'carries us abruptly away with him with wondrous force through thorn and thicket to a new region of greater beauty'. This Romantic sensibility, Fink suggests, is something that is simply not available to the cultivated Frenchman – indeed, his very cultivation (with its echoes of clipped hedges and arrow-straight allées) necessarily mitigates against an appreciation of this aesthetic.[18]

Fink's appeal to an aesthetic of disruption and contrast in landscape constitutes a late example of a strikingly consistent strand in early nineteenth-century Beethoven criticism; indeed, landscape and garden theory, which had established a vital presence in the contemporary cultural consciousness, embodied precisely the tensions evident in Beethoven's manipulation of the musical fantastic. The picturesque garden problematised the experience of time and timelessness, and of linearity (progress) and circularity (stasis). Likewise, mediating between private and public spheres, it was overtly concerned with freedom, both artistic and, by extension, political.

---

[18] Gottfried Wilhelm Fink, 'Urtheil über Beethoven aus der Revue musicale, verbunden mit unsern Ansichten', *AmZ* 30/11 (12 March 1828), cols. 165–70 and 181–5; in Stefan Kunze, ed., *Ludwig van Beethoven: Die Werke im Spiegel seiner Zeit* (Laaber: Laaber Verlag, 1986), especially 614–15.

II

The dialectic between freedom and formal coherence, played out against the changing social space within which the fantasia operated, dominated the critical discourse on the genre in the first decades of the nineteenth century. Czerny cited English gardens as an analogy for the fantasia in order to reconcile the tensions between the free and the strict, drawing attention to the formal plan underlying an apparently chaotic surface; spontaneity and freedom were to be praised, but the well-executed fantasy, like the successful landscape garden, must cohere around an organised, if concealed, plan. The high status of the 'broad and romantic domain'[19] of fantasy as genre, as well as its complex amalgam of free and strict, emerges with clarity from the *AmZ*'s response in 1802 to Beethoven's Sonatas *quasi una fantasia*, Op. 27 nos. 1 and 2. Describing them as 'some of the best pieces received in recent years', the reviewer labelled them unequivocally as fantasies, explaining that they would deeply move any musical soul and elevate it to 'such heights as can only be achieved through free keyboard music'. But, understanding both sonatas as continuous entities, the reviewer was especially enthusiastic about the second, which he praised for its wonderful unity: 'This fantasy is from beginning to end a solid whole, originating all at once from the entire, profound and fervently agitated soul, as if hewn from a single block of marble.'[20]

Critics extolled fantasies that managed to allow for imaginative scope while displaying unity between their diverse sections. Charming individual sections are not enough without a 'tight hidden thread' which 'runs through the whole and can be perceived, if not by the fleeting beholder, by an experienced lover of art';[21] when done properly, the fantasia's 'subtle connections' would appeal to superior players and listeners, those who 'have the intellect and inclination for the deeper art'.[22] Indeed, fantasia represented something difficult and exceptional, whose 'inner essence' was to be learnt only from the fantasias of C. P. E. Bach; too often critics complained of mistaken attempts at fantasia in which the disparate sections failed to connect, and, for all their individual interest, lacked unity.[23] Such connections, however, were 'the more to be praised the more cleverly they are hidden', and the juxtaposition of affects 'neither too precipitous, whereby the sections would appear all too fragmentary, nor too tame, whereby the whole would become more like a sonata'.[24]

---

[19] Review of J. G. Hässler, 'Fantaisie et Sonate', Op. 17, *AmZ* 5/50 (7 September 1803), col. 831.   [20] *AmZ* 4/40 (30 June 1802), cols. 650–3.

[21] Review of Anton Eberl, 'Caprice et Rondeau', *AmZ* 6/48 (29 August 1804), col. 809.

[22] Review of Johann Nepomuk Hummel, 'Fantaisie', Op. 18, *AmZ* 7/49 (4 September 1805), col. 780.

[23] Review of Anton Eberl, 'Fantaisie et Rondeau', *AmZ* 5/33 (11 May 1803), col. 559.

[24] Review of Franciszek Lessel, 'Fantaisie', Op. 8, *AmZ* 13/31 (31 July 1811), cols. 527–8.

By 1813 the *AmZ* was complaining that 'what we have received under the title of free fantasy in the last decade is in fact almost without exception only a freer kind of sonata', reiterating its much-repeated lament that composers were no longer interested in the free fantasia, and blaming this on a 'new change in the prevailing taste', a concern for the extended elaboration of a given idea (variation) rather than the 'ingenious sketching of original ideas'.[25] Beethoven's *Fantasie*, Op. 77 (1809), however, represented an exceptional remnant of true fantasy in the style of C. P. E. Bach, a fabulous and belated reminder of a fading tradition. Beethoven's Op. 77, the piece which Czerny thought the closest approximation to Beethoven's actual improvisations, represents his most direct response to the Bachian fantasia, and crystallises for us the lineaments of Beethoven's fantastic. In his *Systematic Introduction to Improvisation* Czerny cited Op. 77 as 'the freest form of improvising in fantasy style',[26] a style in which ideas shift with seeming arbitrariness from one to the next following the inclination of the performer; indeed, as if characterising the musical picturesque, with its sudden dislocations and abrupt changes of affect, Czerny emphasised the appropriateness here of whim, wit, the piquant and the Baroque. Wilhelm von Lenz, commenting a little later in the nineteenth century, likewise admired narrative discontinuity and an accompanying fantastic distance in Op. 77, describing the piece as a collection of medieval romances, 'several legends of the Middle Ages recounted by Beethoven'.[27] Tellingly, the anonymous reviewer for the *AmZ* cited the model of 'the wonderful' C. P. E. Bach, in praising this piece as 'truly a free fantasy', remarking on the bold and surprising modulations, the novelty of its many ideas, its learnedness, and especially its discontinuous character, the 'interruptions in the writing' ('im Abgebrochenen der Schreibart').[28] Modern critics, however, have offered conflicted responses. Tovey heard in Op. 77 only a strange mass of 'questions and efforts'; Paul Bekker, by contrast, asserted an 'inner unity' and 'readily recognisable and highly poetic sequence of thought throughout';[29] for Hugh Macdonald, this was to miss the point entirely: arguing that the fantasy is an exercise in bafflement, its principal point 'disunity, diversity, illogicality, inconsistencies and contradictions', Macdonald claimed for this 'violently disconcerting piece' the potential 'to explode the whole network of modern criticism', in its refusal of conventional formal coherence.[30]

---

[25] 'Mittheilungen aus dem Tagebuche eines Tonkünstlers', *AmZ* 15/45 (10 November 1813), cols. 732–3.   [26] Czerny, *Systematic Introduction*, 121.

[27] Wilhelm von Lenz, *Beethoven et ses trois styles* (1852; reprint edn, New York: Da Capo, 1980), 217.

[28] *AmZ* 13/32 (7 August 1811), col. 548. Reprinted in Kunze, ed., *Die Werke im Spiegel*, 211.

[29] Paul Bekker, *Beethoven* (Berlin: Schuster and Loeffler, 1921); trans. and adapted by M. M. Bozman (New York: AMS Press, 1971), 267.

[30] Hugh Macdonald, 'Fantasy and Order in Beethoven's Phantasie op. 77', in *Modern*

The *Fantasie*, Op. 77 is indeed made up of a motley collection of topics, juxtaposed for maximum contrast, each merely a short-lived fragment, a hint of a tale. The piece opens with a snatch of virtuosic cadenza which gives way to a lyrical cadence passage; a serene hymn begins, but, twice interrupted by the virtuosic flourish, is displaced by a naively cheerful folksong; after establishing a hopeful antecedent–consequent pattern, this fades desultorily, and is rudely negated by rapid passagework which introduces what amounts to a *Sturm und Drang* etude;[31] this in turn is abruptly followed by impassioned, if questioning declamation, later fugato, and at last a simple contredanse tune which functions as the theme for a set of variations, in itself a patchwork of changing affects. What Tovey focussed on, and indeed what is perhaps most characteristic about the succession of ideas, is that, unlike the contemporary pot-pourri fantasy which it superficially resembles, no single idea reaches anything approaching a conclusion; indeed, most, until the arrival at the theme and variations, can hardly achieve even an opening statement, a proper antecedent–consequent, let alone a coherent period. Ideas are left open-ended, dissolving into nebulous pauses, less articulate questions than moments of sheer disorientation, as if vision had blurred and the path forward had suddenly disappeared in a haze of uncertainty.

Perhaps the most prominent of such moments occurs in the Allegro ma non troppo in B♭ major (the section beginning at bar 15; see example 6.1); at bar 25, after a complete antecedent–consequent structure has been established for the first time in the fantasy, an extension of the consequent phrase trails off after three bars in a static reiteration of the dominant chord; melodic, harmonic, and then even rhythmic action grind to a halt, as two bars of repeated E♭ chords in quavers slow into two bars of dotted crotchets, accompanied by a gradual fade to pianissimo; in the course of these seventeen repetitions of the E♭ sonority, the chord begins to sound like a tonic, and leads at last, with a simple semitone slide in the outer voices, to a B♭ major 6-5, dominant seventh in E♭. However, rather than confirm the modulation, that chord is itself dismantled, in a canonic bicinium that expands the single sonority this time over seven

Musical Scholarship, ed. Edward Olleson (Stocksfield, Northumberland: Oriel, 1980), 141–50. See also Jürgen Uhde, *Beethovens Klaviermusik*, vol. I: *Klavierstücke und Variationen* (Stuttgart: Reclam, 1968), 113–22; Paul Mies, '. . . quasi una Fantasia', in *Colloquium Amicorum: Joseph Schmidt-Görg zum 70. Geburtstag*, ed. Siegfried Kross and Hans Schmidt (Bonn: BH, 1967), 239–49; Jürgen von Oppen, 'Beethovens Klavierfantasie op. 77 in neuer Sicht', in *Bericht über den internationalen musikwissenschaftlichen Kongress Bonn 1970*, ed. Carl Dahlhaus et al. (Kassel: Bärenreiter, 1971), 528–31; and Elaine Sisman, 'After the Heroic Style: *Fantasia* and the "Characteristic" Sonatas of 1809', *Beethoven Forum* 6 (1998), 67–96.

[31] See Sisman's catalogue of topics that constitute the individual fragments of the *Fantasie*, Op. 77 ('After the Heroic Style', 72–7).

Example 6.1   Beethoven, *Fantasie*, Op. 77, bars 15–37

and a half bars, before coming to a halt on an E♭ major 6–4 chord, also pianissimo. In all, what had seemed a straightforward folksong drastically loses direction, coming to a standstill in twelve and a half bars of empty reverie. In the anti-resolution of shocking juxtaposition that characterises the progress of the fantasy, the static daydream is then brutally interrupted by a sudden leap directly to a fortissimo A major 7 chord, held provocatively under a pause, before a stormy arpeggiated D minor passage drives forward in an entirely different direction.

Such distant tonal shifts are integral to the fantasy, and yet the constant tonal surprises themselves hint at an ordering principle that might underlie the apparent chaos of the surface progress. Perhaps most striking is the device of repetition of entire passages at the distance of a whole tone or semitone; this is boldly presented at the outset, as the opening G minor bars are immediately repeated wholesale in F minor (example 6.2); the device recurs, though somewhat less abruptly, at bar 84, where the repeated-note declamatory figure heard in A♭ major in bars 79–83 is restated in B♭ minor (example 6.3); again, as the fantasy draws to a close, the reprise of the theme of the variation set, originally in B major, is begun, complete with its triplet accompaniment, in the

194

Example 6.2   Beethoven, *Fantasie*, Op. 77, bars 1–5

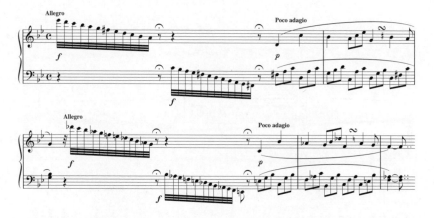

Example 6.3   Beethoven, *Fantasie*, Op. 77, bars 79–91

remote key of C major (bar 222), before a swerve back to B, and a powerful reiteration of the last variation (example 6.4).[32]

In fact, for all its restless shifting among topics and affects, the *Fantasie*, Op. 77 is replete with repetition, restatement and reformulation.
Paul Bekker suggested that the prominent reiterations throughout the

---

[32] Sisman suggests that the direct repetition of a musical idea in a different key was a hall-
mark of free fantasy, and notes its use in Haydn's Capriccio in G major of 1765 (Hob.
XVII: 1) and the fantasia movement from Haydn's E♭ string quartet, Op. 76 no. 6 (1797),
'Repetition, the simplest musical technique, when combined with changes of key, was
simply left out of the array of regular musical structures and relegated to "fantasy"'
('After the Heroic Style', 71).

Example 6.4   Beethoven, *Fantasie*, Op. 77, bars 222–45

piece of the virtuosic scale with which it opens contribute in large part
to the inner unity of the work, as each recurrence of the motive adapts
itself to the prevailing mood, framing the disparate fragments, even
returning in quasi-thematic guise transformed into the B minor fugato
theme at bars 116–50. The motive's appearances are certainly far from
random, for it intrudes consistently at the moments of tonal shift
between melodic fragments, either brashly proposing a new and unrelated key, as at bar 3, or reasserting a key obliquely gained at the end of
the previous section. Yet from the outset the motive is redolent of
paradox: coupled with the lyrical cadence figure at the beginning, it has
the character of cadenza and seems rather to be a gesture of closure

Example 6.5   Beethoven, *Fantasie*, Op. 77, bars 151–60

than opening. At the same time, its recurrences throughout the piece serve less to establish a unifying thread through the apparent chaos, than to draw attention to the fantasy's refusal of tonal stability or structural definition: strangely, this potentially cadential gesture which is continually inserted at the moment at which tonal closure or a point of arrival seem imminent, manages to underscore the fantasy's continual evasion of, and aversion to, cadences. It is still more ironic that the eventual arrival, concluding the variations, at a perfect cadence in the tonic should be achieved, after a moment of hesitation on the dominant seventh in third inversion (bar 236), with nothing other than a hasty iteration of this same virtuosic descending scale. Much too quick to provide a conclusive ending, it merely hints at closure, discharging instead its usual role as an interjection before the unstable coda. The coda wanders from B major towards E minor and even introduces a distant dominant seventh on A, before arriving at a nearly silent F♯ major chord. A hesitant, pianissimo, alternation between V and I follows, and it is only a final iteration in the tonic of the rapid scale motive, that very signifier of instability now, ironically, enacting the confirmatory gesture of the final cadence, that can bring the fantasy to a close (example 6.4).

While motivic recurrence of this sort turns out to be more of a destabilising than connective force in the fantasy, it is typically paradoxical that, in retrospect, it is the idea of hesitation itself, of momentary loss of direction, that proves to have the most far-reaching implications for the notion of coherence in the piece. The B major variation theme is not merely another unrelated melody, casually arrived at; rather, it is a culmination of what has gone before (example 6.5); characterised by its repeated notes, it originates in the declamatory Adagio fragment first heard in A♭ at bar 79 (example 6.3); the restatement in B♭ minor of this Adagio recitative at bars 84–9 is eventually taken up at bar 151 in a modified version which metamorphoses directly into the variation theme; the relation between the B major variation theme and the Adagio fragment is at last directly asserted in the coda (example 6.4): here the variation theme appears for the final time, Adagio, in a hymn-like homophonic texture which openly declares allegiance to the earlier repeated-note Adagio fragment. But the A♭ Adagio fragment itself, with its insistent repetition of E♭ in the soprano, is an almost magical echo of that quintessential moment of emptiness at which all direction had been lost in the reiterations of E♭ at bars 25–8 (example 6.1). Thus what had appeared to embody aimless wandering and disorientation turns out to have been a moment of seminal importance for the generation of the rest of the work.

In the progress from free fantasy to theme and variations in Op. 77, it is the moment of pure fantasy, of absorbingly absented reverie, that provides the work with its idea of greatest thematic importance – disorientation itself that enables the invention of the subject towards which the apparently random discourse tends and upon which it will eventually elaborate. Beethoven's own jottings on the subject in the sketchbook of 1807–8 uphold this notion of improvisation, and confirm Czerny's assertion that Op. 77 reflects Beethoven's actual improvisation practice. That the fantasy originates in an absented and freely emotional state is borne out by Beethoven's note that 'One improvises properly only if one doesn't pay attention to what one plays; thus – if one wants to improvise in public the best and truest way – one has to yield oneself freely to exactly what one feels'; yet the fantasia has a goal, working its way towards the variations which constitute the end, and highpoint of the performance.[33] The *Fantasie*, Op. 77, then, while presenting contemporary listeners with capriciousness, abruptness, delightful dislocations, also enacts the process of *Fantasieren* as the term was used by Haydn, not simply as an evocation of wandering and extra licence but as the performance of the process of invention, the precompositional search for ideas upon which the musical discourse will eventually elaborate.[34] Here, brilliantly, invention is itself predicated on that

---

[33] In the sketchbook of 1807–8 Beethoven noted 'varied Lied, at the end a fugue with pianissimo, every Phantasie planned in this way and thereafter performed in the Theater'; and 'on other occasions, the theme will be given, written down, and similarly varied'. Quoted in Helmut Aloysius Löw, 'Die Improvisation im Klavierwerk L. van Beethovens' (Ph.D. diss., Saarland University, 1962), 12; translation from Sisman, 'After the Heroic Style', 75–6.

[34] On Haydn's compositional process, and the sequence *phantasieren, componieren, setzen*, see Hollace Ann Schafer, '"A Wisely-Ordered Phantasie": Joseph Haydn's Creative

very aimless wandering that its inherent teleology appears to counter-act.

While Beethoven's *Fantasie,* Op. 77 was received with enthusiasm, critics were less comfortable with the composer's strange excursions into the fantastic mode in other genres. By 1817, Ernst Ludwig Gerber could go so far as to claim that, thanks in large part to Beethoven, the fantasia had managed to infiltrate contemporary musical taste and compositional style to such an extent that it constituted a new, tyrannical regime:

It appears to me as if the fantasy, like a despot, has seized absolute power over music . . . One can no longer perceive either any definite musical forms or any limits to the influence of the fantasy. Everything goes in all directions but to no fixed destination; the madder the better! The wilder and stranger, all the more novel and effective. In such a way we hear and play nothing but Fantasies. Our sonatas are Fantasies, our overtures are Fantasies and even our symphonies, at least those of Beethoven and his like, are Fantasies.[35]

Beethoven's musical fantastic is characterised by an interchange of form and formlessness, of significance and semantic emptiness – portentous dreams and shapeless reveries. Its abrupt harmonic shifts, changing affects and formal disruptions play themselves out against a backdrop of absence and recall, a narrative of odd circularity; repetition, of the kind that demands reinterpretation and generates momentum in the sonata-allegro paradigm, results in stasis, and it is dislocation itself that, paradoxically, initiates narrative drive.

Such perturbing moments of formal/temporal dislocation find a prototype in the *Sonata quasi una Fantasia* in Eb, Op. 27 no. 1 (1800–1); here the frantically driven Rondo finale is interrupted, just as the main theme should be stated for the last time, by a return of the theme of the preceding Adagio con espressione (bar 256, example 6.6); the effect is suddenly to deflate the busy energy of the Rondo, even, in under-cutting it with a solemn reverie spoken by a voice from the past, to recast it as an exaggerated bombast.[36] Op. 27 no. 1 as a whole explores the tension between sonata and not-sonata (in its allusion to fantasia), with its 'attacca' indications between movements gesturing towards

Process from the Sketches and Drafts for Instrumental Music' (Ph.D. diss., Brandeis University, 1987); see also Sisman, 'After the Heroic Style', 75; and above, chapter 3 (p. 85).

[35] Letter from E. L. Gerber to C. H. Rinck, 1817, in Friedrich Noack, 'Eine Briefsammlung aus der ersten Hälfte des 19. Jahrhunderts', *Archiv für Musikwissenschaft* (1935), 326. Quoted in Peter Schleuning, *The Fantasia,* II, 15.

[36] Karol Berger writes that 'The effect . . . is that of a mind all of a sudden lost in a recollected past and . . . the return to the here and now is somewhat forced.' Berger, 'Beethoven and the Aesthetic State', *Beethoven Forum* 7 (1999), 17–44.

Example 6.6   Beethoven, *Sonata quasi una fantasia*, Op. 27 no. 1, bars 250–69

the fantasia's sequence of contrasting sections rather than the sonata's independent movements, and its quirky first movement quasi-variation form; even in this context the inserted Adagio fragment has a curiously destabilising effect, and, coming so close to the end, seems to colour the whole piece, introducing as it does a curiously hasty, over-emphatic and unsatisfactory ending. It was the ending to this piece to which the *AmZ* reviewer objected in 1802, finding it commonplace and noisy, a misjudged *lieto fine*; the unconventionality of the sonata's formal procedures, though, aroused little comment, unsur-

Example 6.7   Beethoven, Sonata, Op. 101, i, bars 1–6

prising as they are in the context of fantasia to which their title points.[37]

Not so the Cello Sonatas, Op. 102 (1815), which prompted the response that 'everything is different, completely different from what could be expected, even from this composer', and that 'a few things . . . are shaped *in order that* they appear very strange'.[38] Op. 102 no. 1 reprises Op. 27 no. 1's use of reminiscence, with the Tempo d'Andante which recollects the lyrical opening of the first movement interpolated between the Adagio introduction to the finale and the Allegro vivace finale itself; in so doing it both transforms the first movement theme and subtly alters the character of the finale itself, contextualising it as the outcome of contemplation of the past rather than unambiguously confident progress into the future.[39] But the Piano Sonata, Op. 101 (1816) offers a much more far-reaching example of this procedure, in a work that is imbued with the dislocations and surprises of fantasia. The first movement is an exercise in ambiguity. It opens *in medias res* on the dominant, and unfurls in a long lyrical line that shuns perfect cadences, avoiding conventional development as it does so (example 6.7).[40] The movement has a dreamlike, suspended quality that is enhanced by the strangely halting syncopated repetitions in the central section, bars 29–51, whose rhythmic displacements conceal and deflect the beat (example 6.8).

[37] That they were understood as fantasies (rather than, or as much as, sonatas) is borne out by the designation of Op. 27 no. 2 as the 'Fantasie in C♯ minor' in the review of Beethoven's sonata Op. 57 that appeared in the *AmZ* 9/27 (1 April 1807), col. 435.

[38] *AmZ* 20/45 (11 November 1818), cols. 792–4. Cited in Kunze, ed., *Die Werke im Spiegel*, 341–2.

[39] See William Kinderman, *Beethoven* (Berkeley and Los Angeles: University of California Press, 1995), 'Its thematic substance seems to be plumbed, and the fourth G–C – the main motif and point of departure of the finale – is discovered as an outcome of contemplative reminiscence' (182).

[40] Carl Dahlhaus speaks aptly, of 'the wellnigh insolubly difficult task of a formal analysis of the movement' though his analysis manages, through identifying subtle 'subthematic' processes, to unite the principle of sonata development with the seemingly contradictory one of lyricism. See Dahlhaus, *Ludwig van Beethoven: Approaches to his Music*, trans. Mary Whittall (Oxford: Oxford University Press, 1991), 211.

Example 6.8   Beethoven, Sonata, Op. 101, i, bars 29–40

The lively F major second movement presents a jarring contrast to the first, with its jagged, almost grotesque profile, its incessantly driven dotted rhythms, and its flirtation with two-part canonic artifice. The tendency towards contrapuntal archaism is pursued outright in the trio, the main body of which is written in exact imitation at the octave, creating an effect at once stark and bizarre. The juxtaposition of style and affect gestures towards fantasy, but more profoundly fantastical is the sudden retreat at the heart of this harrumphing movement into a delicate and idealised distance.[41] At bar 30 the action is suddenly suspended, on arrival, hauntingly, at D♭ (example 6.9); as if out of nowhere (yet evoking the opening melody of the first movement) a gently rising legato line, piano, reaches up to the pianissimo climax at bar 33, a high f^3 sustained in a new stillness, before the entry in the bass of the minim D♭. This bass note initiates a slow oscillation, in minims, between D♭ and C, still static, as bars 34 and 35 are repeated – but as the bass arrives at a C pedal the activity and tension build to the vertiginous tumble back to the tonic at bar 44. Now the harmonic implications of the dreamy D♭ interlude, a quintessential moment of disruption and dislocation, are realised as an intensification of the return to the dominant, and eventually the tonic; on the two successive rehearings engendered by the repetitive structure of the movement, this section will continue both to transport the discourse, for a moment, out of the present to another, timeless, realm, and yet, simultaneously, to heighten the (intensely teleological) tension of the dominant preparation that it initiates.

---

[41] A move that brings to mind C. F. Cramer's image of sideslips into 'hidden romantic regions', in his review of 'Six Sonatas . . . by Charles Frederick Horn', *Magazin der Musik* 2/2 (24 April 1787), 1283. See above, chapter 2, p. 41.

Example 6.9 Beethoven, Sonata, Op. 101, ii, bars 28–40

But it is with the introduction to the Finale that the sonata paradigm is most radically called into question, and here that the generic boundaries between sonata and fantasia become most blurred. The *Langsam und sehnsuchtvoll* introduction to the last movement, which conjures again the inward mood of the first movement, comes to rest on a rich E major chord whose sonority and register are exactly those of the opening of the first movement (example 6.10).[42] And indeed, what follows is not the Finale, but, strangely and disorientatingly, a recollection of the opening bars of the first movement, a return to the beginning of the sonata; it is as if, for a moment, the piece has looped back on itself in an unlikely circle, only now the first movement, no longer ambiguously emerging from nothing, is contextualised and concretised by its own slow introduction. Yet the impression of having taken a wrong turning (like a disastrous memory lapse in performance) lasts for only a fleeting moment; the lyrical melody begins almost

---

[42] Kinderman writes: 'this soft chord, which represents the end of the descending progression and the termination of the Adagio, also embodies the *a priori* condition for the first movement, since it presents the exact sonority, in the precise register, out of which the opening of that movement has sprung' (*Beethoven*, 196).

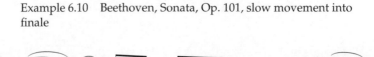

Example 6.10   Beethoven, Sonata, Op. 101, slow movement into finale

immediately to metamorphose and fragment, wrenched towards something bolder, more affirmative – indeed it is the agent, at last, of a triumphant perfect cadence in the tonic that establishes the confident assertions of the final Allegro. The Finale itself, in sonata form, constitutes a virtuosic display of contrapuntal technique. As if taking up on the topic of the second movement, the musical argument here displays canon, invertible counterpoint, fugue proper, alongside stretto, inversion and all attendant devices. But from the subject of the contrapuntal play itself, to the raucous end of the development, with its stretti, dis-

Example 6.11   Beethoven, Sonata, Op. 101, iv, bars 112–28

located off-beat accents and crazed chase through the dominant to the recapitulation, this is strange stuff – a movement which incorporates not only the academic but also the sweetly lyrical (the *dolce* second subject), and even a rollicking oom-pah tune, also part of the second subject.

The sonata as a whole is imbued with the fantastic confusion of past and present, the eruptions from memory and imminent narrative circularity that mark the fantasia. The first movement theme literally haunts the work, not just offering a seductive fantasy of another world at bars 30–5 of the second movement, or appearing with disconcertingly clear focus at the beginning of the Finale, but also later in the last movement: eight pianissimo bars interpolated between the end of the exposition and beginning of the development (bars 114–19) both recall that opening theme and create an effect of sudden absence from the surrounding activity, a moment of reverie and reminiscence that is violently interrupted by the abrupt modulation to the remote key of C major in which the fugal development begins (example 6.11). Such turns and returns have become intrinsic to the work's discourse by the time the coda to the Finale openly confronts the ghost of the first movement: at the start of the coda (bars 305–11) the theme reemerges, *dolce*, and here the soprano line twice quotes the pitches, if not the rhythm, of that first movement opening (example 6.12). Both Karol Berger and William Kinderman have drawn attention to the interplay between past and present, between anticipation of the future and memory of the past in this work; fleeting reminiscences conjure an escape into memory and the imagination, even drawing attention, at times, to the difficulty inherent in moving forward at all.[43] Berger describes such moments as

---

[43] Berger, 'Beethoven and the Aesthetic State', 27–8: 'In such cases [of recollections of music from earlier movements] the mind of the protagonist is not just threatened with losing its grip on the here and now, but actually loses it and shifts its attention from its "real" present to its "imaginary" past.'

Example 6.12   Beethoven, Sonata, Op. 101, iv, bars 297–318

having the effect 'of a mind that wanders off from its present concerns into an imaginary recollected world and that can tear itself away from this other world only with effort'. Here sudden dislocation and erring attention threaten to negate the forward drive that underlies the teleology of form.

III

The tropes of wandering and of momentary disorientation are familiar ones from the critical discourse on the fantasia, and recur with remarkable consistency in the early nineteenth-century reviews of Beethoven's most fantastic moments, a critical literature which grapples with Beethoven's fantasy in the newly fashionable and highly sophisticated terms of the English landscape garden and the picturesque. One of the most extended reflections on the matter of the incursion of fantasy into Beethoven's sonata structures appeared in the *AmZ* in 1815, its author the Leipzig critic and professor of philosophy Amadeus Wendt. Wendt's judgement of Beethoven as fantasist is far from entirely negative, for fantasy, when that of a great artist (Wendt cites Shakespeare and Jean Paul), is the signal of inspiration and genius. But, like Jean Paul and Shakespeare, Beethoven the fantasist risks pushing beyond the boundaries of the coherent artwork, obscuring his originality in caprice and arbitrariness. Where modern art, for Wendt, must be conceived as a whole, with a governing idea from which the individual parts develop, fantasy, whether improvised or composed in the spirit of improvisation, presents only a free succession of ideas, the 'unlimited emotional expression of an artistic soul'. It risks its status as art, for art must attempt to represent perfection, and perfection is circumscribed and formed:

> Musical fantasies are usually forgiven the sins against form and rule, when a great spirit governs them . . . But to transfer this characteristic of the fantasy to other pieces of music, and so to *make musical fantasy rule in the region of the musical world*, can only lead to gross errors. Extravagant wealth of ideas and an inexhaustible originality can reveal themselves there, but clarity, comprehensibility and order, through which the artwork is the work not just of a temporary mood but of lasting pleasure, will often be lacking. It is here that I speak of Beethoven's *gross errors*.[44]

Wendt designates Beethoven as an 'instrumental virtuoso', presumably drawing attention to his abilities as an improviser, and asserts that he has created his own 'romantic musical world' in which fantasy rules, to the detriment of proper harmonic coherence and the structured connection of ideas.

Wendt's somewhat ambiguous assessment of the fantasia (potentially marvellous, potentially meaningless) and his concomitant approach to Beethoven's instrumental music, find their quintessential expression in the extended metaphor that concludes this part of his discussion. Suggesting that Beethoven's instrumental music must be understood in terms of fantasy, he offers a picture of what such listening might entail:

> Many of Beethoven's works, e.g. several of his symphonies, sonatas, can only be understood and judged as musical fantasies. In them even the more attentive listener often completely loses sight of the fundamental idea [Grundgedanken]; he finds himself in a marvellous labyrinth, where on all sides luxuriant bushes and wonderfully extraordinary flowers catch the eye, though without the thread with which to regain the restful home; the artist's fantasy flows incessantly onwards, stopping points are seldom granted, and the impression earlier things made is not seldom eradicated by the later ones; the fundamental idea has vanished entirely, or it shimmers forth only out of the obscure distance in the flow of moving harmony.[45]

Wendt, concerned less with fantasia proper than with the fantastic as an interruption into other genres, fixates on the way in which fantasia problematises the notion of coherence, stressing the too-frequent absence of a connecting thread from Beethoven's discourse. Yet far from dismissing the experience offered by such fantasies, he figures it in terms that

---

[44] Amadeus Wendt, 'Gedanken über die neuere Tonkunst, und van Beethovens Musik, namentlich dessen Fidelio', *AmZ* 17/23 (7 June 1815), cols. 385–6. Cited in Kunze, ed., *Die Werke im Spiegel*, 186.   [45] Kunze, ed., *Die Werke im Spiegel*, 186–7.

suggest potentially utopian pleasures: making a fashionable allusion to *Gartenkunst*, Wendt compares Beethoven's music to a park whose multiple beauties and labyrinthine paths threaten to disorientate the visitor who wanders through it – and as contemporary enthusiasm for such gardens demonstrated, the experience of getting lost in such a landscape might, in itself, constitute intense pleasure.

E. T. A. Hoffmann had suggested as much two years earlier in 1813, introducing his review of Beethoven's Piano Trios, Op. 70 with an enthusiastic allusion to landscape gardens; Wendt may well have known this text, which, recasting material from Hoffmann's essay on Op. 70 for the *AmZ* in March of the same year, appeared as 'Beethoven's Instrumental Music' in the *Zeitung für die Elegante Welt* in December of that year, and then the following year as the fourth essay of 'Kreisleriana' in his *Fantasiestücke in Callot's Manier*. Writing in the persona of the eccentric Kapellmeister Kreisler, Hoffmann included in the later version the following passage:

What pleasure I felt on receiving your two splendid trios, Op. 70, for I knew that after they had been briefly rehearsed I would soon be able to savour their glories. And that is exactly what has happened to me this evening; like someone wandering along the labyrinthine pathways of some fantastic park, hedged in by all kinds of rare trees, shrubs, and exotic flowers, and becoming more and more deeply absorbed, I am still unable to extricate myself from the extraordinary twists and turns of your trios.[46]

For the fantasist Hoffmann, to be enveloped by and lost in this wonderful landscape constitutes the rare beauty of Beethoven's music, its artistic end to involve the listener inextricably in a network of ambiguous paths. And yet, as the earlier, more extended version of this essay made clear, Hoffmann conceived the pleasure of literal amazement as supporting the coherence of the artwork: indeed, he expressed absolute confidence in the connecting thread running through the work, whose dimly suspected absence, or only obscure and distant presence, Amadeus Wendt would warily point out.

In the *AmZ* essay, Hoffmann drew repeated attention to the thematic unity in these pieces, adding that their underlying coherence is perfectly detectable, and not only to the expert ear. In Op. 70 no. 1, he writes, the main theme of the first movement 'impresses itself firmly and distinctly upon the listener, who does not then lose sight of it but follows its amazing twists and turns as though it were a silvery stream'. Hoffmann admits that the first movement of Op. 70 no. 2 is more

---

[46] E. T. A. Hoffmann, *Fantasiestücke in Callot's Manier* (Berlin and Weimar: Aufbau-Verlag, 1976), 55. Translation from *E. T. A. Hoffmann's Musical Writings: Kreisleriana, The Poet and the Composer, Music Criticism*, ed. David Charlton, trans. Martyn Clarke (Cambridge: Cambridge University Press, 1989), 100.

complex, its elements 'more heterogeneous' than one might be accustomed to in Beethoven's music, and, indeed, this movement carries special connotations of the fantastic: another sudden moment of abstracted reverie is created by the return of material from the slow introduction in the coda, an interpolation that interrupts the long dominant and for a moment sidetracks the progress towards closure with an unexpected glimpse of an earlier prospect. Nevertheless, for Hoffmann 'it all constitutes a perfect and compelling whole, and the truly musical listener will easily follow the admittedly complicated course of the Allegro, even if many things may not be clear at first to the less practised ear'. The last movement too, for all its bravura, its fantastic amalgam of ideas, in which 'the most fevered imaginings are given free rein', is cited by Hoffmann as a model of tightly worked out, interconnecting ideas: 'Ideas and images rush past in ceaseless flight, coruscating and vanishing like flashes of lightning . . . And yet, this movement is again fashioned from a few short ideas and closely related figures.'[47]

While Hoffmann's alter ego, the crazed Kapellmeister Kreisler, himself an avid improviser and fantasist (as the hilarious and disturbing scene in 'Kreisler's Musico-Poetic Club' confirms), revels in the solitary bafflement and beauty of an intricately laid out landscape park, Hoffmann the critic is able to complement the image with that of the thread through the labyrinth, the signifier of coherence. Indeed, the 'amazing twists and turns' in which Hoffmann so delights, the labyrinthine paths of the composer's imagination, are themselves constituted as precisely that binding 'Ariadne's thread' in the literature from which this topos is taken – that of commentaries on, descriptions of and guides to well-known contemporary landscape gardens. A typical example is provided by Joseph Widemann's account, published in his popular *Mahlerische Streifzüge durch die interessantesten Gegenden um Wien* (*Picturesque Excursions through the Most Interesting Environs of Vienna*; 1805–8), of Neuwaldegg, the first English garden in the vicinity of the Austrian capital:

In soft, pleasing modulations scene upon scene unfolds, one more charming and unexpected than the next. Small hills covered with vivid greenery, open lawns with blooming flowers, dark and gloomy thickets, open pathways with resting places emerge and recede before me. Like Ariadne's thread the track winds away uncertainly, making a thousand alluring twists and turns.[48]

Given the close links in the critical tradition between fantasy and the picturesque, it comes as little surprise to find the Sonata, Op. 101, with

---

[47] Quotations are from the Clarke translation, pp. 300–25.
[48] Joseph Widemann, *Mahlerische Streifzüge durch die interessantesten Gegenden um Wien* (Vienna, 1805–8), III, 210. Cited in Hajós, 'Picture and Poetry in Austrian Gardens', 215–16.

all its allusions to the fantastic, discussed in the *AmZ* in a similar meta-phorical language:

Truly, here in [Beethoven's] Opus 101 amazement and renewed admiration seize us, when we wander so with the great soul-painter down strange, untrod-den paths – as if with Ariadne's thread through labyrinthine turns, where now a cool brook whispers to us, now a precipitous rock face stares at us; where here an unfamiliar, sweetly smelling flower attracts us, and there a thorny track would like to frighten us away. One has to restrain oneself, not to paint [imagine] further these and other images, which force themselves on one, as one follows this wondrous genius in this creation of his: for certainly such outpour-ings are becoming to no-one less than a reviewer.[49]

As if unable to resist the force of that fantastical metaphor, the reviewer cannot help himself hearing this work in picturesque terms (in both general and technical senses). Listening to this surprising and varied sonata is like a tour through the shifting scenes of a landscape, but the analogy goes beyond merely describing the charm of changing emo-tions. Introducing the review as it does, the allusion establishes a context for the whole piece within the generic realm of fantasy and the aesthetic of the picturesque; in so doing, it frames both formal disrup-tions and games with time, as well as the web of subtle linkages, mani-festations of 'Ariadne's thread', that permeate this sonata, despite its unconventional departures from 'normal' formal procedures.[50]

In 1824, when the *AmZ* reviewer considered Beethoven's last three piano sonatas, Op. 109, 110 and 111, sonatas thoroughly imbued with fantastical procedures, he not only began by explaining that these three found their closest precursor in the sonata, Op. 101, but took the oppor-tunity for a lengthy digression into the general musical character of this composer and genius. He mused on Beethoven's creative imagination and its demands on the listener in an extended allusion to *Gartenkunst* which expands and clarifies the earlier appearances of this topos:

One might well compare such a rich artistic life to a magnificent landscape garden, with excellently laid out and often wonderfully meandering paths, which wind their way through copses, meadows, valleys and rock-walled gorges. In a park of that kind there are points, for the most part unexpected, from which spread delightful prospects, to be enjoyed completely, it is true, by the armed eye only; likewise, in such a magnificent musical park [Kunstgarten] as the one Beethoven has created for us there are certain delightful parts that stand out marvellously. In the one as in the other there are times when the path turns abruptly – often at the most captivating resting points – in the opposite

---

[49] *AmZ* 19/40 (1 October 1817), col. 687. Cited in Kunze, ed., *Die Werke im Spiegel*, 334–5.
[50] On the metaphor of Ariadne's thread through the labyrinth, see Thomas S. Grey, '. . . *wie ein rother Faden*: On the Origins of "Leitmotif" as Critical Construct and Musical Practice', in *Music Theory in the Age of Romanticism*, ed. Ian Bent (Cambridge: Cambridge University Press, 1996), 187–210.

direction, so that one may think at first that one is walking back, or that one has been diverted from the direction in which many an enjoyment was to be awaited, the lack of which now fills one with concern. However, in the one as in the other, one should let oneself, willingly and devotedly, be led by the creator (who could be a better guide than he?), and one will find to one's gratification that not every turning point is a point of culmination.[51]

This is the picturesque landscape that featured in earlier Beethoven criticism, with its contrasting scenes, its winding paths and its sudden vistas into the distance, perhaps offering anticipatory glimpses of what is to come, or new perspectives on places already passed through. The labyrinthine twists of the path bring the walker, or listener, to odd moments of disorientation at which the wrong turn seems to have been taken; significantly, the reviewer suggests that complete enjoyment of such games with perspective and direction is for the connoisseur, one familiar with the particular aesthetics of the landscape garden, its theoretical underpinning in the picturesque, and one who ideally allows himself to be guided by the composer himself. But here is the answer to those who would disparage Beethoven's music as bewildering, chaotic and fantastical – it is indeed all those things, just as a landscape garden approximates the irregularity and wildness of nature, but just as such gardens are highly constructed and offer to the connoisseur the sophisticated pleasures of momentary dislocation and shifting perspectives within the frame of a carefully constructed, and concealed, form, so the freedom and fantasy of Beethoven's music encourages immersion, absorption – and a critical ear.

The author goes further in his exploration of the notion of fantasy in this context, with a technical aside on the nature of the imagination, as theorised by Prince Beloselski in his *Dianoiologie, ou Tableau philosophique de l'entendement* (London, 1790). In an extended footnote the author borrows Beloselski's model for the mind itself, expanding the idea of the meandering paths through the labyrinth that both conceal and reveal. The mental faculties, he explains, may be conceived as a number of concentric circles, at the centre of which is to be found 'shapeless inertia' ('die plumpe Trägheit'); next to it, the 'lowest powers of mind', such as recollection. The outermost sphere is the 'sphère d'esprit', and contains 'wisdom, imagination, taste, genius'. Beyond these concentric circles is to be found the unlimited realm of imaginary space ('les espaces imaginaires'), and between any two particular spheres gaps constituting 'spaces of error and folly' ('espaces d'erreurs et de folies').

But, suggests our reviewer, such a model is too abstract, and to make it a little easier to conceptualise, he suggests adopting the metaphor of

---

[51] *AmZ* 26/14 (1 April 1824), col. 214; this long review runs from cols. 213 to 225. Kunze, ed., *Die Werke im Spiegel*, 357–66 (especially 358 and 365).

an endless spiral ('die Spiralrichtung einer endlosen Linie'); such a shape pictures both the interconnectedness of the faculties of mind and their constant push outwards to more distant spheres; likewise, it helps to explain the illusion created by the twist in the path for those who notice only the temporary curve of the next line without having a sense of the whole spiral, and who mistake 'for a retrogression back to a narrower sphere what is in fact a push forward to magnificent expansion'. The winding paths of a landscape garden that appear to mislead are part of a coherent and inexorable, if mysterious, programme. Likewise, the moments of obscurity and bafflement in a sonata by Beethoven are central to the experience of the work and to its overall plan.

Towards the conclusion of his review, the author confirms the importance, to him, of this explication of the workings of the imagination, bringing Beloselski's theory into the main body of the text and reconciling it explicitly with the landscape garden analogy: 'Certainly, the fantasy [imagination] of Hr. v. B. is a sun which is able to break through even the thickest fogs of the lower atmospheres ... The great master will not linger long in the "espaces imaginaires et – d'erreurs" without charming the admirer of his wonderful landscape garden again on paths which turn quickly back to the beautiful, through true excellence.'[52] The spaces of 'imagination and error' are conflated with the subterranean grottoes, and rocky hollows of the landscape garden, and as the landscape of the genius's imagination is figured as an English garden, so the experience of listening to his music is that of wandering through such a park.

IV

But what are we to make of this repeated turn to the language of the picturesque in order to come to terms with Beethoven's fantasy? In the first decades of the nineteenth century in Germany, the English landscape garden functioned as a cultural icon, a sign of both aristocratic privilege and fashionable taste, as well as the mark of a new democratising impulse. It stood as an emblem of aesthetic freedom, a locus of utopian naturalness within the artfully concealed confines of convention; it embodied, and made available to even the casual visitor, a sophisticated tension between nature and artifice – precisely in its careful staging of effects, opening vistas, changing, often dramatically, the scene, it purported to offer nature in all its variety, with its multiple affects ranging between delight and horror. Such landscapes, and the fetishisation of their natural counterparts, provide a well-known

---

[52] Kunze, ed., *Die Werke im Spiegel*, 365.

backdrop to Beethoven's own biography, and to the construction of his image by his contemporaries and successors; that Beethoven preferred the countryside to the city, that he made a habit of composing in the open air, often on the long walks that came to signify the solitary genius finding inspiration for his art in the wilds of nature, that his attitude to nature was one of quasi-mystical reverence, are all tropes of the composer's biography. In a letter to Therese Malfatti, written in the spring of 1810, he proclaimed his almost reverent love of the natural landscape: 'How delighted I shall be to ramble for a while through bushes, woods, under trees, through grass and around rocks! No one can love the country as much as I do. For surely woods, trees and rocks produce the echo which man desires to hear.'[53] Many of Beethoven's friends and patrons were garden enthusiasts, several with famous parks of their own upon which they lavished vast sums of money around the turn of the century (including Count Rasumovsky and Baron Fries), and it is hardly surprising that Beethoven, so regular a walker in many of these gardens, was well versed in their ideology; if his contemporaries are to be believed, references to *Gartenkunst* figured casually in his general conversation. Gerhard von Breuning recounted how Beethoven expressed his distaste for the formal garden in the course of a walk at Schönbrunn: 'When . . . we went for a walk in the gardens, Beethoven, pointing at the shrubs clipped in the French manner to look like walls, said: "All artifice, docked like those old far-thingales. I only feel well when I'm surrounded by wild scenery"';[54] in the same vein, a metaphorical reference to such things was reported by Dr Karl von Bursy in 1816, to whom Beethoven had complained that the text for a cantata written by him for the Congress of Vienna 'had been pruned and cut like a French garden'.[55] Johann Andreas Stumpff accompanied Beethoven on a walk to the popular Helenenthal – natural, but arranged for consumption by the public, 'the haunt of all classes, where the Emperor himself would divert himself with his noble retinue and where one was often obliged to squeeze past people walking in the opposite direction on a narrow path'; there, passing the newly built palace, Beethoven demonstrated his awareness of the aesthetics of landscape design (according to Stumpff): 'Just look at our excellent good taste in choosing the site for a modern palace! The right site for them is at a place where one can see the ruins of some former palace, don't you agree?' Stumpf goes on to

---

[53] Letter to Therese Malfatti, May 1810; in Anderson, ed., *The Letters of Beethoven*, 273. For more on Beethoven's worship of nature, and for a slightly different translation of this letter, see Maynard Solomon, 'Some Romantic Images in Beethoven', in *Haydn, Mozart and Beethoven: Studies in the Music of the Classic Period*, ed. Sieghard Brandenburg (Oxford: Clarendon Press, 1998), 253–81.

[54] In Hamburger, ed., *Beethoven: Letters, Journals and Conversations*, 249.   [55] Ibid., 147.

exhibit his own sensitivity to picturesque aesthetics: 'Now we were approaching a very romantic place. Tall, ancient, splendid trees raised their crests towards the blue sky, dark shrubs drank in the sun's rays and cast them back upon the green carpet of a lawn . . . One could hear a flowing brook, though invisible, which came cascading down from a height.'[56]

Beethoven would likely have been familiar with other famous garden landscapes in the Viennese environs. Count Cobenzl's garden on the Reisenberg was one of the earliest and best known of the English 'natural' landscapes, having been constructed in the 1780s and widely praised for its incorporation of vistas of the external landscape itself, that of the plain of the Danube, into the programme of the garden. A typical description published in 1784 evoked the poetic experience of visiting Cobenzl's 'small lonely places . . . narrow footpaths for the unaccompanied wanderer, who abandons himself to the outpourings and poems of his heart'.[57] Most strikingly, this park boasted a magnificent, manmade grotto, which Mozart had visited and admired in 1781;[58] a waterfall cascaded from a great height into a huge dark cave whose walls were fissured with sudden cracks through which the visitor was able to catch wondrous glimpses of extensive views across the Danube, capturing the quintessential experience of contrast and opposition, claustrophobic darkness enhanced for a moment by intensely brilliant distances (figure 6.2).

The grotto was a vital feature of any English-style garden; such mixtures of rock and water, imposing, even frightening and chilling, constituted climactic points in the garden itinerary, plunging visitors for a moment into chilly darkness before their meandering return to the light. Characteristic tropes of the new landscape architecture, they feature centrally in Mozart's *Die Zauberflöte*, where the climactic trial by fire and water in the second act finale is set in just such a scene: the stage directions call for two rocky hillsides, one of which thunders with a torrential waterfall, the other spits out fire; caves in the rocky foreground are sealed off by iron gates. In this hostile place Tamino is taken by the two men in black armour to a pyramid high in the centre of the scene; in their archaic chorale they intone the inscription to be found on the pyramid: 'He who travels this path with burdens is purified by fire, water, air and earth; if he but conquers the fears of death, he will ascend from earth to

56 Ibid., 221.
57 Description by Johann Georg Adam Forster, quoted in W. Bauer, *Alt-Wien in Briefen und Erinnerungen* (Vienna, 1924), 50f.; cited in Hajós, *Romantische Gärten der Aufklärung*, 158.
58 Mozart wrote: 'Das Häuschen ist nichts, aber die Gegend, der Wald, worinn er eine *Grotte* gebauet, als wenn sie von Natur wäre, das ist prächtig und sehr angenehm.' Letter of 13 July 1781: Emily Anderson, ed., *The Letters of Mozart and his Family*, 2nd edn, 2 vols. (London: Macmillan, 1966), II, 751–2.

Figure 6.2   The Grotto at Cobenzl in 1810

heaven. Enlightened he will then be able to devote himself to the service of Isis.'[59]

At the park at Vöslau belonging to Beethoven's patron Baron Fries, a special grotto-mountain had been built in 1777, with a ruined village at its summit and Egyptian cabinets inside. The park underwent extensive improvements in the English style from 1790 on; it was visited in October 1800 by the garden commentator E. d. P. A. Gaheis, whose description applauds 'semi-wildness' for seeming to have triumphed

---

[59] Jacques Chailly suggests that Mozart may have based the scenography here on the grotto at the park at Aigen near Salzburg, owned by the Freemason Basil von Amann, though the grotto at Cobenzl surely offered similar inspiration. See Chailly, *La Flûte enchantée: opéra maçonnique* (Paris: R. Laffont, 1968), 152. See also Magnus Olausson, 'Freemasonry, Occultism and the Picturesque Garden towards the End of the Eighteenth Century', *Art History* 8/4 (1985), 413–33.

over art, and finely evokes the appeal of the darker sections of such parks. At Vöslau the hermitage, another typical site of quasi-phantasmagoric obscurity in the English garden, held particular significance: 'It is an irregular place, on all sides wild and overgrown . . . Ruins and boulders are entwined with ivy and other dark green vegetation. The whole has a gloomy aspect.' Stepping up to the old ruin, the visitor encountered a mysterious scene: 'The interior constitutes a chamber with a bed and a statue. A deep stillness surrounds this horrible darkness; one has the sense of being in the company of ghosts. Outside the chamber at the edge of the ruin there is a statue made of lead. It holds a vessel, into which water sometimes gushes out of the rocks. – Art is so hidden in this place, and brought so close to nature, that . . . one has no time to think of art and artist.' But more significant than the carved hermit lying on his pallet are the gods who occupy this place, 'Isis and Osiris, and the hieroglyphics that accompany them', whose strangeness both astonish the visitor and seem to transport him to an exotic ancient Egyptian world.[60]

A favourite image for late eighteenth-century garden statuary, the veiled Isis, representing nature in all her mystery, could be discovered in artifical grottoes and ritualistic temples, or surveying more natural groves and garden spaces, in a curiously circular move allegorising, for a moment, those landscapes designed to allegorise her.[61] But the mysterious figure of Isis, like her counterpart the sphinx, was not just the embodiment of the secrets of nature and thus a suitably mythic focus for a 'natural' garden (figure 6.3);[62] for Tamino in *Die Zauberflöte* she symbolised the endpoint of initiation, and indeed, she was a fundamental icon of Masonic ritual. The landscape of the English garden in these cases constituted more than simply the site of aimless wandering for pleasure, or the aesthetic satisfactions of the carefully constructed circuit of contrasts and juxtapositions. Erring and disorientation, while offering pleasures of their own, played a vital role in the quasi-occult practices for which so many of these gardens provided not just allegorical representations, but also actual sites for ritual acts, and which coloured the meanings of such gardens for their contemporary admirers. The design and construction of the picturesque garden in all its complexity, with its fantastic spaces, was intimately

---

[60] Hajós, *Romantische Gärten der Aufklärung*, 164.   [61] See above chapter 1, pp. 1–5.

[62] On the association of the Isis multimammalia and the Sphinx with fertility and the 'secrets of nature' see Pierre Hadot, *Zur Idee des Naturgeheimnisses: Beim Betrachten des Widmungsblattes in den Humboldtschen 'Ideen zu einer Geographie der Pflanzen'* (Wiesbaden: Steiner, 1982) and Hadot and Dirk Syndram, *Ägypten-Faszinationen: Untersuchungen zum Ägyptenbild im europäischen Klassizismus bis 1800* (Frankfurt am Main: Peter Lang, 1990), 216–19.

Theorie

der

Gartenkunst.

Von

C. C. L. Hirschfeld,

Königl. Dänischem würklichen Justizrath und ordentlichem Professor der Philosophie
und der schönen Wissenschaften auf der Universität zu Kiel.

Vierter Band.

Leipzig,

bey M. G. Weidmanns Erben und Reich. 1782.

Verlagsbuchhandlung
PAUL PAREY
Berlin S.W., Hedemann-Str. 10.

Figure 6.3   Frontispiece, cherubs worship in a nocturnal ritual
before the statue of Isis, C. C. L. Hirschfeld, *Theorie der Gartenkunst*,
vol. IV (1782)

imbued, especially in continental Europe, with the ideology and practice of Freemasonry.[63]

The most famous 'English' gardens in France, among them the Désert
de Retz and the Parc Monceau, were the creations of Masonic aristocracy and provided locations for Masonic rites and alchemical experi-
ments. In Germany, one of the first and most famous English-style
gardens, that of the Prince von Anhalt-Dessau at Wörlitz, was constructed, and continually 'improved', in conjunction with an elaborate
Masonic programme. This park boasted another crucial element, the
labyrinth: here, the wanderer was confronted with such inscriptions as
'Choose, Wanderer, your way with judgement', and 'Here the choice
will be difficult, but critical', as the path led from bewildering gloom 'to
the dawning light of day'. The circuit through the garden led via a
Hermit's Cave to the Cell of the Mystagogue, at which point the path
divided into, on the right, the 'thoughtless laborious track of the ignorant uncultured man' and, on the left, the 'secret path of the mystic, the
apprentice in sublime knowledge'.[64] Eventually the initiate would
arrive at the Pantheon (constructed in 1795), which functioned both as
a temple to art and reason and as a chamber of initiation into the obscure
mysteries of nature: the former, bright and classical, and replete with
Greek statuary, formed the main body of the building; the latter, utterly
dark and subterranean, a sort of cellar under the temple, contained
Egyptian figures, including reliefs of Isis and Osiris, and an urn with the
head of an Egyptian god – a reference to the statue of Isis in the
Pantheon at Stourhead in England.[65] In Vienna, most of the famous

---

[63] See Olausson, 'Freemasonry, Occultism and the Picturesque Garden'; Monique Mosser,
'Paradox in the Garden: A Brief Account of *Fabriques*', in *The Architecture of Western
Gardens: A Design History from the Renaissance to the Present Day*, ed. Monique Mosser
and Georges Teyssot (Cambridge, MA: MIT Press, 1991), 263–80; Anthony Vidler, *The
Writing of the Walls* (Princeton, NJ: Princeton Architectural Press, 1987); and Hajós,
Romantische Gärten der Aufklärung, esp. chapter 4, 'Die Freimaurerei und der Englische
Garten in Wien', 45–59.

[64] August Rode, *Beschreibung des Fürstlichen Anhalt-Dessauischen Landhauses und
Englischen Gartens zu Wörlitz* (Dessau, 1788). Quoted in Buttlar, *Der Landschaftsgarten*,
146.

[65] In Schleswig-Holstein, Prinz Carl von Hessen, the provincial Masonic grandmaster,
established a centre for North German Masonry at Louisenlund and had the park
newly shaped by the garden architect Johann Caspar Bechstedt. Built in 1778, the
garden included a *Freimaurerturm* and an *Ägyptisches Portal*; the tower contained an
alchemical laboratory in its basement, in which the prince and the legendary Count of
St Germain experimented, as well as a secret underground meeting room. Brothers
arriving at the estate were met at the Nordic House, from which they were led along
the path to the Half-Moon Lake, and on to a mysterious grotto, with an artificial waterfall. From here the path led to a bark-covered hermitage inside which lay a wooden
hermit on a stall, beside a table equipped with a skull and a crucifix; when the visitor,

English gardens were constructed during the flowering of Freemasonry in the last decades of the century, and most of the important garden patrons, as well as visitors and admirers, were themselves Masons (figure 6.4).[66] As Anthony Vidler has shown, an increasing emphasis on initiatory rites in late eighteenth-century Masonry gradually transformed the geography of the Masonic lodges, their rituals escaping the confines of the buildings and extending into the landscape beyond, 'for a second and equally powerful vision of initiatory space had asserted itself in the late seventies as the corollary to the Egyptian temple: that of the *jardin-anglais*'.[67]

In its uncanny, circular effect on formal structure, then, musical fantasy emerges from the contemporary critical discourse as a picturesque journey through a phantasmagoric, quasi-Masonic landscape; as such, it enacts the mythic quest of the apprentice at the temple of Isis, for whom bewilderment and amazement constitute climactic points on the journey of initiation into the secrets of nature. But such quests were not confined to occult Masonic theory, for in the years around 1800 the image of the veiled Isis represented a shift in the philosophy of nature more generally, so that the notion of her as a symbol of the limits of human reason in the face of nature was fundamentally contested. In Schiller's famous ballad 'Das verschleierte Bild zu Sais' (The Veiled Statue at Sais) (1795) the youth who searches for truth at the temple of Sais lifts the veil of the statue, violating the shrine, and dies, having ignored its famous inscription. Beethoven had copied out and set before him on his desk a version of this inscription, possibly taken from Schiller's earlier essay 'Die Sendung Moses' (1790) or its source, the Masonic book *Die Hebräischen Mysterien oder die älteste religiöse Freymaurerey* (1788) by Karl Leonhard Reinhold, Schiller's colleague and friend at the University of Jena:[68] 'I am all that is. / I am all that is, was and will be and no mortal has lifted my veil. / He originated by himself and to him all things owe

---

or initiate, stepped on a trigger hidden in the floorboards, the hermit sprang up and stared terrifyingly at the intruder. In the vicinity of the hermitage, stones covered in runes, understood as Nordic versions of Egyptian hieroglyphics, were scattered around. See Buttlar, *Der Landschaftsgarten*, 169–70.

[66] See Hajós, *Romantische Gärten der Aufklärung*, 58.

[67] Anthony Vidler, 'The Architecture of the Lodges. Ritual and Symbols of Freemasonry', in *The Writing of the Walls*, 99.

[68] Reinhold, who taught at Jena from 1787, was one of the earliest proponents of Kantian philosophy; he wrote *Die Hebräischen Mysterien* not as a philosopher, however, but as a Freemason addressing fellow Masons; in Vienna, where he lived before accepting the post at Jena, he belonged to the lodge 'Zur Wahren Eintracht' where Mozart and Haydn were members. See Jan Assmann, 'Yehova-Isis: Egypt and the Quest for Natural Religion in the Age of Enlightenment', to be published in *Egyptomania*, ed. Wilfried Seipel.

Figure 6.4   Entrance to the Temple of the Night through a hidden grotto in the garden at Schönau. Engraving by Piringer, 1810

their being'.[69] In the *Critique of Judgement*, which appeared in the same year as Schiller's essay, Kant cited the Saitic inscription as the touchstone of sublimity, the unknowable deity, identified with Nature itself, representing the profound limits of human reason.[70]

But for a younger generation, such secrets merely demanded revelation. Isis unveiled would appear as the frontispiece, and dedication to Goethe, of Alexander von Humboldt's *Ideen zu einer Geographie der Pflanzen* (1807), which, entitled 'The Genius of Poetry Unveils the Statue of Nature', shows Apollo lifting the veil of the multiple-breasted goddess, at whose feet lies Goethe's *Metamorphosis of Plants*. Fuseli's frontispiece to Erasmus Darwin's *The Temple of Nature* (1803) promised similar revelations (figure 6.5). 'It is time to tear off the veil of Isis and reveal the mystery. Whoever is unable to endure the sight of the goddess, let him flee or perish',[71] wrote Friedrich Schlegel; likewise, in the fragmentary novel *Die Lehrlinge zu Sais*, written in 1798–9 by Schiller's student Novalis, the true apprentice must unveil the goddess: 'if according to the inscription, no mortal can lift the veil, we must seek to become immortal; he who does not seek to lift it is no true novice of Sais'.[72] But the act of unveiling the mysterious Isis is not simply a deeper penetration into nature. Novalis proposed two alternative versions of the act of unveiling. One dramatised Romantic yearning and desire, the rediscovery of a familiar love behind the veil of nature (the novice lifts the veil to discover the lover he had earlier abandoned in order to go on the Saitic quest). The other, more far-reaching, represented the moment of unveiling as, paradoxically, an exploration into the mysteries not of

---

[69] The German text reads: 'Ich bin, was da ist / Ich bin alles, was ist, was war, und was seyn wird, kein sterblicher Mensch hat meinen Schleyer aufgehoben / Er ist einzig von ihm selbst, u. diesem Einzigen sind alle Dinge ihr Daseyn schuldig'. See E. Graefe, 'Beethoven und die ägyptische Weisheit', *Göttinger Miszellen* 2 (1971), 19–21.

[70] 'Perhaps there has never been a more sublime utterance, or a thought more sublimely expressed, than the well-known inscription upon the Temple of Isis (Mother Nature), "I am all that is, and that was, and that shall be, and no mortal hath raised the veil from before my face."' Immanuel Kant, *The Critique of Judgement*, trans. James Creed Meredith (Oxford: Clarendon Press, 1952), 179, footnote. Reinhold was an admirer of Kant and, as Assmann suggests, had very likely sent him a copy of his book. See Assmann, 'Yehova-Isis', 20.

[71] Friedrich Schlegel, 'Ideen', *Kritische Friedrich-Schlegel-Ausgabe*, ed. Ernst Behler, Jean-Jacques Anstett and Hans Eichner, 35 vols. (Munich: F. Schöning, 1958–), II, pt. 1, p. 256.

[72] Novalis, *The Novices of Sais*, trans. Ralph Manheim (New York: C. Valentin, 1949), 17. On the figure of the veiled Isis in German Romantic thought see Alexander Gode von Aesch, *Natural Science in German Romanticism* (New York: Columbia University Press, 1941), 97–113; Stuart J. Harten, 'Raising the Veil of History: Orientalism, Classicism, and the Birth of Western Civilisation in Hegel's Berlin Lecture Courses of the 1820s' (Ph.D. diss., Cornell University, 1994); Arnold Schmitz, *Das Romantische Beethovenbild* (Berlin and Bonn, 1927; reprint edn, Darmstadt: Wissenschaftliche Buchgesellschaft, 1978). See also Solomon, 'Some Romantic Images in Beethoven', 253–81.

Figure 6.5   Frontispiece by Henry Fuseli, Erasmus Darwin, *The Temple of Nature, or the Origin of Society* (1803)

external nature but of the self: 'He raised the veil of the goddess of Sais – But what did he see? He saw – wonder of wonders – himself.'[73] To unveil the secrets of nature is to discover that the external world is a mirror of the human mind; elsewhere Novalis wrote that 'We shall

---

[73] Cited in M. H. Abrams, *Natural Supernaturalism: Tradition and Revolution in Romantic Literature* (New York: Norton, 1971), 248.

understand the world when we understand ourselves', and Schlegel that 'If we are searching for the plan of the universe, we may learn that we ourselves are that plan.'[74] The search for truth embodied by the Saitic quest becomes the quest for self – for a purified, higher self such as that implied as late as 1817 by Carl August Eschenmayer in his *Pyschologie*.[75] That the notion of personal quest and purification of the self embodied by the image of Isis had a currency and immediacy for Beethoven (constantly in the process of re-examining and refashioning himself as he was) emerges from a letter written to the Countess Marie Erdödy of 1815: 'We finite beings, who are the embodiment of an infinite spirit, are born to suffer both pain and joy; and one might almost say that the best of us obtain *joy through suffering* . . . May God grant you greater strength to enable you to reach your *Temple of Isis*, where the purified fire may swallow up all your trouble and you may awake like a new phoenix.'[76]

The intense search for a higher sense of self implied by the fetishisation of nature in the figure of Isis played into the fascination at the turn of the nineteenth century with the complex and highly sophisticated landscapes of English-style parks, already overdetermined, perhaps, in their allusions to, or embodiment of, programmes of Masonic, or quasi-Masonic initiation. Indeed, the garden theorist August Hennings, in somewhat less heavy-handed terms, proposed that the improvement of nature in *Gartenkunst* reflects the improvement of the self, so that the contemplation and study of such landscapes becomes an exercise in self-criticism and self-knowledge: improved acquaintance with nature leads us back to our own spiritual nature, so that 'in the most painstaking inspection of it it is as if we look in a mirror in which we see ourselves reflected'.[77] Garden theory at the turn of the nineteenth century posited such spaces, shrines to Isis, as the locus for introspection and the study of, and discovery of, the self. The 'natural' garden, mysterious yet knowable, sublime yet constructed, embodied nature as the ultimate reflection of human art – in such landscapes the human subject is indeed only partially concealed behind the veil of Isis.

V

In the contemporary press Beethoven's Choral Fantasy, Op. 80 (1808, published 1812) received an eager critical response, one that seems both

---

[74] Novalis, *Schriften*, ed. Paul Kluckhohn and Richard Samuel, 6 vols. (Stuttgart: W. Kohlhammer, 1960), II, 331; Schlegel, 'Ideen', 100.

[75] See epigram to this chapter, taken from Carl August Eschenmayer, *Psychologie in drei Theilen als empirische, reine und angewandte* (Stuttgart and Tübingen, 1817), 567, §510. Cited in Aesch, *Natural Science*, 102.

[76] Letter of 19 October 1815 in Anderson, ed., *The Letters of Beethoven*, II, 527–8.

[77] Hennings, 'Über Baummahlerei', 18.

disconcertingly enthusiastic and bizarrely mystical to the eye of the modern reader. And yet it makes perfect sense when read against this discourse of subjectivity and identity, of revelation and illumination. In the review that appeared in the *AmZ* in 1812 the critic held the piece up as the pinnacle and epitome of fantasia, applauding that genre's rejection of all constraints, its return to a sort of natural musical state à la Rousseau, in which 'the genius of the artist is installed again in its inalienable right – older than forms – as creator, as lord in the realm of sound'. Taking for granted the way in which the fantasia entices, disorientates and bewitches the listener, the critic went on to present Beethoven's Choral Fantasy as a fabulous quest, a journey from darkness into light; but this is not just any old circuit through contrasting affects – rather, it is the elaborate embodiment of a mystical journey of self-discovery, from the vaguest mass of unnameable feelings to the purest and most glorious self-consciousness. The freedom of the fantasy is conceived here as the ultimate artistic liberty to express the most 'personal, private feelings'; indeed, were composers only to relinquish their dependence on form and trust to the 'spirit's emancipation in the realm of freedom' then every fantasy would constitute a 'true autobiography'.[78]

This might seem suprising, given the nature of Op. 80 itself. Like the *Fantasie*, Op. 77, Op. 80 is constructed on the model of free fantasia plus variations, and it was cited by Czerny as an example of his first category of more extended 'fantasy-like improvisation', improvisation on a single theme. But while it takes the listener into an admittedly varied landscape, this is far removed from the topography of the fragmented solo fantasy, the 'true' fantasia in the Bachian sense. Indeed, in the terms of free fantasia, the unifying thread running through the work – the theme upon which the variations that make up by far the largest part of the work are based – is all too clear; there are few astonishing harmonic sidesteps, few nebulous, disorientated moments. Moreover, as a staged piece, the Choral Fantasy becomes thoroughly teleological, for far from being lost in a maze of ideas and affects, the listener is constantly aware of, and expecting, the impending entry of the chorus.

Written for solo piano, orchestra and chorus, the Choral Fantasy was composed quickly and embodies the crowd-pleaser variation-fantasy so typical of its period and so frequently disparaged by critics; a relatively short solo piano improvisation opens the work, but gives way quickly to the extended variations between orchestra and piano, and eventually chorus, which constitute the 'Finale'. The work was itself a

---

[78] Review of Choral Fantasy, Op. 80, *AmZ* 14/19 (6 May 1812), cols. 307–11. In Kunze, ed., *Die Werke im Spiegel*, 215–18.

Finale, having been designed as the summation of that epic, freezing 'Akademie' put on by Beethoven in December 1808, a conclusion that would incorporate into a single allegory of harmony all the performing forces employed during the course of the concert, each of whose individual programme elements the Fantasy in some way refers to.[79] And indeed, the patchwork, hodge-podge character of the work, combined with its theatricality, its programmatic nature and its occasional function, has surely contributed to its critical neglect: it is far from the 'pure' intellectual challenge of the other works on that programme, which included the fifth and sixth symphonies, extracts from the *Missa Solemnis*, as well as the solo piano improvisation which may have been the prototype for the *Fantasie*, Op. 77.

Yet for the *AmZ* reviewer, not only was this a perfect example of fantasy, presenting to an audience a private creative vision, but it simultaneously held the promise, or threat, of critical self-reflection for the artist, functioning as a 'mirror of his inner self, whose depth and richness is clearly reflected in it'. The description of Beethoven's Op. 80 which follows traces an extraordinary psychological journey, as 'the whole arises from the mighty soaring up of a profound genius out of the sea of unending harmony to the highest clarity and self-contemplation'. Initially, the opening free improvisation (or imitation of such fantasising) expresses the 'inexhaustible wealth' of the composer's creative imagination, though 'not without chaotic confusion, which causes the listener at first to fear that the spirit might lose itself in self-absorption, and, vanishing in its profusion, never emerge into daylight'. But subsequently a route begins to be traced out, from obscure ignorance to brilliant knowledge, from claustrophobic darkened passageway to capacious, bright hall. It is a route of initiation: 'Pictures and dreams push under and through one another, lose themselves in a tightly entwined change-dance, and the development is kept in reserve – self-consciousness still appears to be lacking. But as this is only a dark entrance hall, out of which the luminous genius will lead us into the true Pantheon of Harmonies, so this Adagio dissolves with a suspension in a figure in the highest octave to a concerted finale.' With the entry at last of the chorus and its quasi-Masonic text, 'the fantasia . . . now proceeds to actual words – as the genius, which has now arrived at self-consciousness, proceeds to display itself in the utmost clarity'. While somewhat undermining the claims to semantic richness of the instrumental free fantasia – ironically, only with the text's ecstatic vision of music does this discourse emerge into clarity – the reviewer

---

[79] See Steven Moore Whiting, '"Hört ihr wohl": Zu Funktion und Programm von Beethovens "Chorfantasie"', *Archiv für Musikwissenschaft*, 45/2 (1988), 132–47.

extols the Choral Fantasy as an intimate, revelatory, psychological portrait of Beethoven.[80]

The fantasy, then, enacts a quest from obscurity to light, a journey into
knowledge; the composer/performer, the protagonist of the fantasy, is
as the initiate/apprentice coming out of ignorance into self-awareness,
discovering at the climax of the journey not the world outside, nature,
but rather a mirror that throws back a now-clear reflection of the artist
himself. But in the strange doubleness of fantasia as public performance,
this private invention of the self is overseen, or overheard, in a voyeur-
istic moment: the fantasia, the artist's monologue and autobiography,
offers what amounts to a titillating glimpse under the veil of secrecy into
the intimate laboratory of the genius' imagination. This is a reading of
fantasy that both replays earlier fantasy criticism, and recapitulates contemporary reception of Beethoven's own improvisations, scenarios of
voyeurism and the intimate revelation of a jealously guarded private
self. At the same time it echoes the explanation by Rochlitz of the mad
musical fantasies of the asylum inmate Karl, through whose improvisations he claims to have come to know 'the exact exterior and interior
history' of the disturbed man. Exploring the untamed musical landscape
is a means not just of musical discovery but also a coming into self-consciousness; although the *AmZ* reviewer of Op. 80 writes of 'the artist',
perhaps distinct from the person 'Beethoven', an underlying conflation
of life and work remains, the Romantic version of *C. P. E. Bachs
Empfindungen*, as music is projected onto the difficult topography of the
self.

This interpretation of fantasy as autobiography, as a mirror in which the
artist is reflected and represented with the utmost clarity, transposes
eighteenth-century notions of fantasy as the unmediated utterance of
genius into the context of early nineteenth-century thought. It is one
that hints, moreover, at further meanings of the figuring of the grotesque and disruptive features of modern music – those designated 'fantastic' in Beethoven's oeuvre – within the aesthetics of the picturesque.
While the fantasy element in Beethoven's works, his late piano music in
particular, was so often understood by his contemporaries in terms borrowed from the picturesque garden, these gardens, and likewise fantasia, carried connotations of that great Romantic quest, the search for
enlightenment at the Temple of Isis which was itself closely wrought up
with contemporary readings of nature.

---

[80] Review of Choral Fantasy, Op. 80, *AmZ* 14/19 (6 May 1812), cols. 307–11. In Kunze, ed.,
Die Werke im Spiegel, 215–18. See Marshall Brown, 'Mozart and After: The Revolution
in Musical Consciousness', *Critical Inquiry* 7/4 (Summer 1981), 689–706; on the Masonic
connotations of the text of the Choral Fantasy see Edward J. Dent, 'The Choral
Fantasia', *Music and Letters*, 8/2 (1927), 111–21.

Novalis found the supreme presence of nature in musical fantasies, fairy tales, and motley assortments of wonderful curiosities, and implied that all approach sublime, if hidden, meaning in their apparent lack of structure: 'A fairy tale is actually like a dream-image – without context. An ensemble of marvelous things and incidents – for example, a musical fantasy – the harmonic products of an Aeolian harp – nature itself.'[81] Likewise, Ignaz von Seyfried took Beethoven's improvisations as 'the mystical Sanskrit language whose hieroglyphs can be read only by the initiated'.[82] Kapellmeister Kreisler, the invention of the Beethoven enthusiast E. T. A. Hoffmann (and perhaps in part based on Rochlitz's account of the inmate 'Karl', which had fascinated Hoffmann), is himself figured in Hoffmann's strange and fragmented text as a journeyman on the road to self-discovery through music, a bumbling and ultimately successful apprentice at the Temple of Sais.[83] The image of the mirror runs through *Kreisleriana*, which continually blurs the identities of Hoffmann's authorial voice and his alter ego Kreisler; only at last, at the gates to the temple, once access to higher wisdom has been attained, is the lifting of the veil re-enacted as the persona of the Master sees in the mirror the persona of Kreisler and indeed signs Kreisler's Certificate of Apprenticeship 'like you' as 'Johannes Kreisler, *cidevant* Kapellmeister'. And, at the (anti-)climax of initiation into the circle of the disciples of Isis, that certificate itself proclaims that 'Music is a universal language of nature; it speaks to us in magical and mysterious resonances; we strive in vain to conjure these into symbols, and any artificial arrangement of hieroglyphs provides us with only a vague approximation of what we have distantly heard.'[84]

The frontispiece to the extended fantastic text, the *Fantasiestücke in Callot's Manier*, which contains the *Kreisleriana*, frames Hoffmann's project itself in terms of the Saitic legend (figure 6.6). In this image, drawn by the author, a medieval troubadour strums a harp, casually perched on a reclining statue, half-shrouded in shade – a figure which merges the sphinx and the figure of Isis. Hoffmann wrote of the vignette 'Do the *mysteries of music* then not speak to you through the sounds of the harp, which ring out at sunrise from the *ancient German troubadour* before the enigmatic image of the *Isis-headed sphinx*?'[85] The Germanic

---

[81] Novalis, chapter 8, 'General Draft' (September 1798 – March 1799), in *Philosophical Writings*, trans. and ed. Margaret Mahony Stoljar (Albany: SUNY Press, 1997), 136. Cited in Sisman, 'After the Heroic Style'. On the Masonic connotations of the text of the Choral Fantasy see Edward J. Dent, 'The Choral Fantasia', *Music and Letters* 8/2 (April 1927), 111–21.   [82] Sonneck, ed., *Beethoven*, 36.

[83] On Hoffmann's interest in Rochlitz's account of Karl see David Charlton's introduction in *E. T. A. Hoffmann's Musical Writings*, 46–8.   [84] Ibid., 165.

[85] Letter to Hoffmann's publisher, C. F. Kunz, 8 September 1813, cited in Charlton, ed., *E. T. A. Hoffmann's Musical Writings*, 30.

Figure 6.6   Frontispiece by E. T. A. Hoffmann to *Fantasiestücke in Callot's Manier* (1814)

bard, supremely represented in Hoffmann's text by Beethoven, is pictured as an initiate, one who attends at the Temple of Isis, having penetrated its hidden mysteries. That Beethoven's musical fantasies in particular should have represented this ultimate penetration into the hidden secrets of the art, a higher understanding, a supreme achievement, for the nineteenth-century imagination is further borne out by a piece of Beethoven iconography dating from the middle of the century. In Ernst Julius Hähnel's designs for the Bonn Beethoven monument (1845), four panels divide and categorise Beethoven's musical oeuvre into 'Die Fantasie', 'Die Symphonie', 'Die Geistliche Musik', and 'Die Dramatische Musik', allegorising each with a female figure, the muse in four different guises (figure 6.7a on next two pages). The first of these was privileged in Schumann's monument to Beethoven, the C major *Fantasie*, Op. 17, a post-picturesque edifice whose first movement was originally, and aptly, entitled 'Ruins'.[86] But 'Die Fantasie' is also given pride of place on Hähnel's monument (figure 6.7b). It is the first in the series of panels, a vibrant depiction of the scope of the genius's imagination, but also, in line with the other three, an illustration of the fantasia as genre. Here, with flowing hair and bared breasts, the muse plays on a harp, her eyes upturned to heaven in what appears to be ecstatic transport. She is riding on the back of a cavorting figure, whose strong lion's body gives way to a voluptuous female torso and wild-maned head, a liberated and volatile version of Hoffmann's Isis-headed sphinx. Beethoven's Fantasia is carried aloft on the flanks of the mysterious Isis.

---

[86] See John Daverio, *Nineteenth-Century Music and the German Romantic Ideology* (New York: Schirmer, 1993), chapter 2.

(a)

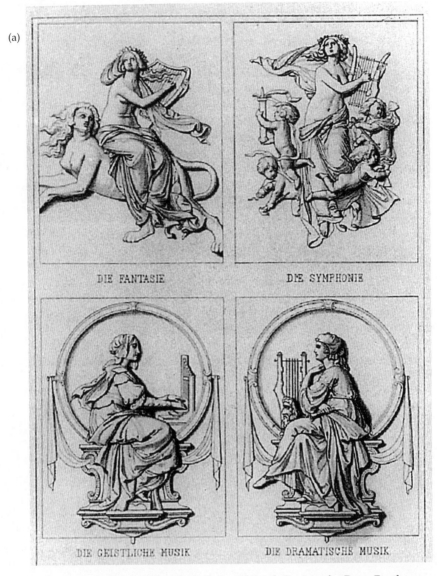

Figure 6.7a and b   Ernst Julius Hähnel, Designs for Bonn Beethoven monument (1845)

(b)

SELECT BIBLIOGRAPHY

Pre-1830

Addison, Joseph. 'The Pleasures of the Imagination'. In *The Spectator*. Ed. Donald F. Bond. Oxford: Clarendon Press, 1965.

Adlung, Jakob. *Anleitung zur musikalischen Gelahrtheit*. Erfurt: J. D. Jungnicol, 1758; reprint edn, Kassel: Bärenreiter, 1953.

Austen, Jane. *Mansfield Park*. London: Printed for T. Egerton, 1814.

Avison, Charles. *Essay on Musical Expression*. 2nd edn, London: Printed for C. Davis, 1753; reprint edn, New York: Broude Bros., [1967].

Bach, Carl Philipp Emanuel. *Versuch über die wahre Art das Clavier zu spielen*. 2 vols., Berlin: C. F. Henning, 1753, 1762; reprint edn, Wiesbaden: Breitkopf & Härtel, 1954.

Essay on the True Art of Playing Keyboard Instruments. Trans. William S. Mitchell. London: Eulenburg, 1974.

Die sechs Sammlungen von Sonaten, freien Fantasien und Rondos für Kenner und Liebhaber. Leipzig: Breitkopf & Härtel, 1954.

Fantasie C. P. E. Bachs Empfindungen (Erstdruck); Abschied vom Silbermannschen Clavier. Ed. Alfred Kreutz. Mainz: Schott, 1953.

The Letters of C. P. E. Bach. Ed. and trans. Stephen L. Clark. Oxford: Clarendon Press, 1997.

Beattie, James. *Essays on Poetry and Music as They Affect the Mind; On Laughter and Ludicrous Composition; On the Usefulness of Classical Learning*. 3rd edn. Edinburgh: E. and C. Dilly, 1779.

Becker, Wilhelm Gottlieb. *Taschenbuch für Garten Freunde*. Leipzig: Voss und Compagnie, 1795–9.

Bossler, Heinrich Philipp Carl, ed. *Musikalische Real-Zeitung für das Jahr 1789*. Speyer, 1789; reprint edn, Hildesheim: Olms, 1971.

Burke, Edmund. *A Philosophical Enquiry into the Origin of Our Ideas of the Sublime and the Beautiful*. London: R. and J. Dodsley, 1757.

Burney, Charles. *The Present State of Music in Germany, the Netherlands and the United Provinces*. London: T. Beckett, J. Robson and G. Robinson, 1773. Reprint of 2nd edn (1775), New York: Broude Bros., 1969.

Carl Burney's . . . Tagebuch seiner musikalischen Reisen. Trans. J. J. C. Bode and C. D. Ebeling. Hamburg, 1773.

A General History of Music from the Earliest Ages to the Present Period (1789). Ed. Frank Mercer. New York: Dover [1957].

Busby, Thomas. *A Complete Dictionary of Music*. London: R. Phillips, 1801.

A Musical Manual, or Technical Directory. London: Goulding & D'Almaine, 1828; reprint edn, New York: Da Capo Press, 1976.

Bibliography

Chambers, William. *A Dissertation on Oriental Gardening*. London: Printed by W. Griffin [etc.], 1772.

Designs for Chinese Buildings, Furniture, Machines and Utensils, engraved from the originals drawn in China; to which is annexed, A Description of their Temples, Houses, Gardens, etc. London: Published for the author, 1757.

Claudius, Matthias. *Botengänge: Briefe an Freunde*. Ed. Hans Jessen. Berlin: Eckart, 1965.

Clementi, Muzio. *Clementi's Selection of Practical Harmony*. London: Clementi [etc.], 1803.

[Combe, William]. *The Tour of Dr. Syntax in Search of the Picturesque: a poem*. 9th edn, London: R. Ackermann's Repository of Fine Arts, 1819.

Cozens, Alexander. *A New Method of Assisting the Invention in Drawing Original Compositions of Landscape*. London, 1785; reprint edn, with introduction by Michael Marqusee, London: Paddington Press, 1977.

Cramer, Carl Friedrich, ed. *Magazin der Musik*. Hamburg, 1783–9; reprint edn, Hildesheim: Olms, 1971.

Crotch, William. *Specimens of Various Styles of Music, Referred to in a Course of Lectures on Music Read at Oxford and in the Metropolis*. 3 vols., Oxford, [1807?]–1822.

Substance of Several Lectures on Music, Read in the University of Oxford and in the Metropolis. London: Longman, Rees, Orme, Brown and Green. 1831.

Czerny, Carl. *Systematische Anleitung zum Fantasieren auf dem Pianoforte*, Op. 200. Vienna: Diabelli, 1829. Trans. Alice L. Mitchell, as *A Systematic Introduction to Improvisation on the Pianoforte*. New York: Longman, 1983.

Schule der praktischen Tonsetzkunst, Op. 600. Vienna: Diabelli, 1839. Trans. John Bishop, as *School of Practical Composition*, Op. 600. London: Cocks, c. 1848.

Diderot, Denis. *The Paradox of Acting, and Masks or Faces? by William Archer*. Trans. Walter Herries Pollock. New York: Hill & Wang, 1957.

Duff, William. *An Essay on Original Genius*. London: Printed for Edward and Charles Dilly, 1767.

Engel, Johann Jakob. *Über die musikalische Mahlerey*. Berlin, 1780.

Eschenmayer, Carl August. *Psychologie in drei Theilen als empirische, reine und angewandte*. Stuttgart and Tübingen, 1817.

Forkel, Johann Nikolaus. *Über die Theorie der Musik, insofern sie Liebhabern und Kennern nothwendig und nützlich ist*. Göttingen: Im Verlag der Wittwe Vandenhoeck, 1777.

Musikalisch-kritische Bibliothek. Gotha: C. W. Ettinger, 1778–9; reprint edn, Hildesheim: Olms, 1964.

Musikalischer Almanach für Deutschland. Leipzig: Schwickert, 1782–4, 1789; reprint edn, Hildesheim: Olms, 1974.

Gerard, Alexander. *An Essay on Genius*. London and Edinburgh: W. Strahan, T. Cadell and W. Creech, 1774.

Gilpin, William. *A Dialogue upon the Gardens of the Right Honourable the Lord Viscount Cobham at Stowe in Buckinghamshire*. London: Printed for B. Seeley, 1748.

Observations on the River Wye, and Several Parts of South Wales, etc., relative chiefly to Picturesque Beauty; made in the Summer of the Year 1770. London: R. Blamire, 1782.

Remarks on Forest Scenery, and other Woodland Views. London: R. Blamire, 1791.

Three Essays: – on Picturesque Beauty; on Picturesque Travel; and, on Sketching Landscape: to which is added a Poem, on Landscape Painting. London: R. Blamire, 1792.

Girardin, René Louis, marquis de. *De la composition des paysages sur le terrain, ou, des moyens d'embellir la nature autour des habitations champetres* . . . 3rd edn, Paris: Mayer, 1795.

Goethe, Johann Wolfgang von. *The Sorrows of Young Werther; Elective Affinities; Novella.* Trans. Victor Lang and Judith Ryan, ed. David E. Wellberry. New York: Suhrkamp, 1988.

Griesinger, Georg August. *Biographische Notizen über Joseph Haydn.* Leipzig: Breitkopf & Härtel, 1810.

Grohmann, Johann Gottfried. *Ideenmagazin für Liebhaber von Gärten, Englischen Anlagen und für Besitzer von Landgütern und Gärten.* Leipzig, 1779–1805.

Hayes, William. *The Art of Composing Music by a Method entirely New, suited to the meanest Capacity, whereby all Difficulties are removed, and a Person who has made never so little Progress before, may, with some small Application, be enabled to excel.* London: J. Lion, 1751.

Heeley, Joseph. *Letters on the Beauties of Hagley, Enville and the Leasowes.* 2 vols., London, 1777.

Hennings, August. 'Über Baummahlerei, Garten Inschriften, Clumps und Amerikanischen Anpflanzungen'. In *Der Genius der Zeit* 10/1 (Altona, 1797).

Hiller, Johann Adam, ed. *Wöchentliche Nachrichten und Anmerkungen die Musik betreffend,* July 1766–December 1770. Leipzig: Im Verlag der Zeitungs-Expedition, 1766–70; reprint edn, Hildesheim: Olms, 1970.

Hirschfeld, Christian Cajus Lorenz. *Anmerkungen über die Landhäuser und die Gartenkunst.* Frankfurt and Leipzig: Weidmanns Erben und Reich, 1779.

Theorie der Gartenkunst. 5 vols., Leipzig: Weidmanns Erben und Reich, 1779–85; reprint edn, Hildesheim: Olms, 1973.

Home, Henry (Lord Kames). *Elements of Criticism.* 9th edn, Edinburgh: A. Millar, 1817.

Hoyle, John. *A Complete Dictionary of Music.* London: H. D. Symonds, 1791; reprint edn, Geneva: Minkoff, 1976.

Johnson, Samuel. *A Dictionary of the English Language.* London, 1755.

[Junker, Karl Ludwig, ed.] *Musikalischer und Künstler Almanach auf das Jahr 1782.* Freyburg, 1784.

Kant, Immanuel. *The Critique of Judgement.* Trans. James Creed Meredith. Oxford: Clarendon Press, 1952.

Klein, Johann Joseph. *Versuch eines Lehrbuches der practischen Musik.* Gera, 1783.

Knecht, Justin Heinrich. *Kleines alphabetisches Wörterbuch der vornehmsten und interessantesten Artikel aus der musikalischen Theorie.* Ulm, 1795.

Knight, Richard Payne. *The Landscape: a didactic poem in three books, addressed to Uvedale Price.* London: W. Bulmer, 1794.

An Analytical Inquiry into the Principles of Taste. 2nd edn, London, 1805.

Koch, Heinrich Christoph. *Musikalisches Lexicon.* Offenbach am Main: A. Hermann dem Jüngern, 1802.

Versuch einer Anleitung zur Composition. Leipzig: A. F. Böhme, 1781; reprint edn, Hildesheim: Olms, 1969.

Lenz, Jacob Michael Reinhold. *Werke und Schriften*. Ed. Britta Titel and Hellmut Haug. Stuttgart: Goverts, 1966.

Lessing, Gotthold Ephraim. *Laocoön: An Essay on the Limits of Painting and Poetry*. Trans. Edward Allen McCormick. Baltimore: Johns Hopkins University Press, 1984.

Hamburg Dramaturgy. Trans. Helen Zimmerman. New York: Dover, 1962. Originally published 1769.

Löhlein, Georg Simon. *Klavier-Schule, oder kurze und gründliche Anweisung zur Melodie und Harmonie, durchgehends mit practischen Beyspielen erkläret*. 4th edn, Leipzig and Zullichau, 1782.

Longinus. *On the Sublime*. Trans. W. Smith. London: B. Dod, 1752.

Loudon, J. C. [John Claudius]. *A treatise on forming, improving, and managing country residences; and on the choice of situations appropriate to every class of purchasers*. London: Longman, Hurst, Rees, and Orme, 1806.

Marshall, William. *A review of The landscape, a didactic poem; also of an Essay on the picturesque: together with practical remarks on rural ornament. By the author of 'Planting and ornamental gardening; a practical treatise'*. London: G. Nicol [etc.], 1795.

Planting and ornamental gardening: a practical treatise. London: J. Dodsley, 1785.

Mason, William. *An heroic epistle to Sir William Chambers . . . author of a late Dissertation on oriental gardening: enriched with explanatory notes, chiefly extracted from that elaborate performance*. 7th edn, London: Printed for J. Almon . . ., 1773.

Michaelis, Johann Christian Friedrich. 'Ueber das Humoristische oder Launige in der musikalischen Komposition'. *AmZ* 9/46 (1807), cols. 725–9.

Nägeli, Hans Georg. *Vorlesungen über Musik, mit Berücksichtigung der Dilettanten*. Stuttgart and Tübingen: J. G. Cotta, 1826.

Novalis [Friedrich von Hardenberg]. *The Novices of Sais*. Trans. Ralph Manheim. New York: C. Valentin, 1949.

Petri, Johann Samuel. *Anleitung zur praktischen Musik*. 2nd edn, Leipzig: J. G. I. Breitkopf, 1782; reprint edn, Prien am Chiemsee: Emil Katzbichler, 1969.

Price, Uvedale, Sir. *An Essay on the Picturesque, as Compared with the Sublime and the Beautiful; and, On the Use of Studying Pictures, for the Purpouse of Improving Real Landscape*. London, 1794.

Essays on the Picturesque, As Compared with the Sublime and the Beautiful; and, on the Use of Studying Pictures, for the Purpose of Improving Real Landscape. London, 1810.

Pückler-Muskau, Hermann Ludwig Heinrich, Fürst von. *Gartenkunst und Denkmalpflege*. Ed. Joachim Fait and Detlef Karg. Weimar: H. Böhlau, 1989.

Hints on Landscape Gardening. Trans. Bernhard Sickert, ed. Samuel Parsons. Boston and New York: Houghton Mifflin, [1917].

Quantz, Johann Joachim. *Versuch einer Anleitung die Flöte traversiere zu spielen*. Berlin: J. F. Voss, 1752; reprint of 3rd edn (1789), Kassel: Bärenreiter, 1953. Trans. Edward Reilly as *On Playing the Flute*. New York: Schirmer, 1975.

Rees, Abraham, ed. *The Cyclopaedia; or, Universal Dictionary of Arts, Sciences and Literature*. London: Longman, Hurst, Rees [etc.], 1802–19.

Reichardt, Johann Friedrich. *Briefe eines aufmerksamen Reisenden die Musik betreffend*. 2 vols., Frankfurt and Leipzig, 1774–6; reprint edn, Hildesheim: Olms, 1977.

Musikalisches Kunstmagazin. Berlin: J. Reichardt, 1782–91; reprint edn, Hildesheim: Olms, 1969.

Vertraute Briefe aus Paris geschrieben in den Jahren 1802 und 1803. Hamburg: Hoffmann, 1804.

'Noch ein Bruchstück aus Johann Friedrich Reichardt's Autobiographie: Sein erster Aufenthalt in Hamburg'. *AmZ* 16/2 (1815), cols. 31–2.

Repton, Humphry. *The art of landscape gardening, including his Sketches and hints on landscape gardening and Theory and practice of landscape gardening*. Ed. John Nolen. Boston: Houghton Mifflin, 1907.

An Enquiry into the changes of taste in landscape gardening, to which are added some observations on its theory and practice including a defence of the art. London: J. Taylor, 1806.

Fragments on the theory and practice of landscape gardening: including some remarks on Grecian and Gothic architecture, collected from various manuscripts in possession of the different noblemen and gentlemen, for whose use they were originally written. London: Printed by T. Bensley and Son . . . for J. Taylor . . . 1816.

The landscape gardening and landscape architecture of the late Humphry Repton, esq., being his entire works on these subjects. London: Longman, 1840.

The Red Books of Humphry Repton. [Ed.] Edward Malins. London: The Basilisk Press, 1976.

Reynolds, Joshua. *Discourses on Art*. Ed. Pat Rogers. London: Penguin, 1992.

Richter, Jean Paul. *Vorschule der Aesthetik: nebst einigen Vorlesungen in Leipzig über die Parteien der Zeit*. Hamburg: Friedrich Perthes, 1804.

Horn of Oberon: Jean Paul Richter's School for Aesthetics. Trans. Margaret R. Hale. Detroit: Wayne State University Press, 1973.

Rochlitz, Friedrich. 'Der Besuch im Irrenhause'. *AmZ* 6/39 (1804), cols. 645–54.

Schlegel, August Wilhelm von. *Vorlesungen über schöne Literatur und Kunst*. Ed. J. Minor. Heilbronn: Henninger, 1884.

Schubart, Christian Friedrich Daniel. *Ideen zu einer Ästhetik der Tonkunst*. Ed. Ludwig Schubart. Vienna: Degen, 1806; reprint edn, Hildesheim: Olms, 1973.

Gesammelte Schriften und Schiksale. 8 vols. in 4, Stuttgart: Scheible, 1839; reprint edn, Hildesheim: Olms, 1973.

Sckell, Friedrich Ludwig von. *Beiträge zur bildenden Gartenkunst für angehende Gartenkünstler und Garten Liebhaber*. Worms: Wernersche Verlagsgesellschaft, 1982.

Sorge, Georg Andreas. *Anleitung zur Fantasie oder: Zu der schönen Kunst das Clavier wie auch andere Instrumente aus dem Kopfe zu spielen*. Lobenstein, 1767.

Sterne, Laurence. *The Life and Opinions of Tristram Shandy, Gentleman*. 9 vols. in 5, London, 1760–7.

Sulzer, Johann Georg. *Allgemeine Theorie der schönen Künste*. 3rd edn, Leipzig: M. C. Weidmanns Erben und Reich, 1786–7. Reprint of expanded edn of 1792, Hildesheim: G. Olms, 1994.

Triest, Johann Karl Friedrich. 'Bemerkungen über die Ausbildung der Tonkunst in Deutschland im achtzehnten Jahrhundert'. *AmZ* 3/24 (1801), cols. 405–10.

Türk, Daniel Gottlob. *Klavierschule, oder, Anweisung zum Klavierspielen für Lehrer und Lernende*. Leipzig: Schwickert, 1789; reprint edn, Kassel: Bärenreiter, 1967. Trans. Raymond H. Haggh as *School of Clavier Playing, or, Instructions in Playing the Clavier for Teachers and Students*. Lincoln: University of Nebraska Press, 1982.

Unger, Johann Friedrich. *Entwurf einer Maschine wodurch alles was auf dem Clavier gespielt wird, sich von selber in Noten setzt. Im Jahr 1752, an die Königl. Akademie der Wissenschaften zu Berlin eingesandt, nebst dem mit dem Herrn Direktor Euler darüber geführten Briefwechsel*. Braunschweig, 1774.

Vogler, Georg Joseph. *Betrachtungen der Mannheimer Tonschule*. 3 vols., Mannheim, 1778–81; reprint edn, Hildesheim: Olms, 1974.

Walpole, Horace. *Essay on Modern Gardening*. Strawberry Hill: Printed by T. Kirgate, 1785; reprint edn, London: Brentham Press, 1975.

[Whately, Thomas]. *Observations on Modern Gardening*. London, 1770.

Wolf, Georg Friedrich. *Kurzgefaßtes musikalisches Lexicon*. Halle: Hendel, 1787.

Young, Edward. *Conjectures on Original Composition in a Letter to the Author of Sir Charles Grandison*. Dublin: Printed for P. Wilson, 1759.

Zimmermann, Johann Georg. *Solitude Considered, with respect to its influence upon the mind and the heart*. Trans. from the French by J. B. Mercier. London: C. Dilly, 1791.

Post-1830

Abrams, M. H. *The Mirror and the Lamp: Romantic Theory and the Critical Tradition*. Oxford: Oxford University Press, 1953.

Natural Supernaturalism: Tradition and Revolution in Romantic Literature. New York: Norton, 1971.

Adorno, Theodor W. *Über einige Relationen zwischen Musik und Malerei. Die Kunst und die Künste*. Anmerkungen zur Zeit, no. 12, Berlin: Akademie der Künste, 1967.

Quasi una Fantasia: Essays on Modern Music. Trans. Rodney Livingstone. London: Verso, 1992.

Aesch, Alexander Gode von. *Natural Science in German Romanticism*. New York: Columbia University Press, 1941.

Anderson, Emily, ed. *The Letters of Beethoven*. 3 vols., New York: St. Martin's Press, 1961.

The Letters of Mozart and his Family. 2nd edn, 2 vols., London: Macmillan, 1966.

Andrews, Malcolm. *The Search for the Picturesque: Landscape Aesthetics and Tourism in Britain, 1760–1800*. Aldershot: Scolar Press, 1989.

Aristotle. *The Complete Works of Aristotle: The Revised Oxford Translation*. Trans. W. D. Ross, ed. Jonathan Barnes. Princeton, NJ: Princeton University Press, 1984.

Baetjer, Catherine, ed. *Glorious Nature: British Landscape Painting 1750–1850*. New York: Hudson Hills Press, 1993.

Balet, Leo and E. Gerhard. *Die Verbürgerlichung der deutschen Kunst, Literatur und Musik im 18. Jahrhundert*. Frankfurt am Main: Ullstein, 1973.

Baltrusaitis, Jurgis. *Aberrations: An Essay on the Legend of Forms*. Trans. Richard Miller. Cambridge, MA: MIT Press, 1989.

Barbier, Carl Paul. *William Gilpin: His Drawings, Teaching, and Theory of the Picturesque.* Oxford: Clarendon Press, 1963.

Barford, Philip T. 'A Fantasia by C. P. E. Bach'. *Monthly Musical Record* 85 (1955), 144–50.

Barrell, John. *The Idea of Landscape and the Sense of Place, 1730–1840: An Approach to the Poetry of John Clare.* Cambridge: Cambridge University Press, 1972.

The Dark Side of the Landscape: The Rural Poor in English Painting, 1730–1840. Cambridge: Cambridge University Press, 1980.

Barrell, John, ed. *Painting and the Politics of Culture: New Essays on British Art 1700–1850.* Oxford: Oxford University Press, 1992.

Becker, Max. *Narkotikum und Utopie: Musik-Konzepte in Empfindsamkeit und Romantik.* Kassel: Bärenreiter, 1996.

Bekker, Paul. *Beethoven.* Berlin: Schuster & Loeffler, 1921.

Benary, Peter. 'Sonata quasi una Fantasia. Zu Beethovens opus 27'. *Musik-theorie* 2/2 (1987), 129–36.

Berg, Darrell. 'The Keyboard Sonatas of C. P. E. Bach: An Expression of the Mannerist Principle'. Ph.D. diss., State University of New York at Buffalo, 1975.

'C. P. E. Bach's Character Pieces and his Friendship Circle'. In *C. P. E. Bach Studies.* Ed. Stephen L. Clark. Oxford: Clarendon Press, 1988. 1–32.

Berger, Karol. 'Toward a History of Hearing: The Classic Concerto, a Sample Case'. In *Convention in 18th- and 19th-Century Music: Essays in Honor of Leonard Ratner.* Ed. Wye J. Allenbrook, Janet M. Levy and William P. Mahrt. Stuyvesant, NY: Pendragon Press, 1992. 405–29.

'Beethoven and the Aesthetic State'. *Beethoven Forum* 7 (1999), 17–44.

Berger, Willy Richard. *China-Bild und China-Mode im Europa der Aufklärung.* Cologne and Vienna: Böhlau, 1990.

Bermingham, Ann. *Landscape and Ideology: The English Rustic Tradition, 1740–1850.* Berkeley: University of California Press, 1986.

'System, Order, and Abstraction: The Politics of English Landscape Drawing around 1795'. In *Landscape and Power.* Ed. W. J. T. Mitchell. Chicago and London: University of Chicago Press, 1994. 77–101.

Bicknell, Peter. *Beauty, Horror and Immensity: Picturesque Landscape in Britain, 1750–1850.* Cambridge: Cambridge University Press, 1981.

Bitter, Karl Herman. *Carl Philipp Emanuel Bach und Wilhelm Friedemann Bach und deren Brüder.* Berlin: Wilh. Müller, 1868.

Bloom, Harold, ed. *Poets of Sensibility and the Sublime.* New York: Chelsea House, 1986.

Bodsch, Ingrid, ed. *Monument für Beethoven: Zur Geschichte des Beethoven-Denkmals und der frühen Beethoven-Rezeption in Bonn.* Bonn: Stadtmuseum Bonn, 1995.

Bonds, Mark Evan. 'Haydn, Laurence Sterne, and the Origins of Musical Irony'. *Journal of the American Musicological Society* 44/1 (1991), 57–91.

Wordless Rhetoric: Musical Form and the Metaphor of the Oration. Cambridge MA: Harvard University Press, 1991.

'The Symphony as Pindaric Ode'. In *Haydn and his World.* Ed. Elaine Sisman. Princeton, NJ: Princeton University Press, 1997. 131–53.

Brauchli, Bernard. *The Clavichord.* Cambridge: Cambridge University Press, 1998.

Brennan, Matthew. *Wordsworth, Turner, and Romantic Landscape: A Study of the*

Traditions of the Picturesque and the Sublime. Columbia, SC: Camden House, 1987.

Brown, A. Peter. 'The Earliest English Biography of Haydn'. *Musical Quarterly* 59/3 (1973), 339–56.

'Joseph Haydn and C. P. E. Bach: The Question of Influence'. In *Haydn Studies: Proceedings of the International Haydn Conference, Washington DC, 1975*. Ed. Howard Serwer, Jens Peter Larsen and James Webster. New York: Norton, 1983. 158–64.

'The Sublime, the Beautiful and the Ornamental: English Aesthetic Currents and Haydn's London Symphonies'. In *Studies in Music History Presented to H. C. Robbins Landon on his Seventieth Birthday*. Ed. Otto Biba and David Wyn Jones. London: Thames and Hudson, 1996. 44–71.

Brown, Marshall. *The Shape of German Romanticism*. Ithaca, NY: Cornell University Press, 1979.

Preromanticism. Stanford: Stanford University Press, 1991.

'Mozart and After: The Revolution in Musical Consciousness'. *Critical Inquiry* 7/4 (Summer 1981), 689–706.

Butler, Gregory G. 'The Fantasia as Musical Image'. *Musical Quarterly* 60 (1974), 602–15.

Buttlar, Adrian von. *Der Landschaftsgarten: Gartenkunst des Klassizismus und der Romantik*. Cologne: DuMont, 1989.

Castle, Terry. *Masquerade and Civilization: The Carnivalesque in Eighteenth-Century English Culture and Fiction*. Stanford: Stanford University Press, 1986.

The Female Thermometer: Eighteenth-Century Culture and the Invention of the Uncanny. New York: Oxford University Press, 1995.

Chailly, Jacques. *La Flûte enchantée: opéra maçonnique*. Paris: R. Laffont, 1968.

Charlton, David, ed. *E. T. A. Hoffmann's Musical Writings: Kreisleriana, The Poet and the Composer, Music Criticism*. Trans. Martyn Clarke. Cambridge: Cambridge University Press, 1989.

Chrysander, Friedrich. 'Eine Klavier-Phantasie von Karl Philipp Emanuel Bach mit nachträglich von Gerstenberg eingefügten Gesangsmelodien zu zwei verschiedenen Texten'. *Vierteljahrsschrift für Musikwissenschaft* 7 (1891), 1–25.

G. F. Händel. 3 vols., Leipzig: Breitkopf & Härtel, 1858.

Clark, Kenneth. *Landscape into Art*. 2nd edn, New York: Harper and Row, 1976.

Clark, Stephen L., ed. *C. P. E. Bach Studies*. Oxford: Clarendon Press, 1988.

The Letters of C. P. E. Bach. Oxford: Clarendon Press, 1997.

Cohen, Ralph, ed. *Studies in Eighteenth-Century British Art and Aesthetics*. Berkeley and Los Angeles: University of California Press, 1985.

Comini, Alessandra. *The Changing Image of Beethoven: A Study in Mythmaking*. New York: Rizzoli, 1987.

Cone, Edward T. *Musical Form and Musical Performance*. New York: Norton, 1968.

Copley, Stephen and Peter Garside, eds. *The Politics of the Picturesque*. Cambridge: Cambridge University Press, 1994.

Dahlhaus, Carl. *Nineteenth Century Music*. Trans. J. Bradford Robinson. Berkeley and Los Angeles: University of California Press, 1989.

Ludwig van Beethoven: Approaches to his Music. Trans. Mary Whittall. Oxford: Clarendon Press, 1991.

The Idea of Absolute Music. Trans. Roger Lustig. Chicago: University of Chicago Press, 1989.

Daverio, John. *Nineteenth-Century Music and the German Romantic Ideology.* New York: Schirmer, 1993.

De Bolla, Peter. *The Discourse of the Sublime.* Oxford: Blackwell, 1989.

De Voogd, Peter J. 'Laurence Sterne, the Marbled Page, and "the Use of Accidents"'. *Word and Image* 1/3 (1985), 279–87.

'Tristram Shandy as Aesthetic Object'. In *Interactions: A Selection of Papers Given at the 2nd International Conference on Word and Image, Universität Zürich, August 27–31, 1991.* Ed. Martin Hensser. Basel: Weise, 1993. 383–9.

Dennis, Jonas. *The landscape gardener; comprising the history and principles of tasteful horticulture.* London: James Ridgway and Sons, 1835.

Deutsch, Otto Erich. 'Ink-Pot and Squirt-Gun, or "The Art of Composing Music in the New Style"'. *The Musical Times* 93 (1952), 401–3.

Douglas, Mary. *Implicit Meanings: Essays in Anthropology.* London: Routlege, 1975.

Fabricant, Carole. 'Binding and Dressing Nature's Loose Tresses: The Ideology of Augustan Landscape Design'. In *Studies in Eighteenth-Century Culture,* vol. VIII. Ed. Roseann Runte. Madison: University of Wisconsin Press, 1979. 109–135.

'The Aesthetics and Politics of Landscape in the Eighteenth Century'. In *Studies in Eighteenth-Century British Art and Aesthetics.* Ed. Ralph Cohen. Berkeley and Los Angeles: University of California Press, 1985.

Fletcher, Angus. *Allegory: The Theory of a Symbolic Mode.* Ithaca, NY: Cornell University Press, 1964.

Fox, Pamela. 'Melodic Nonconstancy in the Keyboard Works of C. P. E. Bach'. Ph.D. diss., University of Cincinnati, 1984.

Freedman, William. *Laurence Sterne and the Origins of the Musical Novel.* Athens, GA: University of Georgia Press, 1978.

Frieden, Ken. 'The Eighteenth-Century Introjection of Genius'. In *Poets of Sensibility and the Sublime.* Ed. Harold Bloom. New York: Chelsea House, 1986. 55–69.

Friedländer, Max. *Das deutsche Lied im 18. Jahrhundert.* Stuttgart and Berlin, 1902; reprint edn, Hildesheim: Olms, 1962.

Frye, Northrop. 'Towards Defining an Age of Sensibility'. In *Poets of Sensibility and the Sublime.* Ed. Harold Bloom. New York: Chelsea House, 1986. 11–18.

Gerndt, Siegmar. *Idealisierte Natur: Die literarische Kontroverse um den Landschaftsgarten des 18. und frühen 19. Jahrhunderts in Deutschland.* Stuttgart: J. B. Metzler, 1981.

Ginsburg. R. 'The Aesthetics of Ruins'. *Bucknell Review* 17 (1970), 89–102.

Goehr, Lydia. *The Imaginary Museum of Musical Works.* Oxford: Oxford University Press, 1992.

Gombrich, E. H. *Art and Illusion: A Study in the Psychology of Pictorial Representation.* Bollingen Series 35:5. 2nd edn, Princeton, NJ: Princeton University Press, 1989.

Grey, Thomas S. '. . . *wie ein rother Faden*: On the Origins of "Leitmotif" as Critical Construct and Musical Practice'. In *Music Theory in the Age of Romanticism.* Ed. Ian Bent. Cambridge: Cambridge University Press, 1996. 187–210.

Grimm, Jacob and Wilhelm. *Deutsches Wörterbuch.* 33 vols., Leipzig: S. Hirzel, 1854; reprint edn, Munich: Deutscher Taschenbuch Verlag, 1984.

Günther, Harri, ed. *Gärten der Goethezeit*. Leipzig: Edition Leipzig, 1993.

Hadot, Pierre. *Zur Idee des Naturgeheimnisses: Beim Betrachten des Widmungsblattes in den Humboldtschen 'Ideen zu einer Geographie der Pflanzen'*. Wiesbaden: Steiner, 1982.

Hadot, Pierre and Dirk Syndram. *Ägypten-Faszinationen: Untersuchungen zum Ägyptenbild im europäischen Klassizismus bis 1800*. Frankfurt am Main: Peter Lang, 1990.

Hagstrum, Jean H. *The Sister Arts: The Tradition of Literary Pictorialism and English Poetry from Dryden to Gray*. Chicago: University of Chicago Press, 1958.

Hajós, Géza. *Romantische Gärten der Aufklärung: Englische Landschaftskultur des 18. Jahrhunderts in und um Wien*. Vienna: Böhlau, 1989.

'Picture and Poetry in Austrian Gardens of the Late Eighteenth Century'. In *Garden History: Issues, Approaches, Methods: Dumbarton Oaks Colloquium on the History of Landscape Architecture XIII*. Ed. John Dixon Hunt. Washington DC: Dumbarton Oaks Research Library and Collection, 1992. 203–218.

'The Gardens of the British Isles in the Diary of the Austrian Count Karl von Zinzendorf in the Year 1768'. *Journal of Garden History* 9/1 (1989), 40–7.

Hallbaum, Franz. *Der Landschaftsgarten: Sein Entstehen und seine Einführung in Deutschland durch Friedrich Ludwig von Sckell, 1750–1823*. Munich: H. Schmidt, 1927.

Hamburger, Michael, ed. *Beethoven: Letters, Journals, and Conversations*. London: Thames and Hudson, 1984.

Harten, Stuart J. 'Raising the Veil of History: Orientalism, Classicism, and the Birth of Western Civilisation in Hegel's Berlin Lecture Courses of the 1820s'. Ph.D. diss., Cornell University, 1994.

Hartmann, Günter. *Die Ruine im Landschaftsgarten: Ihre Bedeutung für den frühen Historismus und die Landschaftsmalerei der Romantik*. Worms: Werner'sche Verlagsgesellschaft, 1981.

Head, Matthew William. 'Fantasy in the instrumental music of C. P. E. Bach'. Ph.D. diss., Yale University, 1995.

Helm, Eugene. 'The "Hamlet" Fantasy and the Literary Element in C. P. E. Bach's Music'. *Musical Quarterly* 58 (1972), 277–96.

Hennebo, Dieter and Alfred Hoffmann, eds. *Geschichte der deutschen Gartenkunst*. 3 vols., Hamburg: Broschek, 1962–5.

'Tendencies in Mid-Eighteenth-Century German Gardening'. *Journal of Garden History* 5/4 (1985), 350–70.

Hipple, Walter John. *The Beautiful, the Sublime, and the Picturesque in Eighteenth-Century British Aesthetic Theory*. Carbondale: Southern Illinois University Press, 1957.

Hoffmann, Alfred. *Der Landschaftsgarten*. Hamburg: Broschek, 1963.

Hörwarthner, Maria. 'Joseph Haydn's Library: An Attempt at a Literary-Historical Reconstruction'. In *Haydn and his World*. Ed. Elaine Sisman. Princeton, NJ: Princeton University Press, 1997. 395–461. Originally published as 'Joseph Haydns Bibliothek – Versuch einer literarhistorischen Rekonstruktion', in *Joseph Haydn und die Literatur*, ed. Herbert Zeman. Eisenstadt: Institut für österreichische Kulturgeschichte, 1976. 157–207.

Hosler, Bellamy. *Changing Aesthetic Views of Instrumental Music in 18th-Century Germany*. Ann Arbor, MI: UMI Research Press, 1981.

Hunt, John Dixon. 'Emblem and Expressionism in the Eighteenth-Century Landscape Garden'. *Eighteenth-Century Studies* 4/3 (1971), 294–317.

The Figure in the Landscape: Poetry, Painting, and Gardening during the Eighteenth Century. Baltimore: Johns Hopkins University Press, 1976.

'Ut Pictura Poesis, Ut Pictura Hortus, and the Picturesque'. In *Word and Image* 1/1 (1985), 87–107.

Gardens and the Picturesque: Studies in the History of Landscape Architecture. Cambridge, MA: MIT Press, 1992.

Hunt, John Dixon, ed. *Garden History: Issues, Approaches, Methods.* Dumbarton Oaks Colloquium on the History of Landscape Architecture XIII (1989). Washington, DC: Dumbarton Oaks Research Library and Collection, 1992.

Hunt, John Dixon and Peter Willis, eds. *The Genius of the Place: The English Landscape Garden 1620–1820.* London: Paul Elek, 1975.

Hussey, Christopher. *The Picturesque: Studies in a Point of View.* London: Putnam, 1927.

English Gardens and Landscapes, 1700–1750. London: Country Life, 1967.

Iser, Wolfgang. *The Act of Reading: A Theory of Aesthetic Response.* Baltimore: The Johns Hopkins University Press, 1978.

Jackson, John Brinckerhoff. *The Necessity for Ruins.* Amherst: University of Massachusetts Press, 1980.

Jackson, Wallace. *Immediacy: The Development of a Critical Concept from Addison to Coleridge.* Amsterdam: Rodopi NV, 1973.

Kahl, Willi. *Selbstbiographien deutscher Musiker des XVIII. Jahrhunderts.* Cologne: Staufen, 1948; reprint edn, Amsterdam: Frits Knuf, 1972.

Kalib, Sylvan. 'Thirteen Essays from the Three Yearbooks Das Meisterwerk in der Musik by Heinrich Schenker: An Annotated Translation'. Ph.D. diss., Northwestern University, 1973.

Kaut, Hubert. *Wiener Gärten: Vier Jahrhunderte Gartenkunst.* Vienna: Bergland Verlag, 1964.

Kayser, Wolfgang. *The Grotesque in Art and Literature.* Trans. Ulrich Weisstein. New York: Indiana University Press, 1963.

Kehn, Wolfgang. *Christian Cay Lorenz Hirschfeld, 1742–1792: eine Biographie.* Worms: Wernersche Verlagsgesellschaft, 1992.

Kinderman, William. *Beethoven.* Berkeley and Los Angeles: University of California Press, 1995.

Kirkpatrick, Ralph. *Domenico Scarlatti.* Revised edn, Princeton, NJ: Princeton University Press, 1983.

Knox, Brian. 'The English Garden in Poland and Bohemia'. In *The Picturesque Garden and its Influence outside the British Isles.* Ed. Nikolaus Pevsner. Washington DC: Dumbarton Oaks, Trustees, for Harvard University, 1974. 99–116.

Kramer, Richard. 'The New Modulation of the 1770s: C. P. E. Bach in Theory, Criticism, and Practice'. *Journal of the American Musicological Society* 38 (1985), 551–92.

Krille, Annemarie. *Beiträge zur Geschichte der Musikerziehung und Musikübung der deutschen Frau (von 1750 bis 1820).* Berlin: Triltsch & Huther, 1938.

Krüger, Renate. *Das Zeitalter der Empfindsamkeit: Kunst und Kultur des späten 18. Jahrhunderts in Deutschland.* Vienna and Munich: Schroll, 1972.

Kunze, Stephan, ed. *Ludwig van Beethoven: Die Werke im Spiegel seiner Zeit*. Laaber: Laaber Verlag, 1986.

Landon, H. C. Robbins. *Mozart and the Masons: New Light on the Lodge 'Crowned Hope'*. Walter Neurath Memorial Lectures, 14. New York: Thames and Hudson, 1982.

Haydn: Chronicle and Works. 5 vols., Bloomington and London: Indiana University Press, 1976–80.

Larsson, Roger Barnett. 'The Beautiful, the Sublime and the Picturesque in Eighteenth-Century Musical Thought in Britain'. Ph.D. diss., State University of New York at Buffalo, 1980.

Lebensztejn, Jean-Claude. *L'Art de la Tache*. Montélimar: Editions du Limon, 1990.

Le Huray, Peter and James Day, eds. *Music and Aesthetics in the Eighteenth and Early Nineteenth Centuries*. Cambridge: Cambridge University Press, 1981.

Lenz, Wilhelm von. *Beethoven et ses trois styles*. 1852; reprint edn, New York: Da Capo, 1980.

Lepenies, Wolf. *Melancholy and Society*. Trans. Jeremy Gaines and Doris Jones. Cambridge, MA: Harvard University Press, 1992.

Leppert, Richard. *Music and Image. Domesticity, Ideology and Socio-cultural Formation in Eighteenth-century England*. Cambridge: Cambridge University Press, 1988.

The Sight of Sound: Music, Representation, and the History of the Body. Berkeley and Los Angeles: University of California Press, 1993.

Leppert, Richard and Susan McClary, eds. *Music and Society: The Politics of Composition, Performance and Reception*. Cambridge: Cambridge University Press, 1987.

Levy, Janet. '"Something Mechanical Encrusted on the Living": A Source of Musical Wit and Humor'. In *Convention in 18th- and 19th-Century Music: Essays in Honor of Leonard Ratner*. Ed. Wye J. Allenbrook, Janet M. Levy and William P. Mahrt. Stuyvesant, NY: Pendragon Press, 1992.

Lochhead, Ian J. *The Spectator and the Landscape in the Art Criticism of Diderot and his Contemporaries*. Ann Arbor, MI: UMI Research Press, 1981.

Loesser, Arthur. *Men, Women and Pianos: A Social History*. New York: Simon and Schuster, 1954.

Longyear, R. M. 'Beethoven and Romantic Irony', *Musical Quarterly* 56 (1970), 647–64.

Löw, Helmut Aloysius. 'Die Improvisation im Klavierwerk L. van Beethovens'. Ph.D. diss., Saarland University, 1962.

Macdonald, Hugh. 'Fantasy and Order in Beethoven's Phantasie op. 77'. In *Modern Musical Scholarship*. Ed. Edward Olleson. Stocksfield, Northumberland: Oriel, 1980. 141–50.

Maduschka, Leo. *Das Problem der Einsamkeit im 18. Jahrhundert*. Weimar: Alexander Duncker, 1933.

Malins, Edward. *English Landscaping and Literature, 1660–1840*. London: Oxford University Press, 1966.

Manwaring, Elizabeth Wheeler. *Italian Landscape in Eighteenth Century England: A Study Chiefly of the Influence of Claude Lorrain and Salvator Rosa on English Taste, 1700–1800*. New York: Oxford University Press, 1925.

McClary, Susan. *Feminine Endings: Music, Gender and Sexuality*. Minneapolis: University of Minnesota Press, 1991.

McVeigh, Simon. *Concert Life in London from Mozart to Haydn*. Cambridge: Cambridge University Press, 1993.

Meredith, William. 'Beethoven's Creativity: Improvisations'. *The Beethoven Newsletter* 1/2 (Fall 1986), 25–8.

Michelsen, Peter. *Laurence Sterne und der deutsche Roman der 18. Jahrhundert*. Göttingen: Vandenhoeck & Ruprecht, 1962.

Mies, Paul. *Das instrumentale Rezitativ: von seiner Geschichte und seinen Formen*. Abhandlungen zur Kunst-, Musik- und Literaturwissenschaft, vol. LV. Bonn: H. Bouvier, 1968.

'. . . quasi una Fantasia'. In *Colloquium Amicorum: Joseph Schmidt-Görg zum 70. Geburtstag*. Ed. Siegfried Kross and Hans Schmidt. Bonn: Beethovenhaus, 1967. 239–49.

Miesner, Heinrich. *Philipp Emanuel Bach in Hamburg: Beiträge zu seiner Biographie und zur Musikgeschichte seiner Zeit*. Heide: Holst, 1929; reprint edn, Wiesbaden: M. Sändig, 1969.

Miller, Mara. *The Garden as an Art*. Albany, NY: State University of New York Press, 1993.

Mitchell, Timothy F. *Art and Science in German Landscape Painting, 1770–1840*. Oxford: Clarendon Press, 1993.

Mitchell, W. J. T., ed. *Landscape and Power*. Chicago and London: University of Chicago Press, 1994.

Monk, Samuel. *The Sublime* [1935]. Ann Arbor, MI: UMI Research Press, 1962.

Morson, Gary Saul. *The Boundaries of Genre: Dostoevsky's Diary of a Writer and the Traditions of Literary Utopia*. Austin: University of Texas Press, 1981.

Mosser, Monique. 'Paradox in the Garden: A Brief Account of *Fabriques*'. In *The Architecture of Western Gardens*. Ed. Mosser and Teyssot. 263–80.

Mosser, Monique and Georges Teyssot, eds. *The Architecture of Western Gardens: A Design History from the Renaissance to the Present Day*. Cambridge, MA: MIT Press, 1991.

Motte, Diether de la. *Musikalische Analyse, mit kritischen Anmerkungen von Carl Dahlhaus*. Kassel: Bärenreiter, 1968.

Neubauer, John. *The Emancipation of Music from Language: Departure from Mimesis in Eighteenth-Century Aesthetics*. New Haven and London: Yale University Press, 1986.

Neupert, Hans. *Das Klavichord: Geschichte und technische Betrachtung des 'eigentlichen Claviers': mit einem Anhang 'Von der wahren Güte der Clavichord' (nach einem Manuskript von J. N. Forkel)*. Kassel: Bärenreiter, 1948. Trans. Ann P. P. Feldberg as *The Clavichord*. Kassel: Bärenreiter, 1965.

Newcomb, Anthony. 'Schumann and Late Eighteenth-Century Narrative Strategies'. *19th Century Music* 11/2 (Fall 1987), 164–74.

Newman, William S. 'Emanuel Bach's Autobiography'. *Musical Quarterly* 51 (1965), 363–72.

Olausson, Magnus. 'Freemasonry, Occultism and the Picturesque Garden Towards the End of the Eighteenth Century'. *Art History* 8/4 (1985), 413–33.

Oppé, A. P. *Alexander and John Robert Cozens*. London: Adam & Charles Black, 1952.

Oppen, Jürgen von. 'Beethovens Klavierfantasie op. 77 in neuer Sicht'. *Bericht über den internationalen musikwissenschaftlichen Kongress Bonn 1970*. Ed. Carl Dahlhaus et al. Kassel: Bärenreiter, 1971. 528–31.

Ottenberg, Hans-Günter. 'Zur Fantasieproblematik im Schaffen Carl Philipp Emanuel Bachs'. In *Studien zur Aufführungspraxis und Interpretation von Instrumentalmusik des 18. Jahrhunderts – Die Einflüsse einzelner Interpreten und Komponisten des 18. Jahrhunderts auf das Musikleben ihrer Zeit*, no. 13. Ed. Eitelfriedrich Thom. Blankenburg, Harz: Institut für Aufführungspraxis Michaelstein (Kultur- und Forschungsstätte), 1981. 74–80.

C. P. E. Bach. Trans. Philip J. Whitmore. Oxford: Oxford University Press, 1987.

Ottenberg, Hans-Günter, ed. *Der Critische Musicus an der Spree: Berliner Musikschrifttum von 1748 bis 1799: Eine Dokumentation*. Leipzig: Philipp Reclam, 1984.

Paul, Steven E. 'Comedy, Wit and Humor in Haydn's Instrumental Music'. In *Haydn Studies: Proceedings of the International Haydn Conference, Washington DC, 1975*. Ed. Howard Serwer, Jens Peter Larsen and James Webster. New York: Norton, 1981.

Paulson, Ronald. *Emblem and Expression: Meaning in English Art of the 18th Century*. London: Thames and Hudson, 1975.

Park und Garten im 18. Jahrhundert: Colloquium d. Arbeitsstelle 18. Jh., Gesamthochschule Wuppertal, Würzburg und Veitshöchheim, 26.-29. September 1976. Heidelberg: Winter, 1978.

Parshall, Linda. 'C. C. L. Hirschfeld's Concept of the Garden in the German Enlightenment'. *Journal of Garden History* 13/3 (1993), 125–71.

Pevsner, Nikolaus, ed. *The Picturesque Garden and Its Influence Outside the British Isles: 2nd Dumbarton Oaks Colloquium on the History of Landscape Architecture (1974)*. Washington, DC: Dumbarton Oaks, 1974.

Preston, John. *The Created Self: The Reader's Role in Eighteenth-Century Fiction*. London: Heinemann, 1970.

Price, Martin. 'The Picturesque Moment'. In *From Sensibility to Romanticism: Essays Presented to Frederick A. Pottle*. Ed. Frederick W. Hilles and Harold Bloom. New York: Oxford University Press, 1965. 259–92.

Pugh, Simon. 'Received Ideas on Pastoral'. In *The Architecture of Western Gardens*. Ed. Mosser and Teyssot. 253–61.

Reading Landscape: Country, City, Capital. Manchester: Manchester University Press, 1990.

Ratner, Leonard G. *Classic Music: Expression, Form and Style*. New York: Schirmer, 1980.

Rave, Paul Ortwin. *Gärten der Goethezeit*. Leipzig: Koehler & Amelang, 1941.

Ribeiro, Alvaro, ed. *The Letters of Charles Burney*. Oxford: Clarendon Press, 1991.

Robinson, Sidney K. *Inquiry into the Picturesque*. Chicago: University of Chicago Press, 1991.

Rorschach, Kimerly. *The Early Georgian Landscape Garden*. New Haven: Yale Center for British Art, 1983.

Rosen, Charles. *The Classical Style: Haydn, Mozart, Beethoven*. London: Faber, 1971.

Sonata Forms. Revised edn, New York: Norton, 1988.

The Romantic Generation. Cambridge, MA: Harvard University Press, 1995.

Ross, Stephanie. *What Gardens Mean*. Chicago and London: University of Chicago Press, 1998.

Russell, Tilden A. 'Minuet, Scherzando, and Scherzo: The Dance Movement in Transition. 1781–1825'. Ph.D. diss., University of North Carolina, Chapel Hill, 1983.

'On '"Looking over a Ha-ha"'. *Musical Quarterly* 71/1 (1985), 27–37.

'"Über das Komische in der Musik": The Schütze–Stein Controversy'. *Journal of Musicology* 4/1 (1985–6), 70–90.

Sayre, Robert. *Solitude in Society: A Sociological Study in French Literature*. Cambridge, MA: Harvard University Press, 1978.

Schafer, Hollace Ann. '"A Wisely Ordered Phantasie": Joseph Haydn's Creative Process from the Sketches and Drafts for Instrumental Music'. Ph.D. diss., Brandeis University, 1987.

Schafhäutl, Karl Emil von. *Abt Georg Joseph Vogler: Sein Leben, Charakter und Musikalisches System*. Augsburg: Huttler, 1888; reprint edn, Hildesheim: Olms, 1979.

Schenker, Heinrich. *Ein Beitrag zur Ornamentik. Als Einführung zu Ph. E. Bachs Klavierwerken*. Vienna: Universal, 1908.

'A Contribution to the Study of Ornamentation: An Introduction to the Keyboard Works of Carl Philipp Emanuel Bach'. Trans. Hedi Siegel. In *The Music Forum* vol. IV. Ed. Felix Salzer and Carl Schachter. New York: Columbia University Press, 1976. 1–139.

Schepers, Wolfgang. *Hirschfelds Theorie der Gartenkunst, 1779–1785*. Worms: Werner'sche Verlagsgesellschaft, 1980.

Schering, Arnold. 'C. P. E. Bach und das redende Prinzip in der Musik'. *Jahrbuch der Musikbibliothek Peters* 45 (1938), 13–29.

Schleuning, Peter. 'Die Fantasiermaschine: Ein Beitrag zur Geschichte der Stilwende um 1750'. *Archiv für Musikwissenschaft* 27 (1970), 192–213.

The Fantasia. Trans. A. C Howie. Cologne: A. Volk Verlag, 1971.

Die Freie Fantasie: Ein Beitrag zur Erforschung der klassischen Klaviermusik. Göppingen: Kümmerle, 1973.

Das 18. Jahrhundert: Der Bürger erhebt sich. Reinbek bei Hamburg: Rowohlt, 1984.

Die Sprache der Natur: Natur in der Musik des 18. Jahrhunderts. Stuttgart and Weimar: J. B. Metzler, 1998.

Schlichtegroll, Friedrich von. *Musiker-Nekrologe*. Edited by Richard Schaal. Kassel: Bärenreiter, [1954].

Schmid, Ernst Fritz. *Carl Philipp Emanuel Bach und seine Kammermusik*. Kassel: Bärenreiter, 1931.

'Joseph Haydn und Carl Philipp Emanuel Bach'. *Zeitschrift für Musikwissenschaft* 14/6 (1932), 299–312.

Schmidt, Erika, Wilfried Hansmann and Jörg Gamer, eds. *Garten, Kunst, Geschichte: Festschrift für Dieter Hennebo zum 70. Geburtstag*. Worms am Rhein: Werner, 1994.

Schmidt, Jochen. *Die Geschichte des Genie-Gedankens 1750–1954*. 2 vols., Darmstadt: Wissenschaftliche Buchgesellschaft, 1985.

Schmitt, Ulrich. *Revolution im Konzertsaal: Zur Beethoven-Rezeption im 19. Jahrhundert*. Mainz: Schott, 1990.

Schmitz, Arnold. *Das Romantische Beethovenbild*. Berlin and Bonn, 1927; reprint edn, Darmstadt: Wissenschaftliche Buchgesellschaft, 1978.

Schroeder, David P. *Haydn and the Enlightenment: The Late Symphonies and their Audience*. Oxford: Clarendon Press, 1990.

Schulenberg, David. *The Instrumental Music of Carl Philipp Emanuel Bach*. Ann Arbor: UMI Research Press, 1984.

Sillitti, Giovanna. *Tragelaphos: Storia di una metafora e di una problema*. Naples: Bibliopolis, 1981.

Siren, Osvald. *China and Gardens of Europe of the Eighteenth Century*. New York: Ronald Press, [1950].

Sisman, Elaine. 'Haydn's Theater Symphonies'. *Journal of the American Musicological Society* 43 (1990), 292–352.

'After the Heroic Style: Fantasia and the "Characteristic" Sonatas of 1809'. *Beethoven Forum* 6 (1998), 67–96.

'Haydn's Solo Keyboard Music'. In *Eighteenth-Century Keyboard Music*. Ed. Robert Marshall. New York: Schirmer, 1994.

Sloan, Kim. *Alexander and John Robert Cozens: The Poetry of Landscape*. New Haven: Yale University Press, 1986.

Smeed, J. W. '"Süssertönendes Klavier": Tributes to the Early Piano in Poetry and Song'. *Music and Letters* 66/3 (July 1985), 228–40.

Solomon, Maynard. *Beethoven*. New York: Schirmer, 1977.

'Some Romantic Images in Beethoven'. In *Haydn, Mozart and Beethoven: Studies in Music of the Classic Period*. Ed. Sieghard Brandenburg. Oxford: Clarendon Press, 1998.

Sonneck, O. G., ed. *Beethoven: Impressions by his Contemporaries*. New York: Schirmer, 1926.

Stafford, Barbara Maria. 'Toward Romantic Landscape Perception: Illustrated Travels and the Rise of "Singularity" as an Aesthetic Category'. *Art Quarterly* NS 1 (1977), 89–124.

Voyage into Substance: Art, Science, Nature, and the Illustrated Travel Account, 1760–1840. Cambridge, MA: MIT Press, 1984.

Body Criticism: Imaging the Unseen in Enlightenment Art and Medicine. Cambridge, MA: MIT Press, 1991.

Stewart, Brian Douglas. 'Georg Philipp Telemann in Hamburg: Social and Cultural Background and its Musical Expression', Ph.D. diss., Stanford University, 1985.

Strommer, Roswitha. 'Die Rezeption der englischen Literatur im Lebensumkreis und zur Zeit Joseph Haydns'. In *Joseph Haydn und die Literatur seiner Zeit*. Ed. Herbert Zeman. Eisenstadt: Institut für österreichische Kulturgeschichte, 1976. 123–55.

Suchalla, Ernst, ed. *Briefe von Carl Philipp Emanuel Bach an Johann Gottlob Immanuel Breitkopf und Johann Nikolaus Forkel*. Tutzing: H. Schneider, 1985.

Carl Philipp Emanuel Bach: Briefe und Dokumente, Kritische Gesamtausgabe. 2 vols., Göttingen: Vandenhoeck & Ruprecht, 1994.

Thayer, Harvey Waterman. *Laurence Sterne in Germany: A Contribution to the Study of Literary Relations of England and Germany in the Eighteenth Century*. New York: Columbia University Press, 1905.

Todd, Janet. *Sensibility: An Introduction*. London and New York: Methuen, 1986.

Todorov, Tzvetan. *The Fantastic: A Structural Approach to a Literary Genre*. Trans. Richard Howard. Ithaca, NY: Cornell University Press, 1975.

Townsend, Dabney. 'The Picturesque'. *Journal of Aesthetics and Art Criticism* 55/4 (Fall 1997), 365–76.

Turner, Roger. *Capability Brown and the Eighteenth Century English Landscape*. New York: Rizzoli, 1985.

Uhde, Jürgen. *Beethovens Klaviermusik*. Stuttgart: Reclam, 1968.

Vidler, Anthony. *The Writing of the Walls*. Princeton, NJ: Princeton Architectural Press, 1987.

Wade, Rachel W. *The Catalog of Carl Philipp Emanuel Bach's Estate*. New York: Garland, 1981.

Waldvogel, Nicolas Henri. 'The Eighteenth-Century Esthetics of the Sublime and the Valuation of the Symphony'. Ph.D. diss., Yale University, 1992.

Wallace, Robin. *Beethoven's Critics: Aesthetic Dilemmas and Resolutions during the Composer's Lifetime*. Cambridge: Cambridge University Press, 1986.

Watkin, David. *English Vision: The Picturesque in Architecture, Landscape and Garden Design*. London: John Murray, 1982.

Webster, James. *Haydn's 'Farewell' Symphony and the Idea of Classical Style: Through Composition and Cyclic Integration in his Instrumental Music*. Cambridge: Cambridge University Press, 1991.

  'The Creation, Haydn's Late Vocal Music, and the Musical Sublime'. In *Haydn and his World*. Ed. Elaine Sisman. Princeton, NJ: Princeton University Press, 1997. 57–102.

Wheelock, Gretchen. *Haydn's Ingenious Jesting with Art: Contexts of Musical Wit and Humor*. New York: Schirmer, 1992.

Whiting, Steven Moore. '"Hört ihr wohl": Zu Funktion und Programm von Beethovens Chorfantasie'. *Archiv für Musikwissenschaft* 45/2 (1988), 132–47.

Wiebenson, Dora. *The Picturesque Garden in France*. Princeton, NJ: Princeton University Press, 1978.

Williams, Raymond. *The Country and the City*. New York: Oxford University Press, 1973.

Wimmer, Clemens Alexander. *Geschichte der Gartentheorie*. Darmstadt: Wissenschaftliche Buchgesellschaft, 1989.

Wollenberg, Susan. 'A New Look at C. P. E. Bach's Musical Jokes'. In *C. P. E. Bach Studies*. Ed. Stephen L. Clark. Oxford: Oxford University Press, 1988. 295–314.

Zádor, Anna. 'The English Garden in Hungary'. In *The Picturesque Garden and its Influence outside the British Isles*. Ed. Nikolaus Pevsner. Washington, DC: Dumbarton Oaks, 1974. 77–98.

Zeman, Herbert, ed. *Joseph Haydn und die Literatur seiner Zeit*. Jahrbuch für österreichische Kulturgeschichte, VI. Eisenstadt: Institut für österreichische Kulturgeschichte, 1976.

INDEX

Adorno, Theodor, 17, 76
André, Johann, 158–60
Aristotle, 99
Artaria, 34, 125
Artemis of Ephesus, *see* Isis
Assmann, Jan, 219 n. 68, 220 n. 70
Aussicht, 61–4
Austen, Jane
  Mansfield Park, 24–5
  Northanger Abbey, 74
autobiography, 148, 175–8, 224–6
Avison, Charles, 89–90, 92

Bach, Carl Philipp Emanuel
  in eighteenth-century criticism, 35–8,
    40–2, 48–9, 66, 95–6
  C. F. Cramer on, 49, 59–61, 71–2,
    97–100, 121–4, 130, 132–3
  in early nineteenth-century criticism,
    135, 191, 192
  Crotch on, 113
  Nägeli on, 138–9
  in twentieth-century criticism, 18–19,
    42, 176–7, 179, 181
  and the clavichord, 149, 151–5
  and Hamburg gardens, 70–1
  and Haydn, 117–18, 125–6, 131–3, 138–9,
    143–4
  and humour, 109, 113–18, 121–5, 131–3,
    135, 140–4
  on improvisation, 40–1, 42–3, 66, 72
  as improviser, 16–17, 34–5, 56, 79
  and the ornamental style, 113–19
  and Sterne, 140–2
  WORKS
  Abschied von meinem Silbermannischen
    Claviere, H. 272, 152–5, 167, 182
  C. P. E. Bachs Empfindungen, H. 536,
    176–82, *180*, 226
  Fantasia in C minor, H. 75/iii, 47–9,
    50–1, 54, 95–100, *97*, 170

Fantasia in G minor, H. 225, 45–6, 48, 54
Fantasia in E♭ major, H. 277, 49, 52–5
Fantasia in A minor, H. 278, 49, 54–5
Fantasia in C major, H. 284, 19, 121–4
Fantasia in B♭ major, H. 289, 20–4, 26,
  49, 54
Fantasia in C major, H. 291, 113–17, 118,
  125
Free Fantasia in F♯ minor, H. 300,
  176–82, 177
Heilig, H. 778, 66–7
Kenner und Liebhaber IV, 34, 49, 55, 59,
  130, 150
Kenner und Liebhaber V, 41, 54, 79
Kenner und Liebhaber VI, 20
Rondo in C minor, H. 283, 54–5
Versuch über die wahre Art das Clavier zu
  spielen, 40–1, 42–5, *43*, *50–1*, 49, 66,
  72, 78, 95
Bach, Johann Sebastian, 37
beautiful, the, *see* sublime, aesthetics of
  the
Bebung, 95, 150–1, 152, 154–5, 156, 163
  see also clavichord, sentiment
Beethoven, Ludwig van
  on gardens, 213–14
  as improviser, 183–4, 192, 198, 226
  and musical comparisons with
    landscape, 190, 206–12, 213
  and musical fantastic, 183, 185, 190–229
    passim
  and Saitic inscription, 223
  WORKS
  Choral fantasy, Op. 80, 185, 223–6
  Fantasie Op. 77, 185, 192–9, 221, 225
  Sonatas, Op. 27, 191, 199–201
  Sonata, Op. 101, 201–6, 210
  Sonatas, Op. 102, 201
  Sonatas, Op. 109, Op. 110, Op. 111,
    210–12
  Trios, Op. 70, 208–9

249

Index

Bekker, Paul, 192, 195
Berger, Karol, 19, 205–6
Bitter, Karl Herman, 139
bizarre, the, 35–6, 48, 131, 132
Bode, Johann Joachim Christoph, 140–2
Bonds, Mark Evan, 18
boredom
  avoidance of in improvisation, 185–6
  picturesque as antidote to, 104–7
Breitkopf, Johann Gottlob Immanuel, 34, 35
Brown, Lancelot 'Capability', 9
Burke, Edmund, 106
Burney, Charles, 34, 72, 78, 141
  on C. P. E. Bach, 16, 35–6, 48–9, 56, 151
  on Haydn, 104
Busby, Thomas, 91
Büsch, Johann Georg, 141

cadenza, 129, 139–40
Chambers, William, 62, *68*
  Dissertation on Oriental Gardening, 8–9, 27 n. 41, 64
chiaroscuro, 89–92
Chodowiecki, Daniel, 30–1, *32–3*
Claude glass, 75
clavichord, 149–55, 163–4, 165–71, 175
  and inspiration, 152
  as medium for fantasy, 56, 95, 166–71, 175, 176–9
  and musical solitude, 31, 149–51
  and sentiment, 150–2, 155–71 *passim*, 177–82
  Silbermann, 151–5
  songs to, 155–71, 165, 167, 182
  see also Bach, Carl Philipp Emanuel;
    Bebung; Cramer, Carl Friedrich;
    Forkel, Johann Nikolaus
Clementi, Muzio, 41, 135
cloudscapes, interpretation of, 93–5, *96*, 98–9
Cobenzl, 214–15
coherence, problem of
  in instrumental music, 89, 93–4, 130–1, 206–9
    Cramer on, 59–61, 98–100
    in fantasia, 17–20, 39, 63–4, 185–6, 191–2, 211; Burney on, 48–9;
      Cramer on, 60–1; Schenker on, 42–3; Wendt on, 207–8
    Forkel on, 36–8
  see also fantasia, instrumental music

colour, musical, 90–2
Combe, William, 73
comic, the, *see* humour
Cone, Edward
  Musical Form and Musical Performance, 64
contrast
  in landscape, 7–8, 27, 64–6, 93
  in music, 7–8, 36–7, 40, 89–92, 93, 130–1
    of Beethoven, 190, 193
    of C. P. E. Bach, 117
    of Haydn, 107–9
  in the ornamental style, 111
  see also chiaroscuro; effects; painting
    and music; picturesque
conversation, 101, 129
Cozens, Alexander
  New Method, 81–5, *86–7*, 94–5, *96*
Cramer, Carl Friedrich, 34
  on C. P. E. Bach, 16–17, 41, 59–62, 71, 79, 97–9, 132–3
  on the clavichord, 149–50
Creed, John, 78
Crotch, William, 109–13, 117–18, 134, 135, 143
  see also ornamental style, the
Czerny, Carl 77
  on Beethoven, 184, 192
  on fantasy and garden, 71, 191
  Systematic Introduction to Improvisation, 71, 185, 191, 192, 224

Dahlhaus, Carl, 201 n. 40
Darwin, Erasmus, 221, 222
Diderot, Denis, 57
digression
  fantasy and, 18, 22–3, 31, 37–8, 59–61, 71, 98, 122–4, 139
  and genius, 59, 171
  harmonic, 40–2, 45–8, 71
  in landscape, 41–2, 62
  narrative and, 31–2, 136
  see also ellipsis
distance
  and Beethoven's Op. 72, 192, 194–5
  and Beethoven's Op. 101, 202
  as metaphor for modulation, 40–1
distance, aesthetic, 26, 74, 119, 139–40, 143, 182
  see also *irony*
Douglas, Mary, 119
dreams, 56–8, 75–6
Duff, William, 59

Index